The Family-Centered Library Handbook

SANDRA FEINBERG
BARBARA JORDAN
KATHLEEN DEERR
MARCELLINA BYRNE
LISA G. KROPP

Neal-Schuman Publishers, Inc.
New York   London

Published by Neal-Schuman Publishers, Inc.
100 William St., Suite 2004
New York, NY 10038

Printed and bound in the United States of America.

The paper used in this publication meets the minimum requirements of American National
Standard for Information Sciences—Permanence of Paper for Printed Library Materials,
ANSI Z39.48-1992.

ISBN-13: 978-1-55570-541-1
ISBN-10: 1-55570-541-3

Library of Congress Cataloging-in-Publication Data

The family-centered library handbook / Sandra Feinberg . . . [et al.].
   p. cm.
  Includes bibliographical references and index.
  ISBN-13: 978-1-55570-541-1 (alk. paper)
  ISBN-10: 1-55570-541-3 (alk. paper)
  1. Libraries and families—United States. 2. Children's libraries—United States.
3. Reading—Parent participation. 4. Family literacy programs—United States. 5. Library
orientation for school children—United States. 6. Information literacy—Study and teaching.
7. Libraries and preschool children—United States. I. Feinberg, Sandra, 1946–
Z711.92.F34F36 2007
027.6—dc22   2006102709

This book is dedicated to the staff and patrons of the
Middle Country Public Library,
the MCL Foundation,
the Americans for Libraries Council
and its programming section,
Libraries for the Future,
and
Family Place Libraries™ nationwide and on Long Island.

Contents

Figures

Preface

Over the last quarter century, librarians have excelled at creating programs to help children master the skills necessary to succeed in school. Family-centered services take libraries beyond early literacy to embrace the entire family unit, to see the link between assisting young children and families and community and economic development, and the importance of collaborative efforts on behalf of children to advocate for a more healthy and literate society. Family-centered librarians broaden their vision to include community health and social services, interactive learning spaces and activities, parent education and support, staff training, and creating culturally and ethnically diverse community libraries.

Developing family-centered services is a gradual process, one that is critically affected by the interaction of professionals from across various disciplines—early childhood, parent education, social and health services, literacy, workforce development. Whether serendipitous or planned, the synergetic process invariably moves in directions that energize and excite (and even sometimes exhaust) the librarians involved. The reward is great. When a public library focuses on family it not only provides a multitude of benefits for all involved; it also improves its viability as an institution and makes it better able to compete in today's society.

The Family-Centered Library Handbook offers a compelling rationale to adopt this type of approach and a variety of practical strategies to optimize services for families of young children. This is a remarkable time of discovery about the significance of early brain development and the process of early learning. Knowing that literacy begins at birth, it is crucial that librarians convey to parents and caregivers the importance of the everyday tasks of reading, storytelling, listening, playing, and interacting with adults.

The Family-Centered Library Handbook challenges children's librarians to:

- focus on the family as a unit
- increase services to babies, toddlers, and the adults who live and work with children
- adopt developmentally appropriate practice
- integrate early intervention and primary prevention strategies
- build coalitions with other family service professionals
- design welcoming spaces and places for young children and their caregivers

The authors encourage librarians to take the ideas presented and make them their own, adopting the basic philosophy and integrating those pieces that especially appeal and make sense in their particular settings.

While targeted to children's services staff, the book is also relevant for administrators, trustees, and outreach professionals who aim to establish the public library as a cornerstone within the local community and seek to win the hearts of the people and the support of elected officials and taxpayers. It serves as a primary text for the Family Place Libraries™ Training Institute and can function as a textbook for public library programs, public library management, public library children's services, parent education, family support, early childhood development, and early intervention courses, as well as a special resource for consultants.

The staff from the Middle Country Public Library in Centereach, New York, with input from other professionals in the fields of family support, developed the underlying philosophy and principles during the past two decades. They culled the majority of programs from Middle Country Public Library, the national model for Family Place Libraries, and other Family Place Libraries throughout the country.

The Family Place Libraries initiative transforms libraries into community hubs for healthy child and family development, parent and community involvement, and lifelong literacy beginning at birth. A comprehensive model for family-centered library service, Family Place focuses on early childhood information, parent education, emergent literacy, socialization, and family support. Key features include programs, collections, and specially designed spaces for parents and children beginning at birth, collaborations with other local agencies to better serve families, outreach to new and underserved audiences, and staff trained in family-centered service philosophy. The Parent/Child Workshop, a five-week program for toddlers and their parents, is the core program of Family Place Libraries. Chapter 8 discusses this national initiative in greater detail.

Organization

The Family-Centered Library Handbook features four basic building blocks:

- "Preparing for a Family-Centered Library"
- "Developing Services for Young Children and Parents"
- "Reaching Out to Special Audiences"
- "Tools for Family-Centered Libraries"

Sixteen chapters cover a broad range of individual topics, including "Forming Coalitions and Collaborations," "Creating Family Spaces and Places," Culturally Diverse Families," and "Programs for Young Children and Parents." Many chapters offer a comprehensive, hands-on list of resources and strategies to facilitate "taking the next step." The chapters may be read cover to cover or used independently as the need arises. The resources relating to each subject are intentionally placed at the end of that particular chapter, making each a complete and practical mini-guide within itself.

In Part I, "Preparing for a Family-Centered Library,"

- Chapter 1 looks at the needs and issues of families with young children in today's society and outlines the underlying principles of family-centered services, with particular regard for how they relate to libraries. It highlights the importance of the family unit and the influence of parents on young children's learning and development. Some of the topics covered include working families and childcare, children and poverty, young children and learning, emergent and family literacy, children with special needs, and the overall need for parent education and support.
- Chapter 2 explains the changing role of the public library and the benefits of adopting family-centered services. Libraries increase their value by investing in young children and families and often increase their political standing and financial support. Initial steps for beginners or those who have already started to explore family services are provided.
- Chapter 3 helps readers to first look at themselves and their own attitudes and values regarding families and young children. Using a personal attitude checklist, a cultural competency checklist, a quality indicator assessment tool, and a self-study checklist, staff members can begin to assess themselves and their organization's readiness. Knowledge-based competencies and professional training opportunities are outlined for further exploration.
- Chapter 4 focuses on coalition building and collaboration. It talks about the benefits of coalitions, looks at the strengths of the public library as a community partner, provides a list of potential partners, and outlines the roles for librarians and partners. Specific examples illustrate the different levels of coalition building: networking, coordination, cooperation, and collaboration.
- Chapter 5 focuses on early childhood development. The first section outlines how a child's brain develops, emotional and social growth, and developmental

milestones, all of which can help librarians better understand the early learn-ing process. The second section looks at play and its role in early literacy and provides librarians with the underlying justification to emphasize play activi-ties when they design services for very young children.

- Chapter 6 provides a basic understanding of how parents develop and outlines different parenting styles and cultural variances. It describes the role of the parent as a child's first teacher and how important it is for librarians to involve parents in our efforts to create a library "habit" in children. One of the major roles for children's librarians who embark on the development of family-centered services is to provide information and referral for parents.

In Part II, "Developing Services for Young Children and Parents,"

- Chapter 7 offers tips and suggestions for designing spaces and areas for very young children and their parents. Topics cover health and safety issues, estab-lishing boundaries, creating interactive activities, space organization and scale, integrating parent resources, and using color and displays. Checklists and a list of questions help readers assess their current space.
- Chapter 8 highlights programs designed for parents and very young children that are offered in Family Place libraries. Each entry provides a short descrip-tion, partnering organizations (if required), some practical tips, supplies and staff needed, contact information, and additional resources. Selected program curricula are provided in Section B of the "Tools for Family-Centered Li-braries" at the end of the book.
- Chapter 9 covers collection development for young children including basic guidelines, books in a variety of formats, videos and DVDs, CDs, materials for children with special needs, and sources for ordering. Specific titles are listed with each type of material.
- Chapter 10 provides guidelines to select, order, catalog, process, and circulate toys. Special sections cover adaptive toys and equipment for children with special needs.
- Chapter 11 provides guidelines for establishing a parents' collection including defining the audience, scope, size, location, management, formats, range of topics, and special items such as kits, brain boxes, and bibliographies. An im-portant component of the chapter includes recommended books, videos and DVDs, magazines, Web sites, and ordering sources.

In Part III, "Reaching Out to Special Audiences,"

- Chapter 12 discusses services targeted to family support providers who work with parents and young children. The importance of providing information and referral, meeting space, professional collections, specially designed kits, and deposit collections are highlighted. Training opportunities and examples of offsite program delivery offered by selected Family Place libraries illustrate a variety of successful ideas.
- Chapter 13 recognizes the importance as well as the challenge of serving limited-literacy and low-income families, with specific strategies recommended for ways

to maximize outreach to this often hard-to-reach audience. It provides recommendations and source information for low-literacy parenting resources and suggestions for programs, services, and partnership opportunities that have proven successful. Family literacy as a particularly successful approach for families with limited literacy is given special attention.

- Chapter 14 responds to the impact of changing demographics on library service across the country, discusses the challenges of finding ways to meet the needs of culturally diverse families, and recommends strategies to respond to the challenges. It describes the programs, collections, and services that have been proven effective, including suggested parenting titles and ordering sources for bilingual, foreign language, and culturally reflective resources.

- Chapter 15 looks at teen parent families. To best serve teen parents, librarians need to consider the needs of both the teens and their children and, in most cases, must work with a community organization to reach and serve this audience. The chapter also lists ordering sources for collections and descriptions of programs some Family Place libraries successfully offer.

- Chapter 16 addresses families and children with special needs. The first part defines inclusion and provides an overview of the law, outlines the needs of these families, and describes how libraries can help to satisfy some of those needs. The major part of the chapter provides resources and ordering sources as well as select programs provided in Family Place libraries for parents of children with special needs.

Part IV, "Tools for Family-Centered Libraries," provides the reader with tools to assist them in their efforts to develop the services. Included in this part are professional development resources, program curriculums, and community surveys.

The Family-Centered Library Handbook looks at families, the role of the library in relationship to parents and young children, and the critical importance of working collaboratively with other family service providers in order to accomplish our goals. A multitude of programs, collections, and services are highlighted to assist readers in their everyday efforts to create family-centered libraries. The authors encourage readers to take these ideas and make them their own, integrate what is offered with what they are already doing to assist families, and join in their efforts to create a community of family-centered libraries across the country.

Acknowledgments

Special appreciation is extended to the staff of Middle Country Public Library, particularly Mary Viggiano and the Children's Services and Community Relations Departments for their contributions to our manuscript. Their dedication to detail provided us with the assurance that the final publication would be accurate and thorough.

Particular recognition is also given to Diantha Schull, the Americans for Libraries Council and their program section, Libraries for the Future, without which Family Place Libraries and family-centered services would not have evolved into a national movement. It has been a dynamic adventure, filled with hard work and exciting activities, that has led to our evolution as a leader and national model for services for parents and children.

Acknowledgment is also extended to all of the libraries and librarians that are part of the national Family Place network for their participation in a community of learners, striving to broaden and extend the reach of children's services in their own libraries. Special thanks to those librarians who provided us with material for our manuscript.

We are especially grateful to all of those community partners that have worked with us and the staffs of the Family Place Libraries around the country to reach and serve parents and children throughout their local communities.

PART I

Preparing for a Family-Centered Library

1

Introducing Family-Centered Services

Young children in our society face many obstacles on their path to attaining the knowledge, skills, and attitudes needed to be successful. The increasing complexity of today's world dictates the need to develop skills in our youth that will enable them to compete in a global economy. The evolving workplace requires employees who can use information and apply problem-solving skills to new and unique situations. Children need to be provided with learning opportunities in school, at home, and in the community to prepare them to acquire and use new knowledge throughout their lifetime. Public libraries are positioned to play an enormously important role in addressing these major societal issues. Family-centered library services can provide the framework from which libraries approach their work with families. An understanding of the developmental data and changes impacting today's families places family-centered library services in a larger context and provides the rationale or "needs statement" necessary to articulate why libraries must be involved for funders, elected officials, policymakers, and administrators.

Best practices developed by early childhood and family support professionals have helped us to understand that healthy development and learning begin at birth. Children who "learn how to learn" and who are able to reason and think creatively will be successful in performing the critical jobs of the future. "Over the past several decades two profound changes have coincided to alter the landscape for early childhood development in the United States. First, an explosion of research in the neuro-biological, behavioral, and social sciences has led to major advances in understanding the conditions that influence whether children get off to a promising or a worrisome start in life. Second, the capacity to use this knowledge constructively has been constrained by a number of dramatic transformations in the social and economic circumstances under which families with young children are living in the United States" (Horsley et al., 2000: viii).

Libraries have the opportunity and responsibility to join together with other family-serving agencies to create family-centered communities. Grounded in a basic respect for individual initiative, quality public library service assumes many of the fundamental tenets and guidelines found in family-centered principles and practice. Committed to lifelong learning and educational enrichment, libraries aim to satisfy the informational, cultural, and recreational needs of patrons, birth through the senior years. Self-initiated learning and respect for diverse cultures go hand in hand with family-centered library services.

Family-centered library services expand traditional children's services by acknowledging the crucial roles that parents and caregivers play in the lives of children; support, respect, and empower parents and caregivers in their roles as teachers, nurturers, mentors, and advocates; encourage libraries and other agencies to work together; and support the creation of community-based programs designed to strengthen parent-child relationships. Family-centered libraries aim to become partners in the family support movement, which strives to transform our society into caring communities of citizens that put children and families first and that ensure that all children and families get what they need to succeed.

Issues and Influences on Today's Families

Understanding the changing structure of families in today's society and some of the major influences that affect the home and learning environments will lay the groundwork for more effective work with families and young children. Significant issues facing families include the need for both parents to work and the difficulty of finding quality, affordable childcare; the mobility of young families resulting in isolation from extended family and close friends; the number of children growing up in poverty; those being raised in single-parent, adoptive, foster care, or blended family situations; the increase in families with limited or no English-language skills; and the lack of public space designed with young children and families in mind. Understanding these issues and supporting families in their efforts to raise healthy children are critical.

Dramatic social, demographic, and economic changes during the past forty years have transformed the American family. For many children and parents the experiences of family life are different today than a generation ago. More than ever before, families are experiencing stress that affects childhood security and healthy growth. Some of the most recent statistics on families and children provided by the Children's Defense Fund (2004) and the Population Reference Bureau (2003) attest to the change in family structures.

More than 9 million children under the age of nineteen in the United States have no health insurance.

1 child in 6 is born to a mother who did not receive prenatal care in the first three months of pregnancy.

1 child in 3 is born to unmarried parents.

1 child in 8 is born to a teenage mother.

1 child in 4 lives with only one parent and 1 in 2 will live in a single-parent family at some point in childhood.

1 child in 24 lives with neither parent.

1 child in 60 sees their parents divorce in any year.

1 child in 139 will die before the child's first birthday.

More than 6 million children—approximately 1 in 12—are living in households headed by grandparents or other relatives.

Working Families and Quality Childcare

In addition to the influence of the family structure in which a child grows, "the economic stability of parents can and will affect the paths open to their children and the choices children will make along the journey. The socioeconomic context of the family setting includes income, parents' education, parents' work, and family structure. For some families, education may take a back seat to priorities such as financial well-being, health, and safety—not by choice, but by necessity or lack of opportunity" (National Center for Family Literacy, 2004).

Two dramatic trends affecting child development are the increased number of mothers who work outside the home and the increased number of working-poor families. Work no longer guarantees economic security and, while work may increase family income, some of that income will necessarily be spent on work-related childcare. This means that the family's resources (time and money) may be distributed differently rather than increasing overall.

In 2002, only 7 percent of all U.S. households consisted of married couples with children in which only the husband worked. "Every day, three out of five children under age six are in childcare, and millions of older children are in after school activities while their parents work. These activities help shape the way children think, learn, and behave for the rest of their lives—but little attention is being paid to the quality of those experiences. There is real cause for concern as parents face great difficulty finding good, quality care they can afford" (Children's Defense Fund, 2004).

Whether families access childcare in group settings or use family members, neighbors, and friends as caregivers, high-quality care closely resembles the qualities of good parenting and vice versa. Far too many American children and families are not getting what they need because quality childcare and after-school activities are unaffordable and difficult to find. Many caregivers lack the information and range of supports they need to fulfill their child-rearing duties including access to early learning materials, knowledge about child development and healthy, safe environments, adequate compensation, and provider education and training opportunities.

Children and Poverty

The family's socioeconomic status and poverty, most powerfully associated with children's cognitive skills when they enter school, can have a long-term impact on language and learning. While low-income parents are working in greater numbers, many families still find major obstacles blocking their path out of poverty. The cost of going to work for poor families—childcare, loss of health insurance and social services, transportation, taxes—takes a disproportionate share of the amount they earn when compared to middle-income families.

Because many low-income families live in economically or geographically isolated neighborhoods within city or rural areas, the cost of food, clothing, furniture, and other basic needs is often inflated and access to good financial services is lacking. Mainstream retailers and financial institutions often steer clear of poor neighborhoods. Housing is limited for poor families who lack the credit or savings to enable home ownership. In the end, many low-income families find it nearly impossible to build the assets and savings that are critical for all families to achieve genuine economic security, leaving them vulnerable to economic catastrophes and entrenched poverty (Kids Count, 2003: 11–20).

In the United States, children (especially minority children) are now the age group most likely to live in poverty. One child in five is born poor, one in three will be poor at some point in childhood, and one in six is poor now. One child in eight lives in a family receiving food stamps and over 2.5 million households with children live in substandard housing. In many parts of the country families with children are the fastest growing segment of the homeless population. Perhaps most disturbing is that the gap between the haves and the have-nots is widening. We have more poor and more rich children in the United States than in the past and a wider disparity between the two than most other Western countries (Horsley et al., 2000: 12; Children's Defense Fund, 2004).

Young Children and Learning

Research has conclusively proven that the brain is remarkably undeveloped at birth. The parts of the brain that deal with cognitive processes like thinking and remembering, as well as those that control emotional and social behavior, become permanently formed during the first years of a baby's life. There is a growing body of evidence that appropriate child development practices in the very early years, including attention to those activities that affect the ability to understand and process spoken and written language, help position the child for success.

The way that brain cells connect and organize is an important factor in determining adult capabilities. Although the formation of connections (synapses) continues to some extent throughout life, these connections are being richly created and "pruned" during the early years of life. It is important to recognize that the number of brain connections made depends on the richness and variety of experiences to which a child is exposed.

Genes, environment, caregiving, and nourishment all play important roles in brain development. About 50 percent of the baby's unique brain function is attributed to nature or genetics and about 50 percent to nurture, or the physical and emotional environment to which a baby is exposed. When considering the nurture component, we have found that there are windows of opportunity for brain development from birth to age three that, if missed, will not present themselves again in the future.

The brain reaches 90 percent of its full adult size capacity and wiring by age three (Stamm, 1999). Although many children can benefit from later intervention, the costs of reversing the effects of a poor start increase as the child grows older and the chance of success diminishes. A lack of development creates deficits that can never fully be made up and, in some cases, are irreversible.

Early Literacy: Early stimulation and relationship building between the parent or caregiver and child make it possible to develop higher-level thinking skills. Playing, reading, listening, and talking create a demand for language—the raw material for thought. Words are tools used to express needs, wishes, and later, hopes and ideas. Without a good command of language, the child will be shut out from much that makes life interesting and worthwhile.

Language skills—listening, speaking, reading, and writing—are basic (and essential) and children acquire them most successfully when they are modeled by caring adults (in close one-on-one relationships). Literacy, truly defined, means acquiring a set of attitudes toward self and others, expectations of self and others, and a sense of self-worth and understanding that may on the surface appear to be quite unrelated to conventional reading instruction (Matthews, 1997: 97).

Children from birth to age five engage in making sense of the world on many levels: language, human interactions, counting and quantification, spatial reasoning, physical causality, problem solving, and categorization. Studies indicate that reading to children, even as infants, improves their language skills, strengthens their family relationships, and enables them to perform better in school. Additional findings show that early reading is the key to school success and that the amount mothers (parents or caregivers) talk to their children is strongly associated with children's vocabulary growth as well as with their performance on measures of emergent and print-related skills. The extent of the child's vocabulary and use of language, understanding of number concepts, letter-sound associations, and executive functioning (sequencing, planning, organizing) skills are the aspects that influence early school performance. "In order for emergent literacy skills to develop, children need to explore language that is sung, spoken, recited and written. It is available, knowledgeable, and willing adults who provide babies and toddlers with the experiences that encourage emergent literacy" (Birckmayer, 2001: 26).

Play experiences provide the foundation for reading and writing skills in young children. Research studies have demonstrated repeatedly that children develop their physical, mental, sensory, social, and other learning skills through play. Despite this knowledge, many parents and caregivers still do not understand or acknowledge the importance of child's play. In a culture based on an orientation toward work, adults often see the play activities and toys of children as frivolous and entertaining, not as intrinsically valuable. And without an understanding of the importance of play, many do not make room for it in their increasingly busy and fragmented lives.

Family Literacy: Other indicators that affect a child's readiness for school and learning include the primary language spoken at home and the literacy level of the parents or caregivers. The specific language that children learn and certain qualities of their language depend on specific features of the cultural environment in which a child grows up. "Children can be at risk in society, not because they do not have mastery of a language, but because they do not have mastery of the dominant language of their society, particularly at the time of formal school entry" (Horsley et al., 2000: 46). According to the Children's Defense Fund (2004), the percentage of five- to twenty-four-year-olds who spoke a language other than English more than doubled between 1979 and 1999 and one child in five has a foreign-born mother.

While difficult to determine, there may be as many as ninety million adults in the United States with limited literacy skills. Many of them are parents. In addition, one child in three is behind a year or more in school; one child in five is born to a mother who did not graduate from high school; and one child in eight never graduates from high school. These statistics reflect the urgency of the situation for children growing up in homes with limited literacy and education.

The family is the strongest influence on children's lives. It is where the cycle of learning begins, where parental attitudes about learning become the educational values of the children (National Center for Family Literacy, 2004). When problems arise, it is less because parents are doing terribly wrong things than because they are *not* doing quite the right things or enough of them, such as talking more, using more elaborate talk, exploring number concepts, reading more often or for longer periods of time, and exploring words and pictures in books.

Children with Special Needs: Today, one in twelve children is born with a disability. Unlike the past when children with disabilities were often placed in residential care, many of these children are now being cared for in the home by parents and caregivers. These families rely on a vast array of professional caretakers and community resources to provide specialized intervention services to help them raise their children at home. While we know that recognition of developmental problems at an early age can lead to intervention when it is most effective, families are often hard pressed to know what to do or where to go for help.

Babies and young children raised by caregivers who lack knowledge about effective child rearing or normal child development may not receive sufficient verbal stimulation, dramatically impairing their brain development and lifelong ability to learn. Whether children lag behind due to a disability with which they are born or as a matter of their environment or social and economic circumstances, they need to be recognized as individuals with specific needs, abilities, and potential aspirations. In many instances, this is not the case.

Children with special needs are often set apart from their typically developing peers. They are denied, in many situations, the opportunity to grow and learn from friends in their neighborhood, schools, and other community settings. This kind of segregation and isolation is detrimental not only for the families and children themselves but for the society as a whole. Children are, by nature, social creatures. They need to play with and observe peers. Being part of a group is almost as important as their need to eat or sleep. Simply put, children want to be included with other children. For children with disabilities, this need is often unfulfilled.

Inclusion and opportunities for normal social experiences during the early years are critical for the healthy development of *all* children. Keeping children with disabilities apart from their typically developing peers only creates larger problems later in life and fails to take advantage of the wonderful openness of young children to new experiences and their nonjudgmental attitude toward differences.

Parent Education and Support

The family and the home environment are the key ingredients to a child's success. "We know that infants thrive on one-to-one interaction with parents, which creates trust and a sense of security. The confidence needed for exploration and the basis of good relationships with others grows from this security. Feeling liked and lovable is the beginning of liking and being able to love, and the foundation for self-esteem. Touching, holding, talking, and reading to the infant are the most effective spurs to later intellectual and emotional development. It is the parents, primary caregivers, and other family members who should provide this basic development for infants and small children" (Matthews, 1997: 97).

Parents who are knowledgeable and feel confident, worthwhile, and supported are better able to engage in healthy child-rearing practices, understand their role as their child's first and most important teacher, and interact effectively with providers and other parents within the community. Lack of access to parenting information, increased mobility of young families, and a dearth of appropriately designed community-based family programs take a toll on infants and toddlers during their most vulnerable stages of development. This lack of support and isolation from extended family and close friends increase the risk factors of isolation, stress, and maternal depression.

Unlike most professionals, parents are not trained or educated on how to raise children. Parenting techniques are often based on family traditions or guesswork influenced by popular media, which often portray the opposite of what educators or child development experts would recommend. Parents need to understand that the parts of the brain that deal with cognitive processes like thinking and remembering, as well as those that control emotional and social behavior, become permanently formed during the first years of a child's life. They need to be aware that the link between parental involvement and the literacy environment of the home leads to a child's success in school. Getting this information to parents and caregivers during the child's early years is critical.

Our understanding of child development and the influence of the home environment has increased during the past half century. Cultural values have a profound impact on how young children learn to interpret and express their emotions and on the behaviors seen as appropriate in various circumstances. While human emotion is rooted in biology and manifested through temperament, it is also significantly developed in the early years of life in the context of social interactions and relationships. Healthy young children gradually transition from extreme dependence to acquiring competence and self-regulation to manage their attention, behavior, and emotion, all of which take place within the cultural context in which the child lives.

Family-Centered Principles and Practices

During the past two decades, many children's librarians have created a variety of early childhood and parenting programs. Some have gotten involved with family support coalitions or outreach to special family audiences. These activities are an important part of family services, and for these librarians and their libraries, family-centered services will be a further development or an extension of what they are already doing. Some children's librarians, however, are just beginning to see themselves as early childhood educators and family support professionals. For those who are well on their way and those who are just beginning, it will help to understand the underlying principles of family-centered practice and how they apply to library settings. This may influence how a current service is provided or introduce a modification that would make the program or service a more effective family support model.

Respect the Importance and Integrity of the Family Unit

The influence of the family on a child cannot be overestimated. The family is a child's first source of information and the model for how a child experiences relationships. It helps a child begin to communicate and to learn personal and cultural values and beliefs. The family teaches a child how to cope in a complex world and provides a child with a sense of belonging and a foundation for self-esteem.

Family-centered librarians will want to reach and actively engage the parent or caregiver and to recognize the family unit as a child's most important relationship, one that will have the greatest impact on the child's learning and educational experiences as well as the child's attitude toward the public library. The design of programs and the role of librarians within those programs will take into account the importance of the family in the evolution of a young child's outlook and engagement with learning.

Treat Parents as Partners and Facilitate Parent/Professional Collaboration

Public librarians have little one-on-one impact on very young children, but they do have the potential and the opportunity to influence those who do—parents and caregivers. Parents have the greatest knowledge and understanding of their own children. Respecting this knowledge can promote communication, trust, and the kind of partnership in which a parent and librarian work together to improve childhood well-being, family literacy, and early learning in the home. Utilizing the parents' knowledge of the child's current development, temperament, and activity level enhances the librarian's ability to recommend resources and materials that best meet the needs of the individual parent and child.

While this holds true for all families, it is particularly vital for families of children with special needs and other families who are at risk. When librarians elicit parents' input, respond and incorporate parental suggestions, and relate to parents as partners in the planning and delivery of library service, parents are empowered and the quality of library service to children and families rises to a new level.

Provide Complete and Unbiased Information

Babies do not come with manuals. In our mobile society parents may be far from their extended families and lack the support and mentoring of loving and experienced family members. Family lore and commonsense parenting techniques may not provide the optimal level of information on best practices or help parents cope with behavior problems or developmental delays. Many families are reluctant to seek out a child psychologist, educator, or family practitioner and parent education classes are few and far between. Where can parents and caregivers obtain the neutral and nonjudgmental information they need to raise healthy children? For many the answer is—or could be—the public library.

Helping people find needed information is at the core of the public library's basic mission. Offering complete and unbiased resources for parents and adults who work with children enhances the role of the children's librarian, provides the community with the support all families need in raising children, and places the library in a key community-building role.

Develop Policies and Services That Facilitate Family Participation and Learning

Infants and young children cannot visit the library independently and need to be accompanied by a parent or caregiver. Children's librarians legally cannot serve in loco parentis. This combination of factors provides a wonderful opportunity for librarians to serve both the parent or caregiver and the child, focusing on the needs of both. Service that reflects a family approach recognizes that the comfort level of the parent or caregiver will be reflected in the comfort level of the child. Librarians have an opportunity to serve as facilitators of family learning, encouraging, supporting, and mentoring parents and caregivers as they fulfill their role as their child's first and most important teacher.

How parents are treated and the ease (or lack thereof) with which library policies and procedures enable parents and caregivers and very young children to participate in library programs, utilize services, and borrow materials directly impact how and how often a family with very young children will visit the library. Flexibility is key. Libraries need to continually examine policies governing such things as library card applications, borrowing procedures, program registration, inclusion of siblings in early childhood programs, meeting room usage, strollers in the library, and noise levels. Removing barriers and promoting ease of use by families and caregivers with very young children are an ongoing process.

Facilitate Parent-to-Parent Support

The integration of parent services within the children's department of public libraries allows children's librarians the opportunity to assist parents and facilitate the development of relationships and networking among parents. Well-designed early childhood and family spaces provide a common neighborhood place where families can meet, socialize, and get to know one another. They can share information, resources, and practical ideas about parenting and child rearing as well as provide mutual support for their own growth and development. Programs such as the Parent/Child Workshop, parent discussion groups, Mother Goose, and parent-child storytimes can stimulate an exchange of ideas among parents and caregivers that can lead to the formation of local play groups and the development of important and supportive friendships. Having a local referral file for parent support groups within a local community, making parents aware of local chapters of the National Association of Mothers' Centers or Mommy and Me programs, and providing meeting space for peer-to-peer parent groups are all natural extensions of traditional children's services.

Build on Family Strengths and Recognize Cultural Diversity

Family-centered principles recognize that all families have competencies and strengths as well as the capacity to grow and develop. Family-centered libraries provide services for people of all cultures, races, ethnic backgrounds, religions, and abilities in ways that acknowledge, reflect, value, and respect the worth of all individuals and protect and preserve their dignity. This is hardly a new concept for public libraries. Since the late nineteenth century, public libraries have served as portals to our democratic society, providing local, free access to information, materials, services, and programs for all residents. The fundamental characteristics of public libraries are reflected and enhanced by family-centered principles and family support practice. This is particularly true in our growing multicultural society with such a wide variety of diverse family backgrounds and needs.

Establish Linkages with Community Services That Serve Families and Children

When the needs of parents and children extend beyond the realm of library service, librarians can play a crucial role as connectors. If they have established meaningful relationships with families, librarians will often find themselves in a position to help parents identify local resources that can assist them with their parenting needs. Sometimes this information is not readily available. Often, it is the librarian's effort to reach out, build coalitions, and network with other family service providers that makes the difference. Networking and coalition building with other community organizations provide librarians with information about other services that are available for families. Through this kind of intentional effort librarians can position themselves to provide families with the information they need, when they need it.

Efforts to build coalitions and networks can be rewarding not only for the parent in need but also for the coalition partners themselves. Librarians become better informed about community resources and enhance their role as information and referral specialists. Community agency providers learn about the vast resources of the library. In many instances, they become advocates and help lead their families to the library—families who may not use the library or are uncomfortable and unknowledgeable about its many resources.

In addition to being a key link between families and the broader family service community, librarians have the capacity to be critical partners in providing coordination and support for family-serving professionals. Utilizing their skills in collection development, management, and organization and access to resources, reference, and information and referral, librarians can enhance community networks. Libraries serve as natural meeting places, a central place to store materials, and a neutral environment in which to share information within the network and broader community.

Design Developmentally Appropriate Services

When designing services to meet the needs of young children, family-centered librarians will integrate the developmental needs of infants, toddlers, and preschoolers into the library environment. Developmentally appropriate practice informs library services to young children. It is not a rigid set of rules and procedures, but a framework or philosophy of service that guides us in providing services that are child centered. Based on data and information about what children are like at different stages of development, appropriate practice ensures a basic respect for a child's developmental needs and cultural background.

There are basic principles of child development that all professionals who work with children need to understand including the predictability of stages, the optimal periods in development, the role of biological and environmental factors, and the importance of individuality. To offer services within a developmentally appropriate framework, family-centered librarians will look at developmental milestones, the relationship of the child to the parent or caregiver at different ages and stages, the child's understanding of his or her environment and surroundings, and the interplay of library resources within the context of the child's experiences.

Become Engaged in Community Efforts That Support Children and Families

Family support practice strengthens and empowers families and communities to foster the optimal development of children, youth, and adult family members.

Family-centered libraries, in tandem with other community agencies, will incorporate family-centered principles as their base. This shared foundation offers the paradigm shift in human service delivery that encourages agencies to work together and to become more preventative, responsive, and flexible. Together they will create community-based programs that are designed to prevent family problems by strengthening parent-child relationships. The family support movement strives to transform our society into caring communities of citizens that put children and families first and that ensure that all children and families get what they need to succeed.

Underlying precepts for family support practice include:

Staff and families work together in relationships based on equality and respect.

Staff enhances families' capacity to support the growth and development of all family members—adults, youth, and children.

Families are resources to their own members, to other families, to programs, and to communities.

Programs affirm and strengthen families' cultural, racial, and linguistic identities and enhance their ability to function in a multicultural society.

Programs are embedded in their communities and contribute to the community-building process. Programs advocate with families for services and systems that are fair, responsive, and accountable to the families served.

Practitioners work with families to mobilize formal and informal resources to support family development.

Programs are flexible and continually responsive to emerging family and community issues.

Principles of family support are modeled in all program activities, including planning, governance, and administration.

Conclusion

Children grow up in families, which have the greatest influence on how they will grow, learn, and develop. Nurturing child-rearing practices leads to healthy development and positions the child for success in school, work, and life. Parents and caregivers, particularly those with young children, need resources, programs, and spaces where they can go to interact and play with their young children, get information and support in their parenting role, become knowledgeable about child rearing and emergent literacy, and gain a better understanding of their role as their child's first teacher.

Family-centered principles and practice provide a framework for understanding the needs of families and young children. Nothing is absolute when applying principles to practice. Librarians can use this framework to examine their programs and practices and determine whether they enhance or diminish the quality of the child's (and family's) experience within the library. Using the principles, librarians can assess the programs they are currently offering as well as initiate new services and programs. By meshing traditional library service with family support principles and family-centered and developmentally appropriate practice, librarians can maximize the learning process, enhance the effectiveness of the family's and young child's experiences within the library setting, and engage the librarian and library in the broader family support community.

References

Birckmayer, Jennifer. "The Role of Public Libraries in Emergent and Family Literacy." *Zero to Three* 21, no. 3 (January): 24–29, 2001.

"Children's Defense Fund: Leave No Child Behind." Washington, DC. Available: www .childrensdefensefund.org, 2004.

Horsley, Kathryn, et al. *The Science of Early Childhood. A Summary Report of From Neurons to Neighborhoods: The Science of Early Childhood Development* (Washington, DC: National Academy of Sciences). Seattle, WA: Public Health—Seattle and King County, 2000.

Kids Count. Baltimore, MD: Annie E. Casey Foundation, 2003.

Matthews, Virginia. "Kids Can't Wait . . . Library Advocacy Now!" *School Library Journal* 43, no. 3 (March): 97–101, 1997.

National Center for Family Literacy. "Frequently Asked Questions: About Family Literacy." Available: http://famlit.org/FAQ/About/shatisfamilit.cfm, 2004.

Population Reference Bureau. "Tabulations from the Census Bureau's 2002 Current Population Survey (March Supplement)." Available: www.AmeriStat.org, 2003.

Stamm, Jill. "Innovator: Jill Stamm." Interview with Jill Stamm by Marilyn Snell in Blueprint: Ideas for a New Century (September). Washington, DC: Democratic Leadership Council, 1999.

2

Initiating Family-Centered Libraries

Over the last two decades, libraries have experienced extraordinary changes in technology, roles, mission, and competition in the delivery of information and services once considered the exclusive domain of libraries. Competitive forces have led to questioning, altering, and reaffirming the role and value of the public library within the community. Judging from competition generated by the Internet, bookstores, educational institutions, not-for-profit agencies, and recreational resources, librarians can expect that continuing private- and public-sector advances will exert even more pressure on public libraries to respond in new ways to the changing needs and expectations of today's clientele. Though tax supported, libraries must compete proactively with public and private entities, continuously challenge themselves to assert their traditional roles, and examine the reasons why libraries exist and how they must be redefined to continue to exist in the future.

To increase their value, libraries must fully examine the needs of targeted audiences to determine how the library can best satisfy those needs, redefine the role of the library and the librarian based on those needs, and integrate the public library's traditional characteristics and strengths into the modern marketplace of educational, social, and cultural trends. This review process begins with an assessment of the library's competitive strengths and weaknesses relative to the audience they are trying to reach, an analysis of the benefits for both the library and

17

the audience, and the development of a plan that identifies objectives, strategies, and practical activities.

Benefits of Library-Based Family-Centered Services

It is well worth the effort for libraries to invest in family-centered services, not only for the benefit of families and young children, but for both the short-term and long-term effects on the health and vitality of the library as a viable institution. Offering early childhood and parent services, integrating emergent literacy and family support principles and practice, and focusing on reading and school readiness increase the importance and value of the public library within the community. Young children and their caregivers benefit from the welcoming environment and supportive activities that family-centered libraries provide. Using and borrowing library materials, playing and interacting with parents and other adults, and engaging in appropriately designed learning activities enhance brain development and reading readiness in young children. Connecting with families of varying ages, stages, and cultures fosters a sense of community and offers parents an opportunity to engage in conversation with each other and library staff. Becoming comfortable with books and reading and learning to use and value the library at an early age give young children a head start toward success in school.

Prepares Young Children for Success

For children the benefits of early education are beginning to be looked at not only from an educational standpoint but also as an economic investment. Studies conducted in the preschool education field "have calculated a 16 percent real internal rate of return on the financial investment for early childhood development programs, which support the development of language, cognitive skills, and other early learning" (Bohrer, 2004: 203). More and more research suggests that the most critical years for learning are the years just after birth. Brain research confirms that providing babies, toddlers, and preschoolers with a rich learning environment of books, toys, songs, stories, and experience, along with a lot of love and nurture, is crucial to their development. Integrating knowledge about brain research and developmentally appropriate practice within children's services programs adds value to the library as an educational resource for early literacy and school readiness—one often overlooked by the educational establishment.

For parents and caregivers, access to information and services during a child's first and most formative years is critical, particularly information about how everyday activities are linked to developing the skills and habits of literacy. "Programs that help parents provide a solid foundation for their children's cognitive, social, and emotional development have proven dividends. Children achieve more in school, act out less, and need fewer services like special education. Both the cost to educate children and the price we pay for poorly educated adults (in terms of welfare, healthcare, and crime) are lowered when resources are allocated to early childhood development" (Bohrer, 2004: 203). Libraries that invest in and train children's librarians in mentoring, coaching, and teaching parents and caregivers about learning strategies that support early literacy add value to an already popular service.

Increases the Effectiveness of Libraries

Libraries that invest in services for young children and families enhance overall library effectiveness. Expanding the age range and developing more programs and services for families add numbers to the library's attendance and circulation records. Reaching out to diverse families attracts new cultural groups that are moving into the community, promotes the library's role as a community center, and creates a powerful image of the library as a leader in early learning, emergent and family literacy, and family support. Working collaboratively with parents, caregivers, and family service providers enhances the librarians' role among professionals who work with families and increases their value as educational and community-building partners. Children who learn to use the library at a young age are most likely to bring their children to the library when they become parents, ensuring ongoing and future support for public libraries.

Positions the Library in the Preschool Market

Libraries have an opportunity to position themselves in the preschool marketplace but need to move aggressively during the next decade. K–12 educators already have targeted the preschool market as evidenced by Universal Pre-K, which is expanding throughout the country. Childcare providers, a necessity for working families, also claim the attention of young children and their families on a daily basis. Restaurant chains, parks, museums, and discovery centers are popping up in many communities and offer fun places to go with young children. Public libraries need to establish their position as a community place for families with very young children to visit and use as an interactive learning space. Children and parents need the kinds of learning resources that the public library can provide, along with stimulating programs to encourage use of these resources.

Librarians need to look for ways to increase recognition of the library as a center for early literacy and parent information. They need to take on leadership roles and form partnerships with community organizations to make the library's early literacy efforts more visible. By becoming more involved with the local school district, childcare, and family support agencies and organizations, the library can establish itself as an integral partner in the development and education of young children. For these partners, the library can transform its image.

Increases Political and Financial Support

Libraries that expand the scope of children's services to embrace the entire family as well as childcare providers often attract additional backing for their already popular services and gain a critical source of political support for the children's department. "In ranking or prioritizing services, public libraries would be loath to cut services to children even in an austerity budget. Service to children is essential, popular and an emotionally charged issue. Family–centered services have the same cost benefit as children's services. They are essential, popular and emotionally or politically important services for all public or government institutions. Selecting family services as a role or strengthening children's services to include service to parents and agencies that serve parents, increases the political worth of the public library" (Feinberg and Feldman, 1996: 2).

Educating adult users on the importance of libraries to families increases the value of the public library in a community. It is not unusual for children's departments to acquire more prestige among administrators, legislators, and funders when the department broadens its audience base and focuses on very young children, their parents and caregivers, and family support providers. Helping families raise healthy children who are ready for school, supporting parents in their role as first teacher, and providing a dynamic community learning space for infants, toddlers, and preschoolers are messages that resonate with supporters of children's services. Parents and providers serve as a solid source of support for the children's librarian and often advocate for more funding and resources for children's services within the library and with outside funders. Bond issues, millage increases, and annual budget votes often get passed with the help of parents and those people who care about children.

Community and family foundations are attracted to the universality and stability of public libraries, particularly if the library is committed to early childhood literacy and parent support as building blocks of community development. Legislators and elected officials, who are beginning to understand that young children's learning is critical to the children's success in school, want to provide families with local resources to help them raise healthy babies and preschoolers. They often jump on the bandwagon when libraries espouse the need for community places for families with young children that emphasize early learning, family literacy, and school readiness. Corporations are increasingly interested in the future workforce and are attracted to what public libraries can offer (for very little money) in the way of preparing even our youngest citizens for future employment.

Grant writing to secure corporate and foundation support can provide potential new revenue for libraries that focus on the needs of families and young children. As ideal institutional partners, whether as initiators or as collaborators in the grant writing process, libraries:

   Provide access to families, public space, varying hours, circulating and online resources, and programming
   Are committed to serving local families who reflect the diverse cultures within the community
   Are stable, well-respected community-based institutions
   Employ librarians with a blend of analytical and customer service skills who bring well-appreciated expertise to the art and science of initiating, writing, and executing the grant process

Traditional Assets as Underpinnings for Family-Centered Services

Clearly the evidence points to public libraries as having utilitarian and educational value for people and communities. They "serve everyone in an open and accessible manner. Their buildings are often at the geographic center of their communities, often feature evening and weekend hours of operation, and are generally physically accessible to those with disabilities. People of all ages, races, socioeconomic backgrounds, and interests meet together in public libraries. Most public libraries have meeting rooms that are used by a wide variety of community groups. Public libraries are a primary source of information on local history and culture and present special programs on these topics. Public libraries work with other organizations to celebrate and improve community life" (McCabe, 2001: 104).

These traditional assets fit well with family-centered services. That parents and children can use the library for no fee at the point of service, that all families are welcome to participate, that involvement in programs and services is voluntary, that the librarian is trained in nonjudgmental and neutral behaviors, and that the library is mandated to serve all ages underscore the concept that traditional library strengths are a good fit with emergent literacy and family support practice.

Builds upon the Role of the Children's Librarian

Historically, children's services focused on the child and did not necessarily include parents, caregivers, and family support providers. Family-centered services stretch the boundaries of the traditional children's department by expanding the age and scope of audiences targeted. "The role of the public library in early childhood learning, parent education and family–centered service empowers librarians to become gatekeepers of the family literacy movement and initiators of the lifelong learning process. 'Reading Begins at Birth,' 'Born to Read,' 'the Preschoolers' Door to Learning,' and 'Every Child Ready to Read' are some of the common themes that run through the public library world and underlie the development of today's service to families and young children. The images of early childhood educator, parent resource and information specialist, and family support professional must be nurtured by the library profession. Public libraries must not only be recognized for the historic contribution that children's librarians, in partnership with parents, have played in 'giving birth to readers,' but beyond this, for a major role in developing language, thinking skills and confidence in children. Library resources can help give context and perspective to young lives" (Feinberg and Feldman, 1996: xv).

Enhances the Role of the Library as a Community Partner

"The history of libraries is a history of collaboration; libraries began as citizens shared their books with each other. The past has been sharing with other libraries and their users. The future is collaboration with other organizations, a more difficult endeavor because of the differences among institutions. These differences range from values and assumptions to policies and procedures. Despite differences, ways must be found to work with other organizations and professions in our quest to create public value while remaining true to the values and expertise of libraries and librarians. This need for collaboration is founded in the understanding of communities as holistic environments, as social systems in which we are part of an integrated whole" (Martin, 2003: 72).

Family-centered services require that the children's librarian work collaboratively with other early childhood and family support providers toward the common good of healthy families and literate children. To assure that children enter school ready to learn, libraries and other agencies must work cooperatively and actively involve parents in the planning, implementation, and evaluation processes.

Many benefits accrue to the library and partnering organizations when they participate in coalition building, networking, and collaboration, including program enhancement, professional development through cooperative training, reaching new and hard-to-reach audiences, promotion of programs and services, joint grant writing, sharing of information and resources, and the creation of new products and services. Establishing relationships with other helping professionals fosters personal satisfaction and helps partners to understand their jobs and their institutions in a broader perspective. Interactions of this type help the librarian and the library to grow and develop into a dynamically innovative and interactive institution.

Ensures the Role of the Library as a Community Center

There is a critical need for places that foster public dialogue and informal social interaction. The deterioration of local community life has increased the importance of those few institutions that continue to serve as community meeting places. Increasingly, public libraries are seen as these gathering places or centers. They require no means test, fees, or purchasing of merchandise, as is the case at a coffee shop or bookstore, and provide opportunities for people who do not necessarily travel in the same occupational, social, political, or economic circles to meet and greet each other. People are looking for social moorings, and libraries—stable, welcoming, venerable, but also modern—make good candidates. Libraries are associated with education and culture and understood as communal property but not too associated with government (Molz and Dain, 1999: 205–6).

Interactive Spaces for Families and Young Children: For parents, caregivers, and children, interactive library space emphasizes learning, exploring, and discovering while having fun. Interactive library space is noisy and free from restrictions and reflects all developmental age levels. Children meet and observe other children. Parents interact with their children in a nonjudgmental educational environment, observe their children's learning styles, and casually meet other adults with young children from the neighborhood. This type of communal space reduces the sense of isolation that parents often experience in today's communities, provides a comfort zone where families of diverse backgrounds can interact, and serves as an indoor learning park or recreation center that is safe and appropriately designed for young children.

Meeting Rooms: As an integral function of most public libraries, the meeting room provides space to enable people to come together. As a function of family-centered services, the library's meeting rooms will go beyond traditional children's programming such as storytimes, movies, magicians, and puppet shows. Registering for child health insurance, sponsoring a fingerprinting session with the police department, using a social services provider to provide a parent education program, providing access to immunizations with health department staff, and conducting a childcare fair with local providers are just some of the many services that may be offered. The library staff in conjunction with other family-serving organizations may use a meeting room for local speakers on topics of interest to professionals and parents or jointly organize a conference that focuses on a particular need of families. Local family support agencies and organizations may use the space for their meetings and staff training or partner with the library to provide their social services onsite. The library may even provide office space for a partnering organization or make space available for displays of their literature and program offerings.

Initial Plans for Getting Started

Libraries that decide to invest in early childhood and family support services will need to compete for the time and attention of the parent and child and aggressively market the library as an influential and valuable service provider. Moving decisively means first assessing the competitors and potential partners. Libraries that intend to become family centered will need to assess the recreational, educational, and cultural activities that are available within their communities, decide on what services the library can provide because they are either not provided at all or they are only available for a fee, look at the skills of current staff and their willingness to change, and create new or parallel services that complement what is already available.

There are many issues to consider, but most important, librarians need to recognize that family-centered services develop over time and often begin first by readjusting what services and resources are already being offered. New services need to be introduced gradually and with a lot of consideration and thought. Satisfying demand and sustainability are major keys to success.

Understand the Audience and Competition

As a first step, the library needs to determine the number of families with young children that reside in the community; how many have library cards and use (or do not use) the library; what barriers may exist for families; strategies to identify, locate, and reach out to families who do not use the library; and what other early childhood and family-serving organizations work within the community.

Work schedules, lack of transportation, cultural values, preconceived notions about libraries, and lack of understanding about the importance of early learning present barriers that libraries need to accommodate or overcome with parents and caregivers.

Many of our potential clients don't know that the library has anything worthwhile for them; others don't come in because they work long hours, are overwhelmed with problems, or have no transportation. Most of the families we don't reach include children and old people. We often learn, to our surprise, that many of these families feel afraid, even threatened, by the library. They see it as not being for them and having the potential to show them up, reject them, or even get them into trouble with the law. Yet these families desperately need the parenting programs, the literacy programs, the early childhood programs and others. Libraries could empower them to help their children learn (McCurdy, 2001: 37).

Before diving into family-centered services, the library must survey the community to determine other existing family resources. Preschool and childcare settings, community schools, family resource centers, bookstores, parks, beaches, discovery centers, parenting programs, museums, restaurant chains, television, and computers actively compete for a child's time and attention. These same resources provide the library with an essential list of potential partners. To start a search:

Look in the yellow pages, search the Web, and contact the school district and other local agencies that serve families and young children. Make a list of programs and resources that are available.

Drive or walk around the neighborhood to locate parks, commercial establishments, or cultural institutions that provide space for children.

Ask parents who are currently using the library where else they go with their children.

Find out if there are any local or regional family or children's coalitions in existence and see how the library can get involved.

Contact local family service agencies. Visit their offices. Discuss potential cooperative programs, shared training services, and mutual promotional opportunities.

Examine Current Library Services for Families and Young Children

Another beginning step is for the library to examine its current mix of programs, services, collections, and other resources that are being offered for families and young children. Are there any programs for babies? Toddlers? Preschoolers? Based on developmentally appropriate practice, are they well designed? How are attendance records? Are parents welcome? Is demand being filled or are there waiting lists? What collections does the library currently have for babies and toddlers? Is there a special space for parents to interact with babies and toddlers? Are there toys and early childhood computers available?

After an initial assessment, librarians may see the need to increase customer convenience despite the fact that libraries exist in only one or a few locations within the community. Providing programs in other locations such as schools or community centers or offering programs in the evenings or on weekends may increase use by working parents or families that have only one car. Assembling materials that create a semblance of the program or providing parents with guidelines on early childhood milestones and literacy skills is another way to reach those families that cannot attend a specially designed program. The key concept is to consider "place" from the users' point of view.

Look at Staff Skills and Education

It is important to recognize that some children's librarians may be uncomfortable serving adult patrons and may have chosen the field of children's services to limit adult interactions. Some do not understand the role of play and social interaction as a first step to reading nor do they see the role of the library in integrating these activities in the library setting. Support staff members may get annoyed at crying babies and noisy spaces. The adult services librarian may claim parents, caregivers, and family service providers as segments of their targeted adult audiences. If a library has a tight budget, departments can struggle over the amount of money for materials and staff. The popularity of family services may cause resentment among library staff members.

In addition to overcoming these attitudes (which may or may not exist), the library staff needs to take a proactive approach to gaining knowledge about early childhood development, parenting, and family service programming. Utilizing traditional research skills to locate reading materials, the library staff can easily begin the self-education process. After their initial outreach to community resource providers, librarians may be able to identify several professionals who have expertise and are willing to share their knowledge with library staff. This could be the best time to begin the sharing process between agencies. After the library staff gets involved with local or regional coalitions and networks, many cooperative training exchanges can occur, some for free and some for a small honorarium. In any case, take advantage of local expertise and experience. They are invaluable.

Consider New Ways to Promote Existing Services

During the initial stages, the administration and children's department may need to look at ways in which the library communicates now and what new strategies may need to be employed. Changing the image of the library can be an uphill battle depending on how the public views the institution and what types of customer service and public relations resources are already in place. Newsletters, brochures, flyers, bulletin board notices, and press releases may need to be redesigned to create a family-friendly look and feel. Speaking with parents who already use the library is an effective initial strategy for finding out where local families "hang out."

Local agencies and organizations provide mutual promotional opportunities. Partners who are familiar with library programs can, and often do, encourage their families to use the library. In some cases, they may bring the families to the library themselves. It is important for children's librarians to form relationships with agency providers and educate them on the resources of the library. Often, the providers themselves lack knowledge about library resources and it is only through personal contact and relationship building that this image—over time—changes. Likewise, the librarian needs to be knowledgeable about what each agency has to offer. In this way, duplication is avoided and usage of resources will increase.

Budget for Family-Centered Services

Libraries that decide to focus on family-centered services soon recognize that, in most cases, the need is great and demand will ensue. Be prepared. Libraries that have moved in the direction of early childhood and family services have either re-allocated their budgets or increased their budgets through grant writing or garnering political support.

To begin the funding process, it may be enough to reallocate current resources, for example, to devote a portion of the current book budget for toys, to reallocate money from the adult collection to provide parenting materials for the children's room, or to identify funds from the budget to provide training opportunities for children's staff. It can be beneficial to assess the costs of programs and services—for both the library and the patron—and how they are currently being used. Librarians may need to adjust program offerings, the times services are offered, where they are offered, and the types of collections, programs, and services that are most convenient and most needed.

From the library's perspective, children's programming costs staff time, materials, and space allocation. From the patron's perspective, the costs may include any or all of these factors: time and transportation to bring the child, aggravation created by a long wait in line or no parking, time of day that is inconvenient, or a room that is too small or too noisy to enjoy the program. Reviewing each program and service in this manner provides strategic knowledge to the librarians about what might prevent a family from returning to the library or a potential customer from attending the program or why attendance figures are low. It may also lead to the types of programs and services that need to be offered, eliminated, or increased.

The most critical element of developing family-centered services is found in the actual quality of the customer service provided as resources are developed and subsequently offered to the community. It is important to remember that early childhood and family services are very popular, often take center stage, and create demands that must be met. Parents and caregivers will request that programs be repeated or that more toys and learning materials be made available. If they like the programs and services (which inevitably they will), information about the program will spread very quickly by word of mouth. It may be best to offer fewer services well done rather than a wide variety that the library cannot afford to fully support.

Eventually, to be successful, there will need to be an increase in the children's services' budget. Departments will need additional resources (collections, staff, public floor space, meeting room space) to satisfy their larger customer base. Adding shelves for a parents' collection, providing adult seating in the children's room, and setting up early learning stations (dollhouse, train, puppet stage, puzzles, blocks, dress-up corner, writing center) and computers with dedicated early childhood software often require a fresh look at space allocation throughout the entire library. More programming may require increased money for parent education and early childhood resource professionals. When children's services expand to include parents, caregivers, and family service providers, the department often needs additional staff to satisfy the reference and programming needs that ensue.

Conclusion

Public libraries are and have always been a cornerstone of the community. In today's society they need to look closely at what their mission is, the roles they need to play, and the audiences they need to reach. Understanding their audiences and creating value in the eyes of those audiences are paramount. How public libraries satisfy their audiences' needs is pivotal to their future success.

Among the library's targeted audiences, and perhaps the most important, are young children, parents, caregivers, and family support providers. By designing welcoming and appropriate spaces for infants, toddlers, preschoolers, parents, and caregivers, libraries can reinvent themselves as exciting destinations for families. By integrating early childhood and family support principles and early brain research, librarians can become specialists within their local communities on emergent literacy, early learning, and reading and school readiness. Making effective use of traditional assets, libraries are especially beneficial to parents and community groups that work with families.

Family-centered services can start very modestly, but in most cases will result in a larger budget for an expanded children's services department. This is the point at which the cycle begins. Popular and political support for the services will hopefully result in successful increases in the operating budget or point to an increase in grant-funded opportunities. By considering all of the information outlined above—promoting the benefits of family-centered services for families and libraries, emphasizing the assets that already exist in public libraries, and planning for the gradual transformation of children's services into a family-centered department to enhance the role of the library within the community—libraries and librarians can make it happen.

References

Bohrer, Clara N. "The Economics of Literacy." *Public Libraries* 43, no. 4 (July/August): 203, 2004.

Feinberg, Sandra, and Sari Feldman. *Serving Families and Children Through Partnerships.* New York: Neal-Schuman, 1996.

Martin, R. S. "Keynote Address: What Is Our Leading Edge?" *Library Administration and Management* 17, no. 2 (Spring): 71–73, 2003.

McCabe, R. B. *Civic Librarianship: Renewing the Social Mission of the Public Library.* Lanham, MD, and London: Scarecrow Press, 2001.

McCurdy, Virginia M. "Head 'Em Up, Move 'Em Out: Four Blessed Bossies in Our Way." *American Libraries* 31, no. 11 (December): 36–38, 2000.

Molz, R. K., and P. Dain. *Civic Space/Cyberspace: The American Public Library in the Information Age.* Cambridge, MA: MIT Press, 1999.

3

Assessing Staff Competencies and Skills

Adopting family-centered library services is a gradual and developmental process during which staff and administration undergo a philosophical change in attitude and behavior. While a library may have effective policies, resources, and collections and offer a variety of programs for babies, toddlers, and parents, these are just a beginning. Library staff and administration will need to have a genuine understanding of and commitment to family-centered principles and practices that can best be achieved through a reexamination of attitudes, expectations, skills, and competencies. Children's librarians, generalists assigned to children's departments, managers of large children's departments, or direct service staff from other library departments have an opportunity to become role models and advocates for family-centered services. This chapter focuses on the competencies and skills the library staff needs to fulfill this role and outlines some training and professional development resources that will help to attain them.

Guidelines for Family Support Professionals

All human service professionals, as well as professionals (such as police) who have regular contact with families, greatly benefit from training in human growth and development and in understanding the responsibilities of professionals to promote family development and the integrity of the family unit. Professionals also have some responsibility to help parents deal with the institutions that influence child and family development.

Trainings such as those mentioned above increase staff capacity to work effectively with parents. The following guidelines emerged from the family support movement and are especially relevant to libraries implementing family-centered services.

1. Professionals need to be responsive and sensitive but not aggressive about offering their advice and information to parents. Professionals need both preservice and in-service training which includes the following elements: how to avoid cultural bias, how to increase sensitivity to the needs of parents and children—including the special needs of nontraditional family types such as single-parent families, and how to enhance parents' understanding of the operation of institutions and how to improve the relationship among institutions, professionals, and parents.

2. In addition to enhancing the roles of professionals in parent education, policies should encourage development of community support systems. Family support professionals need to serve as family advocates by identifying actual needs of parents and communities and by trying to identify and delineate what support systems are already available.

3. Use of media and electronic resources needs to be expanded to provide widespread information on subjects of concern to parents, for example, health, nutrition, education, and so on.

4. Schools and libraries need to take a proactive role in providing parent education.

5. Evaluation and reporting requirements should be built into all programs providing for parent education so that the strengths and weaknesses of various models are consciously addressed and documented.

6. The development of new roles and jobs for professionals working with families and the creation of new models of parent involvement in public and private programs need to be undertaken.

It Begins with Attitude: Staff Self-Assessment

When embarking on any new service model, a critical first step is to conduct an assessment of resources currently in place. What we look for shapes what we see. This is true in our work with families and it is also true in how we view our libraries. By applying a family-centered service philosophy, such an assessment would utilize an asset model, focusing on existing strengths on which to build, rather than a deficit model which focuses on what is missing. This chapter focuses on the most important resource a library possesses: its staff.

What are the staff resources available? How does the staff relate to very young children, parents, and caregivers? Is the staff adaptable to change and flexible about accepting new ideas? What are the barriers to the staff that must be overcome?

Every staff member brings his or her personality, life experience, and comfort level to the workplace. For some, adopting family-centered services will require major change. Others may view it simply as an expansion of current services that represents some changes in program planning, service delivery, training, and evaluation. No matter where the staff is on the continuum of family-centered service development, some degree of change is inevitable. Change is never easy, especially change in perceptions and attitudes.

To begin the process, librarians serving families will have to honestly assess their perceptions, attitudes, and behaviors:

Does the staff believe all families have competencies and strengths as well as the capacity to grow and change?

Can librarians shift their view of parents from recipients of service to one of true partners?

Do librarians see themselves as role models, mentors, coaches, and teachers for early literacy?

Does the staff see the need for and benefits of working collaboratively with other family-serving agencies?

Does the staff believe that libraries have a role to play in providing family support and building community? What role should that be?

Personal Attitude Checklist

The Personal Attitude Checklist (Figure 3-1) and the corresponding Response to Staff Issues and Concerns which follows serve as catalysts for the exploration of feelings and attitudes and guide staff members toward an understanding and awareness of their own feelings and attitudes regarding family-centered services.

Response to Staff Issues and Concerns

Attitude: As a librarian, I am not sure it is the library's responsibility to ensure children enter school ready and able to learn—isn't this the job of early childhood educators? Most libraries consider literacy a major objective and one of their significant roles to help children and adults learn to speak, read, and write as part of the larger community-wide network of literacy supports. An essential mission of public libraries is to ensure that young children receive services and support that help them prepare for success in school and become lifelong learners. Children who enter school ready to learn have experiences rich in language, listening, play, and print in the home and within the community. Since the 1960s, public libraries have nurtured this readiness by providing age-appropriate literature and programs. Family-centered services expand and heighten this mission by providing a holistic model beginning when a child is born. Family-centered services in-

3-1:   Personal Attitude Checklist

		AGREE	DISAGREE
1.	As a librarian, I'm not sure it's the library's responsibility to ensure children enter school ready and able to learn—isn't this the job of early childhood educators?	_____	_____
2.	I became a librarian because I care about children and books. If I had wanted to be an early childhood or parent educator, I would have become a teacher.	_____	_____
3.	If my library embraces family-centered services, the activities and noise level may be disturbing to other library users.	_____	_____
4.	I became a children's librarian because I want to work with children. I'm uncomfortable interacting with parents and having them attend the programs.	_____	_____
5.	My first priority must be to serve families already frequenting the library. This leaves little or no time to participate in coalitions and engage in outreach activities.	_____	_____
6.	I treat all families, regardless of age, education, language, and economics with equal respect.	_____	_____
7.	Including parents in the planning, implementation, and evaluation of programs and services is not realistic for public libraries.	_____	_____

tegrate and enhance the resources and expertise of family-serving community agencies, the library, and parents and caregivers to ensure that *all* children have the quality early learning experiences necessary to enter school ready and able to learn.

Attitude: I became a librarian because I care about children and books. If I had wanted to be an early childhood or parent educator, I would have become a teacher. Teaching and learning are not activities confined to a classroom. Learning begins at birth and people of all ages are continually learning in all types of environments. Librarians have always played a major role in lifelong learning. Through reference interviews, information and referral, reading guidance, programs, material and information displays, and instructional workshops, librarians have served as educators. Children's librarians in particular provide early childhood and parent education—during programs and one-on-one on the public floor—by providing access to and guidance in the use of age-appropriate learning materials, modeling enjoyable and effective early literacy activities, and imparting information to parents on how activities assist children in gaining specific skills.

Thanks to recent advances in neuroscience, we now know how young brains develop and how early experiences influence that development. This knowledge provides an opportunity for librarians to assess their programs and services, identify those elements already in place that support early brain development, and incorporate new elements based on the latest research. In addition to offering developmentally appropriate programs, librarians are in a key position to share this information with parents and caregivers, forming a natural bridge between theory and practice, research and application. According to Dr. Jill Stamm, president of the New Directions Institute for Early Infant Brain Development, "Librarians are 'middlemen' between scientists/neurologists and parents and daycare providers" (Stamm, 2003). By providing programs rooted in research, sharing the research behind these programs with parents and caregivers, and modeling ways to put research into practice, librarians maximize their impact as coaches, mentors, and educators.

Attitude: If my library embraces family-centered services, the activities and noise level may be disturbing to other library users. Many public places have become more "family friendly" in the past two decades. It is not uncommon to see specially designed spaces for families with young children at airports, museums, and other public facilities. When young children are engaged in enjoyable, age-appropriate activities, they are more content and, in most cases, less noisy and demanding. Libraries often offer programs for babies and toddlers in segregated meeting rooms but may lack an appropriately designed learning space on the public floor. Carving out an area for families encourages interactive learning with young children, provides a gathering place for parents and caregivers, and acts as a visible venue to educate adults on the important role libraries play in providing family support and encouraging early literacy development. It may be better to provide a quiet space for adult users and students, reversing the idea that the entire library is a quiet place and furthering the concept of the library as a community learning center.

Attitude: I became a children's librarian because I want to work with children. I'm uncomfortable interacting with parents and having them attend the programs. Parents and caregivers are children's first and most important teachers and as such impact a child's learning much more than any program provided by the library. Literacy begins at home and it is the home and childcare settings that libraries need to impact. Research indicates that immersing children in pleasurable language experiences results in increased brain capacity that prepares them for later reading and writing. It also indicates children learn best through routine and repetition in a secure, loving, and nurturing atmosphere, and parents and caregivers who enjoy books together with children help those children develop an attitude toward books and reading that will likely have a positive effect later in life. Library programs in isolation have minimal direct or long-term impact on very young children. By shifting the focus from child-centered to family-centered, library programs can more positively influence the knowledge and behaviors of parents and have a profound and lasting impact on the social, emotional, language, and cognitive development of young children.

Attitude: My first priority must be to serve families already frequenting the library. This leaves little or no time to participate in coalitions and engage in outreach activities. When a library decides to reach out to a new audience, some staff members feel it is taking resources away from those patrons already using the library. This was most likely true when libraries first began to serve children and share resources with adult services. Today few would question the benefits of providing library service to children. In fact, in addition to serving children within the library, it is common for the library staff to reach children through class visits, programs, and presentations at agencies that serve children such as schools, preschools, and recreation centers. Children's staff members eagerly collaborate with school personnel to coordinate and maximize the impact of programs such as summer reading clubs and homework help.

Outreach to and collaborations with agencies and organizations serving young children and families, particularly those from hard-to-reach or at-risk populations, are essential for quality family-centered library services. Collaborations and partnerships enable libraries to reach a broader segment of the community and often enhance and expand the programs and services being offered to all families—those already frequenting the library as well as new users. These outreach efforts reinforce the library as a significant and vital institution and solidify its role as a key player in community development. Through outreach and coalition building, libraries gain prestige in their partnering capacities, are recognized as a place to meet and offer services, and are better understood as a place of access, a public venue in which all families can interact and learn.

Attitude: I treat all families, regardless of age, education, language, and economics, with equal respect. This is an ideal that every person working with families must constantly work toward. The nature of public libraries is one of neutrality, acceptance, and respect for individuals. Librarians pride themselves on being nonjudgmental and providing equal access to users. It is important, however, to be aware that, as human beings, we perceive the world through our own individual lenses, which are colored by our values, belief systems, and life experiences. When working with families and family situations that differ from our own orientation and experiences, librarians must be aware of their inner lenses and how they may inadvertently have a negative impact on building relationships with families. A checklist, adapted from the National MultiCultural Institute's Cultural Influences on Communication Worksheet as presented at the Family Support America Conference workshop, "Envisioning Cultural Competency" (2004), provides a framework to begin this process (see Figure 3-2).

Attitude: Including parents in the planning, implementation, and evaluation of programs and services is not realistic for public libraries. While librarians may not identify it as such, they have been responding to parental input since service for children began. Informal conversations with parents have provided information on such things as service needs and program interests and feedback on such issues as the best time to schedule programs or new books to order. Information parents share about their child's temperament, interests, and abilities influences interac-

3-2:   Cultural Influences on Communication Checklist

I get uncomfortable when someone:

___ Speaks a language other than English in the workplace.
___ Speaks English with a foreign accent.
___ Does not take initiative.
___ Agrees with everything I say, even if he/she doesn't understand or agree with me.
___ Constantly challenges me.
___ Stands too close to me during a conversation.
___ Stands too far away from me during a conversation.
___ Fails to acknowledge what I say or show understanding.
___ Insists on bringing the entire family to all programs.
___ Male answers questions for the female.
___ Is never on time for programs.
___ Does not make eye contact.
___ Speaks very softly.
___ Speaks very loudly.
___ Giggles and smiles at "inappropriate" times.

tions and can be a key factor in whether or not the child and family have a positive library experience.

In addition to informal input, many libraries utilize structured information-gathering techniques such as program evaluation questionnaires, community surveys, and focus groups. Engaging parents in the process by eliciting and utilizing their input lets them know they are valued and important to the library and the community. We all recognize young children do not come to the library by themselves. Parents make a conscious decision to bring them. With so many demands and so little time, that decision is often based on the perceived value and enjoyment of the library experience for the child and parent and whether the program fits into the family's schedule. The more informed and engaged parents are, the more likely they will develop positive perceptions of library activities. This is particularly important for families unfamiliar with a library who may not feel comfortable. Engaging parents in library activities empowers them and increases their comfort level when utilizing library services and programs. For libraries wanting to develop quality programs and services, soliciting parents' input is essential for success.

The public library has long been dubbed the "people's university," providing access to the knowledge people need to succeed in our society. As early as the 1900s librarians were reaching out to new Americans by bringing baskets of books to families living in urban ghettos, helping them learn to read, write, and speak English. The connection between literacy and one's economic well-being and quality of life has long been evident. It is even more so today, in our constantly changing technological society. Libraries are in a unique position to support families in developing strong relationships between parents and their young children, nurturing parents in their role of child's first teacher and supporting adults in their own lifelong learning. The results are stronger, more self-sufficient families, children who start school ready and able to learn, and confident, capable parents who are true partners in their children's education—all hallmarks of healthy communities.

Quality Indicator Assessment Tool

The Quality Indicator Assessment Tool for Librarians (Feinberg and Feldman, 1996: 215) is an example of a survey that assesses staff attitudes and includes qualities that are most relevant to public libraries serving families (see Figure 3-3). This assessment tool features quality indicators of the current status of individual staff strengths as well as current attitudes regarding the importance of working with parents and community agencies. By matching items of importance to current status, this tool can help identify areas of concern in ensuring that family services develop or continue within a family-centered context, with strong parent involvement and interagency coordination.

Competencies for Family-Centered Services

The introduction to Competencies for Librarians Serving Children in Public Libraries states, "The future of service to children depends on advocacy and professional development. As society changes, so does the public library, and so must the public librarian. Professional growth and development is a career-long process" (Association of Library Service to Children, 1999). Librarians who pursue the development of family-centered services require a broad knowledge base and a specific set of skills. Utilizing the following knowledge-based competencies and skills-based competencies listed, librarians can determine if they require additional training, have achieved competency, or have the ability to train others.

Knowledge-Based Competencies

Knowledge of Clients: Identifying and understanding the characteristics of target audiences are the first steps in developing any new service. Family-centered services focus on four main client groups, which are outlined below and more fully described in later chapters.

VERY YOUNG CHILDREN BEGINNING AT BIRTH: An understanding of the stages of early child development helps the library staff to design appropriate programs and services. Knowledge about social, cognitive, emotional, and physical development; the latest research on brain development; developmentally appropriate policies and practices; and new ideas on space design, furniture and equipment, and quality early learning materials is critical to effective family-centered services.

3-3:   Quality Indicator Assessment Tool

CS=CURRENT STATUS:
1=a strength; 2=needs strengthening; 3=not a strength, would like; 4= not a priority

I=IMPORTANCE:
1=very important; 2=important; 3=somewhat important; 4=not important

	Quality Indicator	
WORKING WITH PARENTS	CS	I
1. Provide parent(s) with pertinent information on programs and services.____		
2. Give parents written materials about the library.____		
3. Establish rapport, giving ample opportunity for parent(s) to ask questions.____		
4. Interact with families in a manner that is respectful of individual and cultural diversity.____		
5. Offer parent(s) choices in programs for their children and themselves.____		
6. Assist parents in obtaining information and services that the library cannot provide.____		
7. Utilize good communication skills (e.g. active listening, questioning, checking of understanding) to develop partnerships with parents.____		
9. Facilitate parent(s) participation in planning for new library services and evaluating existing services.____		
10. Ensure that parent(s) can participate in all programs available for their children.____		
11. Share information, knowledge and skills with families to help them become more knowledgeable, skilled and confident.____		
12. Provide services that reflect parent's preferences for type, location, duration, and frequency.____		
13. Offer parent(s) choices about level of participation in services.____		
14. Offer parent to parent services not only parent-child services.____		
15. Minimize procedures and policies that block parent and child participation.____		
16. Have written policies and plans that support family centered philosophy and practice. ____		
WORKING WITH OTHER AGENCIES	CS	I
1. Share information about formal and informal services for families.____		
2. Participate in the coordination of services.____		
3. Work collaboratively to address service gaps.____		
4. Recognize that parent(s) assume or want to assume responsibility for the services they need.____		
5. Strengthen information and referral service to address family needs.____		
6. Provide services that reflect the agency need for information.____		
7. Offer agencies choice in their level of participation.____		
8. Minimize policy and procedure that block agency participation.____		

Adapted from "Self Assessment and the Change Process: Applications in Early Intervention," Waisman Center UAP, University of Wisconsin, Madison.

PARENTS AND CAREGIVERS: The knowledge and behaviors of parents and caregivers have the greatest impact on young children's development. As the focus of library programs and services is broadened from child centered to family centered, it is important that parents and caregivers be viewed as a client group. Librarians are in the unique position to nurture and support parents, but to do this more effectively, they will work toward understanding the stages of parent development, parenting schemas and styles, the social, emotional, and informational needs of parents, and family and adult literacy and learning styles.

SPECIAL POPULATIONS: In addition to typical family needs and concerns, families with special circumstances have needs and concerns related to their particular situation. Families that have children or parents with disabilities, immigrants, teen parents, foster parents, and relatives parenting young children are some examples of families with special needs. Knowledge of special education laws, family cultural values and support systems, and an understanding of the families' social, emotional, and informational needs are vital when working with families with special needs.

PROFESSIONALS WORKING WITH YOUNG CHILDREN AND FAMILIES: Family support providers are potential library partners, collaborators, coalition builders, and clients. By gaining an understanding of the missions, goals, and needs of family-serving agencies and individual providers, librarians can design services to support agencies, meet individual provider needs, and participate in strong, collaborative relationships and information and referral networks to better serve young children and families.

Knowledge of the Missions and Goals of the Library and Community: A library is not an isolated entity but is part of the larger community it serves. Knowledge of the vision and goals of the broader community and how the library's mission and goals help to support them is needed. In turn, children's services will want to be aware of how their goals support the overall library mission and goals and fit in with the vision and goals of the larger community.

Knowledge of Family Literacy: Family literacy is more than parents reading to young children. Family-centered librarians will want to have an understanding of family literacy which includes supporting adults in their own learning, nurturing communication activities between parents and their children, respecting the variety of learning styles and preferences unique to both children and adults, and strategies to respond to these varied modes of learning.

Skill-Based Competencies

Working with infants, toddlers, young children, parents, caregivers, and other family service providers requires unique skill sets that are complementary to but different from those generally needed to work with older children and requires interactive skills that go beyond working with one's own children and library staff. Family-centered librarians demonstrate the following skills:

Communication, including active listening skills
Communication facilitation
Problem solving
Advocacy and assisting people to identify and secure services
Networking, coordination, and collaboration
Assessing community and library services for young children and families
Presentation and instruction
Facilitating parent-child activities
Facilitating parent support groups
Program planning
Program evaluation
Incorporating research into practice
Grant writing
Collection development and management
Electronic research
Reader's, listener's, and viewer's advisories
Written communication including policy, procedure, and program plans
Outreach
Working with volunteers
Educational consulting
Public relations and marketing
Material development, including curriculum, bibliographies, electronic presentations, and so on
Reference and interviewing negotiation skills

Self-Study for Children's Librarians

It is important for children's staff members assigned to work with children to identify their own strengths and weaknesses. To assist in this process, the Self-Study for Children's Librarians is appended in the Tools section of this book. It is intended that the librarian complete the checklist, seek the technical assistance and training to enhance those skills that need improvement, and offer assistance to others in areas where the librarian feels competent.

Obtaining Knowledge and Skills

Research demonstrates that the level of staff education and training is an important determinant of quality early childhood programs. While graduate library school programs provide training in some of the skills listed above, courses on early childhood development, parenting and family services, interagency cooperation and collaboration, and facilitated learning are not typically offered. Librarians developing a family-centered approach to library services must look elsewhere for this information. Training can be provided in a variety of ways depending on the library's budget, staff size, and need. The following resources provide information and professional training relevant to serving families with young children.

Professional Librarian Training Opportunities

Local, state, and national library organizations offer conference programs and continuing education training related to many of the skills listed above. For children's librarians to gain the full range of skills, they must broaden their workshop attendance to include programs in tracks other than youth services. Those unable to attend a conference can often access select programs electronically via the organization's Web site or obtain printed highlights or summaries published in library journals.

Major program initiatives such as the Public Library Association/Association for Library Service to Children (PLA/ALSC) Every Child Ready to Read Project provide information on the latest research, a toolkit on implementing the program, and certified program instructors available for national, regional, and local training. PLA's New Planning for Results provides information and step-by-step instruction on assessing one's library and community as an initial step in its strategic planning process. In-person training workshops and online courses provide easy access to this information, and discussion lists provide continuing professional support.

Periodically checking state and regional library organizations' Web sites will alert you to training, programs, and information available on a more local level. Checking these sites will also increase your awareness of new and needed topics which are not currently being addressed.

Family Place Libraries: Family Place Libraries, a joint national initiative of Libraries for the Future (program arm of the Americans for Libraries Council) and the Middle Country Public Library (Centereach, NY), provides librarians with comprehensive training and ongoing support and technical assistance. Family Place Libraries provides librarians with the knowledge and skills necessary to develop their libraries into centers for early childhood information, parent education, early literacy, socialization, and family support. The comprehensive four-day Family Place Libraries Training Institute (Family Place Libraries Training Curriculum, 2006) includes the following topics:

History of Family Place Libraries
Family-Centered Services: Overview and Rationale
What Do We Have? What Do We Need? Assets and Needs Assessment
Individual Library Assessments
Who Can I Help? Who Can Help Me? Building Partnerships and Coalitions
Mapping Your Community

Infant Brain Development
Early Childhood Development
Parent Education
Early Literacy and Programming
Parent/Child Workshop, the Signature Program of Family Place Libraries
Space Development and Children's Room Design
Collection Development for: Parents, Professionals Who Work with Very
    Young Children and Families, and Very Young Children
Who's Out There: Identifying and Reaching Out to New Audiences
How to Keep Track: Evaluation and Documentation
Building Your Family Place Library
Developing Your Family Place Plan

Related Disciplines and Professional Development

Looking beyond the library profession to related fields such as early intervention, early childhood education, social work, health, family development, and family support, one can tap into a wealth of knowledge, experience, and training on topics and skills related to family-centered services not readily available in the library arena.

Nationally, Zero to Three, the American Academy of Pediatrics, the National Institute for Learning Disabilities, and the National Association for the Education of Young Children are examples of organizations that provide extensive research information and publications for professionals and parents, as well as continuing education, conference programs, and networking opportunities for family support professionals from diverse disciplines. State and local chapters of national organizations typically offer regional access to additional conferences and workshops.

Cooperative Extension Associations are another rich resource offering statewide research-based training, programs, and materials at the local level for parents and professionals working with families. Cooperative Extension training for family support professionals vary from region to region, running the gamut from half-day programs on such topics as working with grandparents parenting their grandchildren to week-long family literacy institutes. Cornell Cooperative Extension of Suffolk County, New York, in cooperation with the Family Service League of Suffolk, offers an intensive 110-hour Family Development Credential (FDC) training for family support professionals and paraprofessionals. Similar family development training is available in many states through many agencies, helping to redirect the way health, education (library), and human services are delivered to families. This redirection is a change in approach from a professional having all the answers toward an empowerment and family support–based approach, emphasizing prevention, interagency collaboration, and a greater role for families in determining services. Comprehensive training such as this is invaluable for a library staff implementing family-centered services.

Local and online courses through colleges and universities are another source of training. Specific skills can also be obtained through select courses offered through schools of education, family and child studies, social work, and public policy and administration.

Training need not be costly or very time-consuming. Look to your community for expertise and existing training opportunities that may be available in your local area. Head Start, early intervention programs, health departments, childcare councils, school districts, resource and referral agencies, employee assistance programs, and hotlines are just some of the agencies that provide in-service training that addresses many of the skills and competencies listed earlier.

Recognizing that the first and last library staff members that families come in contact with are often not librarians, efforts need to be made to provide all staff members with some basic training. Local agency training may be geared to particular groups of employees (professional, paraprofessional, support staff) and offer opportunities to include various groups of library employees in the family development process.

One-on-one observation of skilled professionals from other disciplines is another valuable training tool. Viewing the interactions among parents and other family support professionals during parent education workshops, parent advisory groups, early intervention programs, and new parent support groups can provide librarians with a variety of service models that utilize a family-centered approach to working with children and families.

Professional Development Resources: A chart provided in the Tools section at the end of this book provides some suggested agencies and organizations that offer resources on family-centered services.

Conclusion

Family-centered library services challenge library professionals to explore personal attitudes, develop new competencies, and expand their roles within their libraries and their communities. By joining together with other family-serving agencies, supporting, nurturing, and empowering parents and caregivers in their roles as children's first teachers, advocates, and lifelong learners, librarians can ensure that libraries fulfill their potential as key players in the development of family-centered communities.

References

Association of Library Service to Children. "Competencies for Librarians Serving Children in Public Libraries." Chicago: American Library Association. Available: http://www.ala.org/ala/alsc/alscresources/forlibrarians/professionaldev/competencies.htm, 1999.

Family Place Libraries Training Curriculum. Centereach, NY: Middle Country Public Library and Americans for Libraries Council, 2005.

Family Support America National Conference. "Envisioning Cultural Competency Workshop," presented by Kinaya Sokoya, Chicago, May 13, 2004.

Feinberg, Sandra, and Sari Feldman. *Serving Families and Children Through Partnerships: A How-To-Do-It Manual for Librarians.* New York: Neal-Schuman, 1996.

Stamm, Jill. *Infant Brain Development: The Critical Intervention Point.* Prepared for and presented as part of the training curriculum for Family Place Libraries at the Middle Country Public Library (Centereach, NY). Phoenix, AZ: New Directions Institute. Video, 2003.

4

Forming Coalitions and Collaborations

Just as we have come to understand that children are inextricably connected to the families from which they come and that children's librarians need to embrace parents and caregivers as parallel constituencies, so too libraries and librarians do not stand alone within their communities. The effectiveness of our outreach efforts and family support services and our ability to maximize the potential of public libraries as community hubs depend on our ability to partner, collaborate, and build coalitions with the larger network of child and family service providers with whom we share common goals. We cannot assume that our potential community partners are aware of the variety of services that libraries offer and how librarians can support and contribute to youth advocacy and family support efforts. Forging connections and partnerships brings a host of benefits for libraries, librarians, and the community.

Benefits for Libraries and Librarians

Having community partners expands the reach of the library to connect with new audiences. Whether we are talking about reaching new immigrant populations, families with limited income or education, childcare providers, parents, local businesses, schools, or community-based service providers, libraries can get tremendous assistance in reaching new constituencies from their community partners.

Networking and coalition building increase librarians' effectiveness as information and referral providers. Information specialist is one of the major roles of public librarians. By expanding the librarians' personal knowledge of community resources through increased networking and coalition-building activities, librarians increase their effectiveness and value as information providers.

Partnerships create new and improved services. Cooperative programming, agency services delivered in library settings, offsite library service delivery, or the development of totally new products, programs, and entities that address community needs are just some of the results of working in partnership with other agencies.

Collaboration stretches limited staff and budgets. Sharing resources and creating win-win exchanges that capitalize on the strengths of partnering organizations are a cornerstone of the collaborative process.

Community partners extend the knowledge base of librarians. Connecting to other professionals who have different skill sets and greater knowledge about child development and family-centered practice provides opportunities for cross-training of staff and expands the knowledge base of all partners. Broader exposure to professionals in other disciplines keeps librarians abreast of trends in youth services, early childhood, and family support that can inform the development of library-based programs, collections, and services.

Forging connections enhances personal satisfaction for librarians. Enjoyment and job involvement increase as the librarian comes to understand his or her job and its strength in a broader perspective, which often leads to greater recognition and stature in the community.

Building coalitions builds support for the library in the community. Increased visibility and awareness of the value of the library and its resources become more apparent as partners work with librarians and express their recognition and support.

Networking in the community increases funding opportunities. Joint grant writing and fundraising efforts evolve naturally, and many funders now require evidence of collaboration when giving grants and allocating resources.

Strengths of Public Libraries as Community Partners

Libraries are safe and trusted community institutions, usually centrally located and accessible, that can offer space for meetings, community programs, and service delivery. Public space is a premium commodity and the neutrality of the library can often help diffuse the turf issues that arise with multiagency initiatives. They provide a natural audience of regular users, an incentive for organizations that need to get their message out. The large numbers of families with young children that visit the library regularly make libraries ideal partners for other family-serving agencies eager to reach this audience.

Libraries are respected as the community's "information place," able to organize and disseminate information to the community in many ways and formats. They present few barriers to access. Their lifelong learning mission allows them to serve all ages, and they are intrinsically democratic in their efforts to provide free and open access to information and services. Their broad mission to support the educational, cultural, and informational needs of its community permits them to embrace most of the interests and issues that community partners are seeking to further. Finally, libraries offer greater flexibility than many other institutions, leaving them free to interpret and redefine their programs, services, and strategies to meet new and changing community needs.

Potential Community Partners

The following programs and services represent some examples of good starting points for potential partnerships. Although most are organizational, do not overlook the potential of key community individuals who share the respect and trust of segments of the population that the library may be particularly interested in reaching.

Early childhood programs (childcare services, nursery schools, Head Start)
Literacy programs (Even Start, Parent-Child Home Program)
Early intervention providers
Public health nurses
School personnel (school nurses, social workers, guidance counselors)
Housing projects and shelters
Hospitals, healthcare clinics, and Women Infant and Child (WIC) sites
Food pantries, parish outreach centers, and family violence programs
United Way Success By Six initiatives
Cooperative Extension programs
Youth agencies
Faith communities
Family-serving community agencies
Business and community leaders
University and college departments of child development, education, and nursing
Teen parent programs

Roles for Librarians and Their Community Partners

Librarians and their community partners stand to benefit mutually from their joint work on behalf of children and families, taking on such roles as:

Assisting each other in reaching new audiences
Marketing each other's programs and services
Serving as resources to each other's programs
Writing joint grants
Cross-training each other's staff
Initiating new programs and services
Developing new products that benefit the community

Planning cooperative programs

Sharing resources (staff, space, materials, translation assistance)

Validating, promoting, and building support for each other's efforts on behalf of families

Promoting greater coordination of family and child services within communities

Extending each other's knowledge base

Assumptions

Certain assumptions underlie the value of working in partnership with others in the community:

Coordination is preferable to competitive, parallel, or duplicative efforts.

Sharing maximizes limited resources and is economically beneficial.

Few families are aware of or utilize all of the community's resources.

The ability to reach new and expanded audiences is improved through combined efforts.

Trust comes only with familiarity and positive experiences over time. Organizations working together can piggy-back on the trust established with diverse constituencies to achieve credibility with new audiences.

Services for families should be available as conveniently and locally as possible.

Many individuals and organizations are unaware of the strengths of libraries as family support partners.

Working collaboratively offers the possibility of accomplishing objectives beyond the scope of single organizations working in isolation.

Working through other family support providers may be the best strategy for reaching families least likely to use the library on a regular basis.

Coalition building is a process that requires time and administrative support.

Working collaboratively leads to change and, almost without exception, results in the development of new collections, programs, and services.

Continuum of Coalition Building

Coalition building is a fluid process than can range from networking meetings and information exchange to formal relationships that create new entities and define the specific financial and programmatic roles of collaborating agencies. The continuum includes networking, coordination, cooperation, and collaboration. Libraries may engage in activities across this continuum as they take a place at the table and become more involved in the fabric of family and child services in their community.

Networking

The first step in coalition building is to facilitate communication among organizations by sharing information and taking advantage of opportunities to get to know each other and promote awareness of existing services. The children's librarian might join an existing coalition, take the lead in convening a group of local family and child service providers, or simply reach out on a one-to-one basis to acquaint local agencies of the library's programs and resources. Agency-to-agency relationships start with individual person-to-person connections, finding that common ground on which to build future collaborations.

The librarian can develop bibliographies of library resources for parents and children on topics determined in consultation with agency personnel. Together they might consider developing a community listing or directory of programs and services for families and children. A collection of brochures and flyers of local resources can be assembled and conveniently sited in the library where parents can learn about family support resources in their community. The library can advertise its family literacy programs, parent-child workshops, storytimes, and other services to agencies that can in turn promote the library to their client group. Many libraries have meeting space, and the neutrality of public libraries makes their meeting rooms perfect for community meetings and events as well as for launching a new alliance of family-serving organizations.

In Saratoga Springs, New York, children's librarian Jim Karge is involved in the local KIDS.NET, trading his service organizing monthly parenting articles for the local newspaper with the opportunity to locate speakers for his library's Parent/Child Workshop. The relationships made through this networking group have paid off, with community agencies now more comfortable using the library and recommending programs to their families. Some have offered to present parenting programs in the library, another step on the coalition-building ladder. Networking lays the foundation on which all future partnerships and collaborations can develop.

Coordination

Once there are mutual recognition and communication between librarians and practitioners from other agencies, a new phase of coalition building may evolve as they work together to coordinate activities and events. Little organizational autonomy is lost and often only modest effort is required to coordinate services.

On Long Island, libraries are sought after as child immunization sites by the local health department, and they are frequently family enrollment sites for New York State's Family and Child Health Insurance programs. Scheduling of meeting room space is coordinated in advance and publicity and promotion are a joint effort. Parent education programs can often be similarly negotiated, utilizing the expertise of the local family service agency or Cooperative Extension association. Libraries offer space and ready access to families. These are win-win arrangements for libraries bringing new services to families in their communities and providers looking for convenient settings in which to deliver their services.

Staff training offers other opportunities for coordinated effort. A library and a community agency may discover a common interest in staff development and together contract with a trainer, getting training for two staffs for the price of one.

They may consider cross-training each other's staff, trading the expertise of the development specialist or parent educator to provide some library staff training in return for early literacy training or Internet searching for parenting resources provided for family agency staff by the children's librarian. These examples of coordinated effort can take on a momentum that involves the whole community.

The PAKRAT Coalition (Parents and Kids Reading Together) in Lyndonville, Vermont, involves the Cobleigh Public Library, Head Start and Early Head Start, Healthy Babies, Success by Six, a local bookstore, the school district, the health department, and a child abuse prevention program. Coordination via the coalition stretches limited resources in this very rural area. Families with newborns are sent a letter inviting them to redeem a Welcome Baby Bag at the library or receive one during a home visit from the Healthy Babies staff. Each bag contains free books for baby and sibling, information on local services, and a certificate to redeem a free book at the local library. PAKRAT agencies making home visits agree to promote all of the organization's services, and together the coalition members identify gaps in services and coordinate joint funding applications. PAKRAT also makes kindergarten transition bags for incoming students and their families in coordination with the local schools and recently initiated a large outreach project to deliver books to childcare programs in this geographically widespread area. From a junkyard van to a state-of-the-art vehicle purchased through an Institute of Museum and Library Services (IMLS) grant, this new service spawned by the PAKRAT Coalition now visits thirty childcare sites per month and reaches more than 300 children. Though focused on early literacy, the coalition's coordinated efforts address many issues and continue to result in new joint initiatives for families and babies (Feldman and Jordan, 2001: 32).

Cooperation

Cooperation requires a higher level of commitment built upon the trust and mutual understanding that develop between organizations over time as they find new strategies for addressing shared goals.

Partners for Inclusion: In the 1990s, a grant-funded initiative in Suffolk County, New York, worked to promote greater inclusion of young children with disabilities in natural community settings. The project fostered cooperative arrangements among public libraries and developmental disabilities agencies in two Long Island communities. The libraries were eager to attract young children with disabilities into their Parent/Child Workshops, and the early intervention agencies working with the families wanted to support the families' efforts to move more into the mainstream of community life. The libraries and agencies agreed to work together to set aside a few slots in each Parent/Child Workshop series to be filled by agency-referred families. Agency personnel sometimes accompanied the families and occasionally served as community resource specialists for all the families in the program, sharing their expertise on early childhood development, early intervention services available, and other areas. Sometimes attendance policies and rules about attending more than one series of workshops had to be waived, but in the end the libraries increased participation of families of children with disabilities who might not otherwise have attended a library program and the agencies met their goal of helping families toward more inclusive community experiences. The partners' flexibility and shared enthusiasm proved the essential ingredients in the success of this cooperative arrangement.

Library-Based Mothers' Centers: The National Association of Mothers' Centers (NAMC), a nationally replicated peer-led support program for parents, saw the potential of public libraries as perfect community settings for Mothers' Center programs. Libraries offered space and age-appropriate early learning resources and often had special collections to support parents' need for information. Middle Country Public Library, providing the leadership for Family Place Long Island, a network of Family Place Libraries committed to serving young families, knew that libraries often had few vehicles for engaging parents in ways that put parents in leadership positions, directing their own activities. At a joint informational meeting, twelve Long Island Family Place Libraries expressed interest in hosting a Mothers' Center. They were willing to commit to working in cooperation with interested parents and NAMC staff to implement a new peer-driven family support program in their communities. The national staffs of NAMC and Family Place Libraries developed a tailored training curriculum for Library-Based Mothers' Centers, and the first group of Library-Based Mothers' Centers was implemented on Long Island—a win-win model of cooperation in action. See Chapter 8 for a detailed look at how to implement a Library-Based Mothers' Center.

Collaboration

Collaboration requires a more formal relationship, sometimes even a written contractual arrangement, and usually implies a joint financial responsibility or the need for joint grant writing or fundraising. Collaboration often results in the development of a total new entity, one unattainable by either agency individually. The amount of staff time required, need to establish a shared vision or goal, need to specify the roles of each collaborating agency, and frequency of face-to-face communication are often the hallmarks of this highest form of coalition-building activity. Collaborations often result in new staff hires and the need for personnel to be clear about chain of command and reporting requirements. Collaborative relationships are complex as each organization strives to maintain individual identities and yet promote a common goal that can be achieved only by working together.

The Safe Children and Healthy Families Are a Shared Responsibility, 2005 Community Resource Packet (http://nccanch.acf.hhs.gov/topics/prevention) cites the need for understanding and respect among collaborators, effective and continuous communication, equitable, but not always equal, sharing of resources, and clearly stated goals and expectations as qualities of successful collaborations. Content areas to consider when developing a memorandum of understanding (MOU) between collaborating organizations may include:

Process for referrals across organizations
Assessment protocols
Parameters of confidentiality
Interorganization training of staff
Organization liaison and coordination
Process for resolving conflicts
Timeline for periodic review of the MOU

The Family Center: Family Service League of Suffolk, Inc. (FSL), one of the oldest and most respected family service agencies on Long Island, had developed several community-based family centers located geographically across Suffolk County, New York, but had no such center operating in the north Brookhaven Township area of the county. The agency had worked on numerous projects and committees with Middle Country Public Library (MCPL) over many years and knew of the library's commitment to families and active involvement in family support initiatives (see Figure 4-1).

Initial conversations about the need for a family center in the library's geographic area led to a series of interagency staff meetings during which the strengths and resources of each organization were analyzed. FSL offered trained social workers and family case managers experienced in crisis intervention, family counseling, family case management, and a track record of serving families most in need, those with limited income and education. The library offered a full range of programs and services typically available in a family center: a drop-in area for families with parent-child activities and programs available for parents and children of all ages; career counseling services for adults as well as English to Speakers of Other Languages (ESOL), General Educational Development (GED), and literacy classes; a wonderful parents' collection; and a resource database with information on health and human services for all of Long Island.

The library staff knew they had families with needs that the library staff did not have the resources or the skills to assist beyond referral to library and community programs, nor was such additional assistance an appropriate role for the librarians, no matter how committed they were to the families. The idea of having a family caseworker available at the library to assist families in a more intensive one-on-one capacity was intriguing. FSL saw at once that many of the resources they had had to develop in their other family centers were already in place at the library. Groups of FSL and MCPL staff paid visits to each other's sites, touring programs and getting to know each other better. A joint grant proposal was written and secured, providing initial funding from United Way of Long Island as part of their Success by Six Initiative. A collaboration was forged and a new entity, the Family Center at Middle Country Public Library, was created.

Building the Family Center Collaboration Step-by-Step:
FSL and MCPL jointly interviewed for a family caseworker position.
Staff members at each agency were identified to get the project off the ground.

4-1: The Family Center @ Middle Country Public Library Brochure

Want to connect with other parents?

Need information & resources?

Family stresses getting you down?

Just want to talk?

Welcome to the Family CENTER

Middle Country Public Library

In Partnership With
Family Service League of Suffolk County

FSL would hire and supervise the staff worker, providing oversight for the case management and counseling activities.

The MCPL librarian assigned to the family center initiative would serve as the key liaison and see that the new staff person was thoroughly introduced to all of the programs, services, and staff at the library.

The library provided desk space, a filing cabinet, phone and computer access, email, and Internet access.

An informational brochure was developed reflecting the joint involvement of FSL and the library.

A simple report format was developed that was distributed monthly to appropriate staff members at both agencies and regular meetings involving all of the staff members involved from both organizations were conducted.

The family center caseworker became a regular feature in Parent/Child Workshops, getting to know families and letting them know of the availability of this new resource to assist them individually with problems and becoming accepted by the library staff members who were encouraged to keep the caseworker's services in mind and pass along referrals.

Childcare, domestic violence, pending divorce, adoption, elder issues, problems accessing services for a disabled child, securing food stamps, and negotiating other entitlement programs all surfaced as concerns that the family caseworker could assist with.

The librarian and the family caseworker together visited local food pantries, churches, health clinics, and school personnel to acquaint them with the family center at the library.

Parents requested an opportunity to get together to discuss discipline and other child-rearing issues on a regular basis, and a weekly Parent Drop-In Discussion Group was formed, led by the family caseworker.

Once the initial funding was depleted and the collaboration deemed a success by both organizations, continued fundraising efforts were needed on the part of both. They separately appealed to government sources that each had relationships with and managed over the next two years to creatively "cobble together" sufficient funding to keep the position funded at a minimal number of hours. Staff turnover and the peculiarities of staffing requirements unique to each agency have necessitated flexibility and patience. Consistent administrative support from the very top of both organizations has been essential. Although the next chapter of this collaboration is yet to be written, the core commitment of both organizations to keeping the Family Center afloat has not wavered and serves as a unique model of collaboration for others to consider.

Putt-ing Families First: Three family support programs on Long Island joined forces to do what no one organization could do alone. The National Center for the Parent-Child Home Program, the National Association of Mothers' Centers, and Middle Country Library Foundation's Family Place project recognized that golf tournaments raised a great deal of money for other local organizations, but all three were small organizations with limited staff to devote to running a major fundraiser (see Figure 4-2). Six years ago they decided to collaborate and share staff resources, board expertise, and corporate contacts to create Putt-ing Families First, a golf tournament fundraising event, the proceeds of which they would share.

A single event committee was formed with representation from all three organizations' staffs, boards, and networks of volunteers. Clear areas of responsibility were delineated to assure that work was distributed equitably among the three organizations and that all tasks were covered. Honesty, openness, communication, and trust continue to be required with money, hard-earned corporate relationships, and staff resources at stake.

Putt-ing Families First is celebrating its eighth annual tournament and has generated as much as $30,000 in one year for each organization. In addition to the financial rewards, the three organizations have gone on to collaborate programmatically at a regional level, and they have produced a joint video that promotes all of their programs. They have elevated awareness about all of their programs in the corporate world through this popular event—succeeding together where no one of them could have succeeded alone.

4-2:   Putt-ing Families First Logo

**Middle Country Library Foundation Family Place
National Association of Mothers' Centers
The Parent-Child Home Program**

Creating the Opportunities for Connection

Opportunities for networking and collaboration abound, but seizing these opportunities and bringing them to fruition on behalf of families and children require the conscious efforts of an individual or organization to take that next step forward.

Join an Existing Coalition

Once the library has made it a priority to reach out beyond its doors and more actively engage the larger community, the fastest route to connectivity is to join an already existing coalition or group.

Port Washington Child Care Partnership: Looking for opportunities to actively involve the library in community-wide efforts to improve services for children and families, the Port Washington, New York, Public Library eagerly joined the Port Washington Child Care Partnership, a community coalition that engaged the schools, local businesses, clergy, childcare providers, the county Child Care Resource and Referral Agency, and elected officials in an effort to make community childcare needs more widely known and understood, improve existing childcare services, and serve as a forum for communication, problem solving, and networking at the community level. Through participation, the library became a major player, cosponsoring events, providing meeting space for the partnership, and finding increased opportunities for collaboration with other partners. The library and the local Pre-K program implemented a special Parent/Child Workshop to reach families that might not otherwise have participated and the Pre-K program helped to identify families with high need and limited resources for the library's Parent Child Home Program, a home-based family literacy program for at-risk families. The partnership still meets monthly and the library considers their involvement a great success story—an opportunity taken that continues to reap rewards.

Rockville Centre Parent Centre: Anita La Spina, head of Children's Services at the Rockville Centre Public Library, New York, has been a board member of the Rockville Centre Parent Centre since its inception. Being involved has fostered connections for the library with all of the local organizations serving parents and families in the community. Participation has brought funding to support programs and furniture for the library's Parents' Corner and, more important, has nurtured the community relationships that put the library at the table when planning, decision making, and the distribution of funding take place.

Seize the Moment: The Serendipity Factor

Being alert to potential opportunities for creative collaboration can pay off in unexpected ways. Seated next to each other at a community luncheon, the librarian got to talking to the administrator of a local domestic violence agency. The administrator described a wonderful new program for children affected by family violence that they were piloting in a school district some miles away. The success of the approach and the need for more such services came up. The librarian suggested the possibility of partnering with the library to widen the geographic reach of the program, an idea that had never occurred to the agency administrator but which met with immediate appeal. A chance encounter turned into a potential new partnership opportunity because the librarian was out and involved and in a position to make potential strategic connections and because she had a "can-do" attitude which left the door open for new possibilities of working together. The serendipity of being in the right place at the right time cannot be predicted, but the openness with which we approach these unanticipated moments needs to be cultivated and encouraged.

Form a Coalition

If no existing group to facilitate networking among family-serving organizations in a community exists, the library can take the initiative to organize one. "If the initiative to form a coalition is taken by the library then the library will have a major role in shaping the coalition's mission. It must be prepared to allocate some resources (staff time, in-kind support or some funds), both initially and as an ongoing commitment. . . . Librarians traditionally thought they could just serve as liaisons to other youth serving agencies. While this activity points to team building and involvement, coalition building points to leadership and commitment. The librarian must be action oriented and have a genuine concern for improving and developing services based on input from the coalition. In this active role, the librarian becomes the catalyst or change agent, providing new information to enhance group communication and an alternative way to serve families" (Feinberg and Feldman, 1996: 23).

Suffolk Coalition for Parents and Children: More than twenty years ago, Middle Country Public Library convened what has become the Suffolk Coalition for Parents and Children, a coalition of more than 1,200 individuals who work with children, youth, and families in Suffolk County, New York (see Figure 4-3). What started as a small interdisciplinary group that included a parent educator from Cornell Cooperative Extension, a speech therapist from a local hospital clinic, a nutritionist, and a Board of Cooperative Educational Services (BOCES) early childhood educator has grown into a loose but ongoing networking and education organization. Members include public health nurses, school personnel, social workers, librarians, and youth agency staff. The library's public space, neutral stance, and ability to identify area resources made it the ideal convener of such a coalition.

Middle Country Library (Centereach, NY) continues to provide the "glue" for this coalition, initially maintaining a mailing list and now an email group; producing the bimonthly meeting notice; and taking the responsibility for convening the biannual organizing meeting. Members are invited to recommend topics that need to be addressed and ten workshop themes are

4-3: Suffolk Coalition for Parents and Children Logo

selected to be covered over a two-year period. Those present commit to organizing the workshops, usually a panel presentation reflecting a broad spectrum of the best resources to be had in the county on the particular subject area. Some topics require repeat coverage every few cycles, such as family violence, perinatal health, single parenting, and raising children with special needs. Other topics reflect emerging issues, such as gangs, cutting and self-mutilation among teens, and depression in young children.

The Suffolk Coalition for Parents and Children has survived for more than two decades because the library took the initiative and maintained the leadership over time. As a result of publicly committing itself to coalition building on behalf of children and families, the library emerged as a player in the arena of child and family services and was eventually invited to be represented on the boards of the Child Care Council, the Suffolk Network on Adolescent Pregnancy, the Family Violence Task Force, the United Way's Success By Six Coalition, the Head Start Advisory Council, and the ECELI (Early Care and Education on Long Island) Network. It cannot be overestimated how important library representation is on these boards and networks which shape services to children and families in every community.

"Taking the time . . . to get acquainted with potential partners by joining community organizations and participating in their activities establishes an important foundation for future collaborations. Often, potential partners don't know enough about each other's mission and need time to become familiar with the ways a relationship could be mutually beneficial. Potential partners who have gotten to know and trust one another are better able to maximize their commitments and rarely feel threatened by issues of 'is it ours' or 'theirs'" (Morrison, S. in Lynch, 1999: vii).

Practical Tips and Suggestions

Coalition building is both an art and a science. Some practical tips include:

Attend community meetings convened about child and family issues and concerns.

Meet and get to know personally the representatives of local agencies, invite them to the library, keep them informed of library services, and ask to be placed on their mailing lists; after the in-person contact is made, follow up with a note or email and stay in touch with occasional phone calls.

Encourage staff representation on the boards of organizations you are strategically interested in partnering with.

Offer the library as a meeting space and distribution site for service information and promote the library's ability to organize and disseminate information and share resources within the community.

Offer to develop resource listings for parents or staff that complement agency priorities and highlight library collections in the process.

Take the lead in suggesting possible joint activities, such as a community resource fair or local services directory.

Go prepared to meetings with business cards and program information that may be a good fit for the group or event.

Learn how to "work a room," setting practical goals for each encounter; for example, plan to initiate a specific number of conversations at a social function; exchange business cards to facilitate follow-up communication; engage in conversation with the person in front of and behind you in the buffet line or seated to your right and left at a meeting; gradually expand your comfort zone to increase your capacity for networking.

Collect business cards, jotting down notes to remind you of information to follow up on or to remind you of what you discussed—refer to them in follow-up calls or correspondence.

Be dependable—if you say you will get back with a piece of information, be sure to follow up—and always express appreciation when others do the same.

The wider your circle of contacts, the more potential for making connections when the need arises—cultivate now to reap the benefits later.

Conclusion

More than just an opportunity, community connectedness is a responsibility for librarians, a goal that is central to the library's mission and critical to the work of supporting families and children. With so much recent attention to the notion of "community building" and "sustainable development," Kathleen de la Pena Mc-Cook, in her book *A Place at the Table*, decries the lack of a library presence on the national community-building landscape and the often passive role relegated to libraries and librarians as reflected in the literature. She cites the need for activism and leadership and describes the critical role of library administrators whose support is needed to permit staff sufficient time to engage in the important work of building community relationships. "Librarians must be given the power to activate their ideals and to take a place at every table where community building occurs. When authorized to do so the inherent energy and commitment librarians possess will be freed to build the communities their neighborhoods deserve" (McCook, 2000: 100).

References

Feinberg, Sandra, and Feldman, Sari. *Serving Families and Children Through Partnerships.* New York: Neal-Schuman, 1996.

Feldman, Sari, and Jordan, Barbara. "Together Is Better: The Role of Libraries as Natural Community Partners." *Zero to Three* 21, no. 3 (December/January): 30–37, 2001.

Lynch, Sherry, Editor. *The Librarian's Guide to Partnerships.* Fort Atkinson, WI: Highsmith Press, 1999.

McCook, Kathleen de la Pena. *A Place at the Table: Participating in Community Building.* Chicago: American Library Association, 2000.

"Safe Children and Healthy Families Are a Shared Responsibility: 2005 Community Resources Packet." Washington, DC: U.S. Department of Heath and Human Services, Administration for Children and Families. Available: http://nccanch.acf.hhs.gov/topics/prevention, 2005.

5

Understanding How Young Children Grow and Learn

Recent research on infant brain development has provided a great deal of crucial information new to the world of science and education, greatly impacting how we understand and nurture children and parents. As children grow and develop from birth, they do so differently, each at his or her own pace. Physical, social, and emotional development occurs simultaneously—but is unlikely to unfold exactly the same way in all children. For those who work with children, some basic understanding of infant brain development, early childhood stages and developmental milestones, and how play impacts early literacy will influence the design of appropriate services, collections, spaces, and programs to best satisfy the needs of babies, toddlers, and preschoolers.

Infant Brain Research

Scientific research has proven that children's brains are most receptive to information between the ages of birth and three years. During this period, amazing transmissions and developments, which have been recognized only recently, occur at a rapid pace that sets the stage for a child's learning capacity and future development. By the child's third birthday, the brain is 90 percent of its adult size. While the brain continues to develop throughout life, this opportunity for parents and caregivers during a child's early years is very brief.

At the New Directions Institute of Infant Brain Development (Phoenix, AZ), Dr. Jill Stamm researches, lectures, advocates, and educates professionals and parents on the findings and implications of infant brain development. For the first time, scientists have technologies that actually allow them to look "inside" the brain of a living person. These new technologies—the PET scan, functional Magnetic Resonance Imaging tests (MRIs), and new, sophisticated EEGs—are coming from the field of medicine, not the field of education. They provide concrete evidence to support the theories and principles of leading cognitive scientists and psychologists that until now were based on mere observation or on results of surgery on diseased or injured brains. The emergence of this scientific evidence presents challenges and possibilities to parents, caregivers, librarians, and educators. As brain research begins to filter into the educational community and ultimately to the general public, its impact will alter the medical, educational, governmental, economic, and social communities (Stamm, 2001).

What does the research show? Through a variety of new technologies, scientists have revealed a number of processes by which the brain develops, grows, and functions. A child is born with one thousand trillion synapses, and yet the brain is only 25 percent "wired" at birth. The forming and reforming of neural connections is the task of early brain development. As a child seeks out and uses the environment to complete this wiring, the process is 75 percent complete by age one.

Exposure to the environment and various stimuli supply the information that forms the connections within the brain. The more that parents and caregivers engage in speaking, singing, reading, touching, and playing with young children, the more connections are formed and the better "wired" the child. With an abundance of brain activity proven to occur in the first year alone, parents and caregivers can begin to understand how these first years of development are most impressionable and have the greatest sustainable impact in the life of a child. The evidence to support libraries' intensive work with families during the earliest years is implicit as well.

The brain forms in three directions: from back to front, bottom to top, and inside out. Figure 5-1 demonstrates the order in which the brain acquires information; in this instance, the single word. The sequence of seeing, hearing, speaking, and generating words begins in the back of the brain and progresses forward so that generating words occurs in the frontal lobe. Until recently, this pattern sat undiscovered.

Neuroscience has also proven that the manner in which a child is cared for affects the development of the infant brain. The level of security a child feels plays a pivotal role in how the child will absorb various information and stimuli. Children who engage in consistent interaction and bonding with a significant adult are more likely to feel safe. In turn, this provides the sense of security the child requires to ingest and process the child's surroundings to the best advantage.

Conversely, children who lack a sense of security as a result of inconsistent engagements or in extreme cases of neglect or abuse are less likely to absorb the environment and reach maximum potential. Simply put, an anxious brain is less

5-1:   Positron Emission Tomographic Studies of the Processing of Single Words

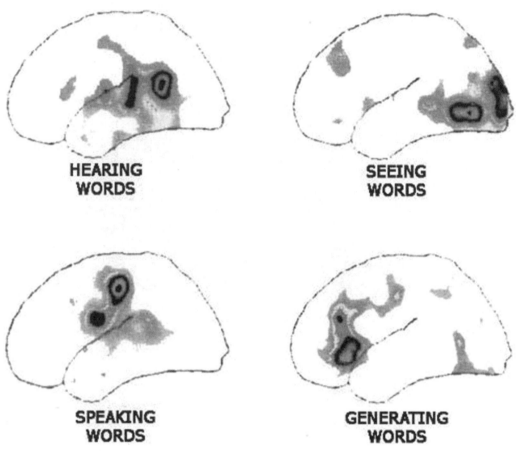

©2000 New Directions Institute. Source: Peterson, S. E., et al., as cited by Stamm, 2002.

receptive than one at ease. How a child is cared for and attended to has a direct impact on the "wiring" of the infant brain and on the future success of the child. Figure 5-2 offers a visualization of the contrast between a normal brain verses a brain that is sensory deprived due to abuse and neglect.

An amazing mass of tissue and nerves, the brain has the ability to continue to learn and to alter previously learned behaviors throughout its entire lifespan. Behaviors that have been reinforced over time and have a strong emotional association to a particular experience can be very difficult to change, but change is possible. The old cliché that "you can't teach an old dog new tricks" has become a scientifically proven untruth. With this new information, the responsibilities to help any child or adult alter negative behaviors or ease emotional distresses are never complete, regardless of how hopeless change may seem.

Developmental Stages

In tandem with knowing how the brain develops, understanding early developmental stages informs adults about what is taking shape within the physical, social, and

5-2:   **Differences in Normal versus Sensory Deprived Infant Brain**

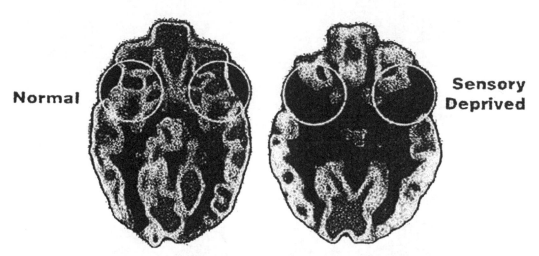

Normal vs. Deprived Brain
of a Three Year Old Child

Normal

Sensory Deprived

©2000 New Directions Institute. Source: Chugani, H. T., as cited by Stamm, 2002.

emotional growth of young children. While many theories exist on the development of early childhood, all reflect the relative extent to which nature and nurture are considered to control the course and outcomes of development during the early years. Psychologist Erik Erikson, a student of Sigmund Freud, expounded on Freud's philosophy, which was based on the idea that the emotional health of adults is shaped by key interactive experiences during the first five years of life. Erikson believed that experiences beyond those first five years (those embarked upon in school-age, teen, adult, and senior years and so on) also had an impact on the emotional and social adaptation of adults. Erikson theorized that eight developmental stages, three of which will be discussed in the following paragraphs, are each set within natural confines upon which nurturing, or lack thereof, can have an influence.

Erikson theorized that in the first developmental stage of infancy (birth to fifteen months), children strive to develop a basic trust and attachment to at least one primary caregiver. By offering responsive care, attention, predictability, and opportunities for bonding, parents satisfy the need in infants to feel safe and secure. During this first stage, librarians can assist parents by offering information that reinforces the importance of the parent-infant bond, referral to local support groups for new parents, a bibliography that covers new parent materials, a rocking chair, and board books in the children's room to facilitate bonding activities, and a Mother Goose lapsit or similar programs for parents and infants to share together.

A sense of autonomy is the objective of toddlers (ages fifteen months to two and a half years). Children at this age are developing a sense of self and desire opportunities to act independently of their parents. Once young children realize they have legs that can take them places, they want to go and do. Toddlers begin to think for themselves and prefer to make their own choices and decisions. While they are more aware of their surroundings, they do not yet fully understand the consequences to their actions and lack the control to police their behavior. A toddler might know that he should not climb onto the countertop but may not realize why. Parental vigilance is necessary and exhausting.

As children this age are becoming their own persons, the toddler years are some of the most difficult years for parents. Helping parents put toddlers' normal developmental behavior into perspective can help parents maintain their own balance and good humor. An understanding of a child's temperament is also beneficial. Identifying the child who observes rather than acts, one who is verbal rather than quiet, or one who is shy versus one who always seems to be in the middle of the action can help us serve the individual child more appropriately. Awareness of acceptable variances in behavior on the part of librarians can ease stress for parents and encourage positive development of the child. Libraries can assist by offering spaces for active and quiet experiences, programs that encourage one-on-one and group activities, large writing tools, and toys that encourage gross motor skills and imaginative play.

Between the ages of two and six, preschoolers begin taking initiative and having pride in their accomplishments and abilities. During this stage, parents will find themselves attending to questions such as "Look what I can do," "Watch me do this," and "Did you see what I built?" Children this age have more refined motor skills and may have the ability to hold a pencil or string a lacing toy with a piece of yarn. They generally have a better understanding of their surroundings and the consequences to their actions. Preschoolers enjoy taking responsibility for their accomplishments and can better judge and police their behavior. The beginnings of self-care such as washing their own hands and face and dressing begin to emerge. Parents can foster positive development by offering encouragement, support, and attention to the many accomplishments and abilities their children are exhibiting. Libraries provide opportunities for language development, dramatic play, expressive art, and group and goal-oriented activities while simultaneously supporting and partnering with parents.

Developmental Milestones

Developmental milestones provide some general characteristics associated with each stage of early childhood development. Being aware of typical behaviors and skills that children will exhibit influences how a program or service may be offered, what should be emphasized or expected of the child, and the materials and activities that librarians may select and use in a program. This awareness also helps the librarian to explain behavior in simple terms to parents, increasing their understanding, lessening their anxieties, and nurturing more realistic expectations.

1–3 Months

Lifts head and chest briefly when on stomach
Turns head toward bright colors and lights
Visually follows moving object with both eyes moving in the same direction
Pays attention to someone's face in his or her direct line of vision
Reacts to sudden sounds and noises
Smiles and coos
Makes fist with both hands; can grasp toys or hair
Wiggles and kicks arms and legs

3–6 Months

Follows moving objects with eyes
Recognizes familiar faces and objects
Turns toward sounds
Turns over from back to stomach
Stretches out arms to be picked up
Babbles and laughs out loud
Reaches for and holds objects; can switch toys from one hand to the other
Helps hold bottle during feeding

6–12 Months

Sits without support
Pulls to a standing position
Creeps or crawls
Finger-feeds self; drinks from a cup
Plays Peek-a-Boo and Patty Cake; waves bye-bye
Looks at person speaking
Uses crying to show different needs
Responds to name; pats and smiles at image in mirror
Knows strangers from family
Uses five or six words like "mama" or "dada"
Holds out arms and legs while being dressed
Picks up objects with thumb and forefinger and looks closely at them; puts objects in containers
Stacks two blocks

12–18 Months

Pushes, pulls, and dumps things
Pulls off shoes, socks, and mittens
Walks with help
Steps off a low object and keeps balance
Follows simple directions (e.g., "Bring the ball," "Give it to me," "Stop!")
Imitates simple words

Likes to listen to music and dance in rhythm to it
Likes to look at pictures
Tries to build and stack objects
Feeds himself or herself
Makes marks on paper with crayon

18–24 Months

Carries something while walking
Feeds self with a spoon
Refers to self by name
Turns pages two or three at a time
Listens to stories with pictures
Uses two- to three-word sentences
Has a vocabulary of 300 words
Says name of toys
Carries on "conversations" with self and dolls
Builds a tower of four blocks
Recognizes familiar pictures
Plays independently for short periods of time
Imitates parents and everyday activities
Identifies hair, eyes, ears, and nose by pointing
Shows affection
Begins to run and jump
Likes to scribble and draw
Puts squares and circles into puzzles

24–30 Months

Kicks a ball
Turns pages one at a time
Cam help to dress and undress
Turns doorknobs and unscrews lids
Feeds self with spoon
Uses many new words
Speaks in short sentences
Names objects in books
Pays attention to activities for longer periods of time (6–7 minutes)
Knows at least one color
Points to parts of the body

30–36 Months

Walks upstairs (alternating feet)
Rides a tricycle
Puts on shoes

Plays with older children for short periods of time
Repeats common nursery rhymes
Says first and last name
Knows whether he or she is a boy or girl
Follows two- or three-step direction given at one time
Begins to count
Begins to draw circles and vertical lines
Uses three- to five-word sentences
Has vocabulary of 1,000 words
Uses words to relate observations, concepts, and relationships
Understands night/day, big/little, summer/winter, yesterday/today
Can stay with one activity for eight to nine minutes

36–48 Months

Speaks in short sentences within the context of a conversation
Asks how many, why, when, what, and where questions
Gradually replaces parallel play with cooperative play
Opens and turns pages of a book
Knows the front and back of a book; can recognize if a book is upside down
Listens to a book with a very simple storyline
Counts using a one-to-one correspondence
Builds a tower with nine blocks
Begins to draw a stick-figure person
Is toilet trained and able to use restrooms with assistance
Is able to dress and undress independently
Is able to put toys or materials away when asked

48–60 Months

Has a vocabulary of about 1,500 words
Understands spatial language (over, under, in, out)
Actively engages in conversations with other children
Follows direction requiring sequential order
Orders objects by size, number, shape
Begins to recognize colors, numbers, and letters
Strings beads in a pattern
Begins to use scissors
Engages in more elaborate and sophisticated dramatic play
Follows a story with a full storyline
Sits in a group for fifteen or more minutes
Separates from parent or caregiver for a short period of time

Librarians can build upon existing programs and services for families by applying what we know about typical child development. In addition to knowing the milestones, it is important to remember other basic growth principles as outlined by Carol Gestwicki (1995: 8–9):

There is a predictable sequence in development.

Development at one stage is the basis for later development.

There are optimal periods of development.

Development results from the interaction of biological factors (maturation) and environmental factors (learning).

Development proceeds as an interrelated whole, with all aspects (physical, cognitive, emotional, and social) influencing others.

Each individual develops according to a particular timetable and pace.

Development proceeds from simple to complex, from general to specific.

Ideally, young children should be engaged in activities that allow them to explore, inquire about, and utilize new concepts, skills, and materials. Any activity or material presented during a program or available in the early childhood area should be developmentally meaningful, engaging, and relevant to the child. Very young children, particularly those age three and under, should be engaged in activities with the parent or caregiver at hand. When designing library-based early childhood programs, it is best to consider the parent-child dyad as the critical factor and recognize that each child needs to move at his or her own pace in any skill acquisition that takes place. The parent is critical to facilitating the child's participation in new activities. The hallmark of good early childhood program practice is always that the process, not the product, is what matters most in a young child's learning.

Play and Literacy

In a culture based on an orientation toward work, it is easy to dismiss the importance of play. Adults often see play activities and toys for children as frivolous and entertaining—not necessarily as intrinsically valuable. Nothing could be further from the truth. Play is the work of young children. It is through interaction with others, manipulation of objects, and exploration through touching, feeling, smelling, seeing, tasting, and physical movement that children learn about their environment, how things work, and the concept of cause and effect. Research studies have demonstrated repeatedly that children develop their physical, mental, sensory, social, and other learning skills through play.

Child-initiated play lays a foundation for learning and academic success. Through play, children learn to interact with others, develop language skills, recognize and solve problems, and discover their potential. In short, play helps children make sense of and find their place in the world. Psychologists Jean Piaget and Les Vygotsky were among the first to link play with a child's cognitive development. Piaget's research shows that play behaviors become more complex and abstract as children progress through early childhood, promoting four major skills that are crucial to the development of literacy: underlying cognitive skills and the ability to learn deliberately; development of symbolic representation; oral language; and introduction of content and related skills and concepts.

Play is critical to the development of early literacy skills and sets the foundation for reading readiness and future success in school. Early childhood play gives children a means to develop and assert their sense of competency. The generalized feeling of competency resulting from play can be seen as children explore both reading and writing. Not only does a child's social, cognitive, and emotional development flourish and grow with play experiences, but these experiences also unify learning and development. Healthy play fosters creativity and builds the base for reading, writing, and mathematical reasoning. Play helps children learn to pick up, hold, move, and carry things; roll over; crawl; stand; walk; run; jump; climb; and more. Children learn how to share, take turns, make choices, solve problems, and understand the feelings of others during play (Playing for Keeps, 2003).

Play appears to have at least two potential links to the development of literacy. Pretend play allows children to develop and refine their capacities to use symbols, to represent experience, and to construct imaginary worlds, capacities they will draw on when they begin to read and write. As an orientation or approach to experience, play can make the various roles and activities of people more meaningful and hence more accessible to young children (McLane and McNamee, 1991).

In their book *Playful Learning and Teaching: Integrating Play into Preschool and Primary Programs*, Judith E. Kieff and Renee M. Casbergue (2000: 9) list the different areas where play provides children opportunities to develop a broad range of skills:

Creative Expression

Improvising
Thinking flexibly
Exploring new options
Extending and elaborating on ideas
Manipulating rhythm, sound, form, and volume
Testing new materials

Cognitive Competencies and Literacy Skills

Developing symbolic capabilities
Practicing newly acquired skills
Attempting novel or challenging tasks
Solving complex problems
Making predictions
Drawing conclusions
Comparing sizes, shapes, and colors
Determining cause and effect
Developing an understanding of time
Enhancing early literacy skills
Energizing and organizing learning
Paying attention to a project until it is done

Social Competence

Interacting with others
Expressing and controlling emotions

Taking on new roles
Sharing
Taking turns
Negotiating to solve a problem
Settling arguments
Cooperating
Having and being friends

Healthy Lifestyle

Refining large motor skills
Refining small motor skills
Understanding safety concerns
Understanding nutrition concepts
Developing trust in one's own capabilities

According to Piaget, there are three categories of play: functional play, symbolic play, and games with rules. Children experience functional play over and over again—usually for the sheer pleasure of the experience. How often have adults watched children pour sand or water in and out of containers? As children participate in this kind of play, their motor skills are developing at the same time as their cognitive skills. Libraries that provide puzzles or cardboard or plastic blocks for children to play with, where children can stack a row of blocks up and then knock them down—over and over again—are providing endless opportunities for children to experience functional play.

Similarly, children can experience symbolic play in a corner of the library that is set up like a post office, a kitchen, or a storefront, for example. Having materials present for parents and children that they can utilize in creative ways helps children explore the concept of symbolic representation. A child who takes a block and pretends that it is a telephone is realizing that he or she can use one object to represent another.

As children grow and develop, their play becomes more complicated and rules begin to emerge. Games with rules show young children that sometimes there are steps that need to be followed in order for something to happen. It is important to keep in mind that rules can easily frustrate a young child. It may be best to present games such as finger plays or rhymes such as "Ring Around the Rosie" where the child learns that everyone will fall down in a big heap at the end of the rhyme. Librarians who are aware of the different categories of play and the important role they play in a child's development can guide and model for parents some of the educational, social, and emotional benefits that their children experience through play, reassuring them that play is indeed "serious business."

Play experiences and supportive parent-child interactions, as well as access to books, print materials, and writing tools, are critical for the emergence of reading and writing skills in young children. Literacy is a dynamic, lifelong, developmental process in which the individual's abilities, relationships with others, and environmental opportunities interact. Play nurtures the four main components of emergent literacy: listening, seeing, speaking, and writing. Early literacy has been defined as "the constellation of skills young children accumulate through hands-on, age-appropriate, playful experiences involving listening, speaking, being read to, handling books and using writing implements before they are ready for formal reading and writing instruction" (Byrne et al., 2003: 42). Increased exposure to print, developmentally appropriate toys, conversation, and social settings provides endless learning opportunities for children that foster early literacy skills and nurture their individual abilities.

Parents who understand the pivotal role of play and its direct association to early literacy, reading readiness, and school success are less likely to dismiss it and more likely to encourage and participate in playful activities with their children. Through modeling, coaching, and teaching, librarians can send the message that play experiences and supportive parent-child interactions as well as access to books, print material, and writing tools are crucial for the emergence of reading and writing skills in young children (Snow et al., 1991; Spodek and Saracho, 1993). A child who begins the chain of positive experiences and interactions at birth is much more likely to fare better in an academic setting later on. Literacy is a dynamic, lifelong, developmental process in which the individual's abilities, relationships with others, and environmental opportunities interact.

Conclusion

From as early as birth, children begin their life's journey of learning. Awareness of recent developments in infant brain development, a basic knowledge of early childhood stages and milestones and how they fit into library programs and services, and an understanding of the importance of play in early literacy challenge librarians to reevaluate their services. "Experience changes the way the brain functions. The more positive experiences children have, the more likely they will acquire knowledge and learn. Libraries can benefit from proven research because it is primary to the mission of libraries" (Diamant-Cohen, Riordan, and Wade, 2004: 12).

Informed librarians, knowledgeable about what early brain development is telling us about the significance of the child's earliest years, can become more informed advocates, reaching as many parents and caregivers as possible with the message. By creating programs, spaces, and collections that nurture positive, stimulating, developmentally appropriate childhood experiences, enhancing parent knowledge and parent-child interactions, libraries demonstrate their commitment to working in partnership with parents to ensure healthy physical, social, and emotional developmental outcomes for their children.

References

Byrne, Marci, Kathleen Deerr, and Lisa G. Kropp. "Book a Play Date: The Game of Promoting Emergent Literacy." *American Libraries* 34, no. 3 (September): 42–44, 2003.

Diamant-Cohen, Ellen Riordan, and Regina Wade. "Make Way for Dendrites: How Brain Research Can Impact Children's Programming." *Children and Libraries: The Journal of the Association for Library Service to Children* 2, no. 1 (Spring): 12–20, 2004.

Gestwicki, Carol. *Developmentally Appropriate Practice: Curriculum and Development in Early Education.* Albany, NY: Delmar Publishers, 1995.

Kieff, Judith E., and Renee M. Casbergue. *Playful Learning and Teaching: Integrating Play into Preschool and Primary Programs.* Boston: Allyn and Bacon, 2000.

McLane, Joan B., and Gillan D. McNamee. The Beginnings of Literacy. *Zero to Three* (September), http://www.zerotothree.org/begin.html, 1991.

Playing for Keeps. "The Promise of Play," www.playingforkeeps.org, 2003.

Snow, Catherine E., et al. *The Social Prerequisites of Literacy Development: Home and School Experiences of Preschool-Aged Children from Low-Income Families.* Cambridge, MA: Harvard University, 1991.

Spodek, Bernard, and Olivia Saracho. "Languages and Literacy in Early Childhood Education." In *Yearbook in Early Childhood Education,* Volume 4. New York: Teachers College Press, 1993.

Stamm, Jill. *Neuroscience Enters the Nursery.* A presentation for the Distinguished Speakers Series at the Middle Country Public Library (Centereach, NY), 2001.

Resources for Professionals

Brain Development

Bruer, John. *The Myth of the First Three Years: A New Understanding of Early Brain Development and Lifelong Learning.* Old Tappan, NJ: Free Press, 2002.

Eliot, Lise. *What's Going On in There? How the Brain and Mind Develop in the First Five Years.* New York: Bantam Press, October 2000.

Gerhardt, Sue. *Why Love Matters: How Affection Shapes a Baby's Brain.* New York: Taylor and Francis, 2004.

Gopnik, Alison, Andrew N. Meltkoff, and Patricia K. Kuhl. *The Scientist in the Crib: What Early Learning Tells Us About the Mind.* New York: Perennial Press, December 2000.

Greenspan, Stanley. *Building Healthy Minds: The Six Experiences That Create Intelligence and Emotional Growth in Babies and Young Children.* Cambridge, MA: Perseus Publishing, 2001.

Hart, Betty, and Todd R. Risley. *Meaningful Differences in the Everyday Experiences of Young American Children.* Baltimore, MD: Brookes Publishing, July 1995.

Hawley, Theresa. *Starting Smart: How Early Experiences Affect Brain Development.* 2nd Edition. Washington, DC: Zero to Three Press, 2000.

Healy, Jane. *Your Child's Growing Mind: Brain Development and Learning from Birth to Adolescence.* New York: Broadway Books, 2004.

How People Learn: Brain, Mind, Experience and School. Washington, DC: National Academy Press, 2000.

Kagan, Jerome, and Norbert Herschkowitz. *Young Mind in a Growing Brain.* Mahwah, NJ: Lawrence Erlbaum Associates, 2005.

Nelson, Charles A., Kathleen M. Thomas, and Michelle de Haan. *Neuroscience of Cognitive Development: The Role of Experience and the Developing Brain.* 5th Edition. Hoboken, NJ: Wiley, 2006.

Posner, Michael I., and Mary Klevjord Rothbart. *Educating the Human Brain*. Washington, DC: American Psychological Association, 2006.

Shonkoff, Jack P. *From Neurons to Neighborhoods: The Science of Early Childhood Development*. Washington, DC: National Academy Press, November 2000.

"Small Wonders: Early Brain Development." (Video) National Center for Family Literacy, 1998.

Shore, Rebecca. *Baby Teacher: Nurturing Neural Networks from Birth to Age Five*. Lanham, MD: Rowman and Littlefield, 2002.

Shore, Rima. *Rethinking the Brain: New Insights into Early Development*. New York: City Families and Work Institute, 2003.

Siegel, Daniel J. *The Developing Mind: Toward a Neurobiology of Interpersonal Experience*. New York: Guilford Press, 1999.

Siegel, Daniel J. *Developing Minds: How Relationships and the Brain Interact to Shape Who We Are*. New York: Guilford Press, October 2001.

Tortora, Suzi, ed. *The Multisensory World of the Infant*. Washington, DC: Zero to Three, 2004.

Zigler, Edward F., Matia Finn-Stevenson, and Nancy W. Hall. *The First Three Years and Beyond: Brain Development and Social Policy*. New Haven, CT: Yale University Press, 2003.

Early Childhood Development

Allen, Eileen, and Lynn Marotz. *Developmental Profiles: Pre-Birth Through Twelve*. 5th Edition. Florence, KY: Thomson Delmar Learning, 2007.

Brazelton, T. Berry. *The Irreducible Needs of Children: What Every Child Must Have To Grow, Learn, and Flourish*. Cambridge, MA: Perseus Publishing, 2000.

Gowen, Jean Wixson. *Enhancing Early Emotional Development: Guiding Parents of Young Children*. Baltimore, MD: Brookes Publishing, 2002.

Harms, Thelma, and Debbie Cryer. *Infants and Toddlers in Out-of-Home Care*. Baltimore, MD: Brookes Publishing, 2000.

Hughes, Fergus P. *Children, Play and Development*. Boston: Allyn and Bacon, 1999.

Levine, Max. *A Mind at a Time*. New York: Simon and Schuster, 2002.

Martin, Sue, and Jennifer Berke. *See How They Grow: Infants and Toddlers*. Florence, KY: Thomson Delmar Learning, 2007.

Miller, Karen. *Ages and Stages: Developmental Descriptions and Activities Birth Through Eight Years*. Marshfield, MA: Telshare Publishing, 2001.

Phillips, Deborah, and Kathleen McCartney, eds. *Blackwell Handbook of Early Childhood Development*. Malden, MA: Blackwell Publishing, 2006.

Porter, Louise. *Young Children's Behavior: Practical Approaches for Caregivers and Teachers*. 2nd Edition. Baltimore, MD: Brookes Publishing, 2003.

Post, Jackie. *Tender Care and Early Learning: Supporting Infants and Toddlers in Child Care Settings*. Ypsilanti, MI: High/Scope Press, 2000.

Slentz, Kristine. *Early Childhood Development and Its Variations*. Mahwah, NJ: Lawrence Erlbaum Associates, 2000.

Talay-Ongan, Ashe. *Typical and Atypical Development in Early Childhood: The Fundamentals*. New York: Teachers College Press, 1998.

Trawick-Smith, Jeffrey. *Early Childhood Development: A Multicultural Perspective*. 4th Edition. Upper Saddle River, NJ: Prentice Hall, 2006.

Play and Literacy

Bardige, Betty. *At a Loss for Words: How America Is Failing Our Children and What We Can Do About It.* Philadelphia: Temple University Press, 2005.

Bardige, Betty, and Marilyn Segal. *Building Literacy with Love.* Washington, DC: Zero to Three Press, 2005.

Barone, Diane M., and Lesley Mandel Morrow. *Literacy and Young Children: Research-Based Practices.* New York: Guilford Press, 2003.

Bennett-Armistead, Susan, Annie Moses, and Nell Duke. *Literacy and the Youngest Learner.* New York: Scholastic, 2006.

Boehm, Helen F. *The Official Guide to the Right Toys.* Bloomington, IN: Authorhouse, 2005.

Early Childhood Consortium. *Play in Practice: Case Studies in Young Children's Play.* St. Paul, MN: Redleaf Press, 2002.

Einon, Dorothy. *How Children Learn Through Play.* Hauppauge, NY: Barron's Educational Series, 2004.

Feierbend, M. John. *First Steps in Music for Infants and Toddlers.* Chicago: GIA Publications, 2000.

Fenichel, Emily, ed. *Language and Literacy in the Earliest Years.* Washington, DC: Zero to Three Press, 2004.

Frost, Joe L., Sue Wortham, and Stuart Reifel. *Play and Child Development.* New York: Prentice Hall, 2004.

Golinkoff, Roberta M. *How Babies Talk: The Magic and Mystery of Language in the First Three Years of Life.* New York: Dutton, 2000.

Hart, Betty. *The Social World of Children Learning to Talk.* Baltimore, MD: Brookes Publishing, 1999.

Jalongo, Mary Renck. *Early Childhood Language Arts.* 3rd Edition. Boston: Allyn and Bacon, 2002.

Jones, Elizabeth, and Renatta Cooper. *Playing to Get Smart.* New York: Teachers College Press, 2005.

McQuillan, Jeff. *The Literacy Crisis: False Claims, Real Solutions.* Portsmouth, NH: Heinemann, 1998.

Oppenheim, Joanne, Stephanie Oppenheim, and Joan Auclair. *Oppenheim Toy Portfolio: The Best Toys, Books and DVDs for Kids, 2007 Edition.* New York: Oppenheim Toy Portfolio, 2007.

Piaget, Jean. *Language and Thought of the Child.* New York: Routledge, 2001.

Piper, Terry. *Language and Learning: The Home and School Years.* 3rd Edition. Englewood Cliffs, NJ: Prentice Hall, 2002.

Rockwell, Robert E. *Linking Language: Simple Language and Literacy Activities Throughout the Curriculum.* Beltsville, MD: Gryphon House, 1999.

Rosenkoetter, Sharon E., and Joanne Knapp-Philo. *Learning to Read the World: Language and Literacy in the First Three Years.* Washington, DC: Zero to Three Press, 2006.

Roskos, Kathy, and James Christie. *Play and Literacy in Early Childhood: Research from Multiple Perspectives.* Mahwah, NJ: Lawrence Erlbaum Associates, 2000.

Seefeldt, Carol. *Playing to Learn: Activities and Experiences That Build Learning Connections.* Beltsville, MD: Gryphon House, 2001.

Singletary, Mary Jones. *Children's Speech, Language and Hearing: The Answer Book.* Kent, OH: Communication Enhancement, 2000.

Whitehead, Marian R. *Developing Language and Literacy with Young Children*. London: Chapman, 2002.

Zigler, Edward F., et al. *Children's Play: The Roots of Reading*. Washington, DC: Zero to Three Press, 2004.

6

Communicating Effectively
with Parents

Parents hear repeatedly that they need to act as their child's first teacher and capitalize on the window of opportunity that is presented in the child's early years. In their quest to help their children grow into healthy adult readers and learners, parents have routinely sought the advice and help of relatives, friends, and professionals. Today, with families scattered across the globe, traditional sources of advice, such as the extended family, are less available, and parents have come to rely on educators and health and human service professionals for child-rearing information and family support. In addition to relying on health professionals, "recent decades have seen a burst of media publications related to parenting" (Rankin, 2005: 1). Indeed, "the percentage of editorial space devoted to child rearing has been increasing in women's magazines, the children and family "beat" is becoming a regular assignment for newspaper reporters, and there has been a boom in parenting magazines" (Rankin, 2005: 2). All this leads to the library, where information specialists collect, make available, and communicate information to parents on a wide variety of topics to support and empower them in their role as their child's first teacher.

Burton White and his associates at Harvard University undertook a thirteen-year study that looked at how children develop in the first six years of life. In their research they were impressed not only by "what some children could achieve in the first years, but also by the fact that a child's own family seemed so obviously central to the outcome. Indeed, we came to believe that the more informal education that families provide for their children makes more of an impact on a child's total education than the formal education system. If a family does its job well, the professional can then provide effective training. If not, there may be little a professional can do to save a child from mediocrity" (White, Burton L., 1985: 4).

Family-centered library services focus on both the individuality of the child and the important role of the family. Partnership and collaboration with parents are essential for the delivery of quality service. Because librarians have only limited contact, they may not be fully aware of the child's overall development or family stress with which caregivers are coping. By developing a general understanding of and sensitivity to the emotional needs of families, practicing active and reflective listening skills, and implementing strategies to encourage parents to trust and partner with the library, library staff can more effectively communicate with parents and gain a better understanding of their and their child's wants and needs.

Understanding Parents

"Parenting is a complex activity that includes many specific behaviors that work individually and together to influence child outcomes. Although specific parenting behaviors, such as spanking or reading aloud, may influence child development, looking at any specific behavior in isolation may be misleading. Many writers have noted that specific parenting practices are less important in predicting child well-being than is the broad pattern of parenting" (Darling, 1999: 1). Just as children go through a number of developmental stages on their journey to adulthood, so too do their parents.

Understanding different stages of parenthood, the influence parents' early childhood experiences have on their child-rearing techniques, and the variety of parenting styles and cultural influences helps librarians to empathize with parents and create a more neutral, supportive, and welcoming library environment. By understanding the various stages of parenthood as well as parent roles of teacher and caregiver, librarians can better assist them in locating appropriate resources, books, community groups, and other information for themselves and their children.

Stages of Parenthood

In her groundbreaking book *The Six Stages of Parenthood*, Ellen Galinsky explored the theory that adults, as parents, go through a series of stages of development. Her research was groundbreaking at the time in its belief that "parents had pictures in their minds of the way things were supposed to go, and of the way that they as parents and their children were supposed to act" (Galinksy, 1987: 8). These images of how life as a parent was supposed to operate were the adult legacy of children's play. Just as a child plays and explores through creative play and expression, parents, too, can role-play at transitional times in their parental development by imagining how things are supposed to be or how they would have changed something if they had the control or ability to do so. Galinksy believed that parents were able to grow and develop as more effective parents through these role-playing sessions.

The Image-Making Stage: The period that prospective parents enter when they begin to gather and go through information about childbirth and child development is the image-making stage. Parents begin to reform their images of what is to come in terms of both the birthing process and parenthood in general.

The Nurturing Stage: The stage from birth to two years brings conflict as parents come to terms with what they thought their child-parenting situation would be like and what the reality is for them. During this period parents form an attachment to their baby, accepting the child that has been born and dealing with the fact that this child may, in fact, be quite different from the one they had been imagining over the past few months.

The Authority Stage: The authority stage occurs during the child's second through fifth year of age. The parents' ability to act as their child's first teacher comes into play during this third stage. How do adults as parents handle the responsibility of power and authority? How do they communicate or make decisions in relation to their child's well-being? How do they handle battleground issues such as sleeping, toilet training, discipline, and nutrition?

The Interpretive Stage: During the child's age from five to twelve years the parents interpret everything surrounding them—their values, their child's values, the school's values, and other aspects of their world. The parents' major task at this stage is to interpret the world to their children, and that entails not only interpreting themselves to their children and interpreting and developing their children's self-concepts but also answering their questions, providing them access to the skills and information they need, and helping them form values.

The Interdependent Stage and the Departure Stage: These final two parenting stages encompass issues that parents face as their children enter adolescence and young adulthood. The interdependent stage is very similar to the authority stage, except that it covers the teenage years. Often parents have the same types of questions regarding rules, permissiveness, and strictness as they do in the younger authority stage. As the child is entering adulthood, parents need to start forming a different kind of relationship with their child.

The sixth and final stage is the departure stage, when the child leaves the family home. Often this is a stage of loss for the parents and brings about a period of self-evaluation. Parents question how good a job they did raising their child and how their image of their child fits with reality. At this time, parents need to accept the child as an adult and to let go of their child.

Parenting Schemas

In *Parenting Schemas and the Process of Change* (Azar, Nix, and Makin-Byrd, 2005: 45–58), the authors contend that schemas guide parents' child-rearing behaviors. Schemas are information structures in memory that help us organize past experiences and respond to novel situations. Parenting schemas include conceptions of the caregiving role, beliefs about one's own functioning in that role, knowledge of children in general (i.e., how they develop and what they should be like), and thoughts about one's own children in particular. Schemas help us predict the behavior of people we encounter on a regular basis and efficiently respond to environmental stimuli. Parenting schemas are the starting point of information processing in child caregiving situations.

Because parenting is a socially constructed role, the society within which mothers and fathers live most likely exerts the strongest influence on parenting schemas. Culturally related customs and practices of child rearing are internalized and become standards against which acceptable parenting practices are judged. Parenting schemas are also shaped by individual experiences parents have as children in their own families and by ongoing experiences parents have with spouses, partners, friends, and other important people in their lives. Parents learn some aspects of their role by talking to and imitating other parents.

When parenting schemas are overly simplistic, they may miss opportunities to help their children master age-salient developmental tasks. Parents need to be able to assess what their children do and do not understand so they can provide optimal scaffolding to enhance competence. By providing a safe, neutral context within the library environment, librarians help parents examine their own parenting schemas and assess their expectations of their child's behavior, developmental levels, and skill expectations. Parents can adapt or modify their own behaviors based on information they learn from books and other resources and knowledge they acquire in group programs or one-on-one interactions with staff and other parents. By modeling and coaching, librarians educate parents about typical child behaviors and developmental tasks. Parents are also afforded opportunities either in programs or when using the drop-in spaces in the children's room to learn by observing and interacting with other parents and children.

Parenting Style

Parenting style is meant to describe normal variations in parenting and revolves around issues of control, assuming that the primary role of all parents is to influence, teach, and control their children. Different styles yield different outcomes for children. Social scientists find that parenting styles affect children's psychological well-being, their school achievement, and other aspects of their social and psychological adjustment (Ballantine, 2001: 46). Most of the research on parenting styles grew out of the work of Diana Baumrind, a developmental psychologist, who ascertained that four main styles of parenting could be observed, based on two important elements: parental responsiveness and parental demandingness.

"Parental responsiveness (also referred to as parental warmth or supportiveness) refers to 'the extent to which parents intentionally foster individuality, self-regulation, and self-assertion by being attuned, supportive, and acquiescent to children's special needs and demands.' Parental demandingness (also referred to as behavioral control) refers to 'the claims parents make on children to become integrated into the family whole, by their maturity demands, supervision, disciplinary efforts and willingness to confront the child who disobeys'" (Darling, 1999: 1).

There are positive parenting behaviors found in both responsiveness and demandingness. The following are lists of those behaviors, taken from the book *Raising Cuddlebugs and Bravehearts Volume II: Adult Temperament and Parenting Styles* (Harkey and Jourgensen, 2004: 233).

Responsiveness—Positive Parenting Behaviors:

Providing warmth and affection to your child
Providing a loving and supportive home environment
Taking a great interest in your child's development at all stages
Speaking and reading to your child early and often
Clearly explaining your reasons for rules and limits
Listening to your child's ideas and openly considering his or her feelings and viewpoints
Encouraging and actively supporting the child's education and special interests

Demandingness—Positive Parenting Behaviors:

Setting reasonable and appropriate behavioral limits and consequences for misbehavior
Confronting misbehavior directly and consistently
Enforcing consequences consistently
Establishing a home environment that is organized and provides routines
Establishing responsibilities for household and school work and monitoring completion
Monitoring the child's world to protect from harmful influences

In addition to responsiveness and demandingness, parenting styles differ in the extent to which they are characterized by psychological control or intrusions into the psychological and emotional development of the child. Baumrind, who believed parents are high or low on parental demandingness and responsiveness, created a typology of four parenting styles, summarized in an article by Nancy Darling (1999):

Indulgent or permissive parents: Indulgent or permissive parents are more responsive than they are demanding. Nontraditional and extremely lenient, they avoid confrontation and allow for considerable self-regulation from the child. Further subdivided, indulgent parents can be classified as democratic, who, though lenient, are more engaged and conscientious, and nondirective, those who are both lenient and not as engaged.

Authoritarian parents: Highly demanding and directive, authoritarian parents expect their orders to be obeyed without explanation. They provide clearly stated rules and highly structured environments. Authoritarian parents can also be subdivided into those who are directive but not intrusive or autocratic in their use of power and those who are directive and highly intrusive and autocratic in their use of power.

Authoritative parents: Authoritative parents are both demanding and responsive to their child's needs. They balance clear, high parental demands with emotional performance, psychosocial development, and problem behavior. They monitor and impart clear standards for their children's conduct, are assertive (but not intrusive and restrictive) and are supportive rather than punitive in their disciplinary methods. They want their children to be assertive as well as socially responsible and self-regulated as well as cooperative.

Uninvolved parents: These parents are low in both responsiveness and demandingness. In extreme cases, this style of parenting can lead to neglect and rejection of a child, though most parents of this type fall within the normal range.

When librarians model various communication strategies based on knowledge about parenting styles and child development, they remain flexible in their approach to helping parents become more effective caregivers and better teachers. Some parents respond to parent-child group programs, while others prefer a lecture on a child development issue. Some parents prefer to research an issue using a book or electronic resource. Acceptance of varying parenting styles and recognition that there is no one way to raise a child build trust between the librarian and parent and models for other parents that there are various ways to raise a child and no one way is appropriate for all parents.

Cultural Differences and Parenting

"As the population of early childhood programs becomes more diverse and as educators seek to provide all children an optimal start in life, there is a growing recognition of the need for strategies that enhance the learning experiences of children of diverse cultures and languages" (Jones and Lorenzo-Hubert, 2006: 188). In communicating and working with parents, librarians should recognize the role that culture, ethnicity, race, and religion play in parenting and child rearing. "Communication is directly influenced by culture and is more than simply linguistic rules or the words that one learns to speak. Language is but one part of communication, and the rules that guide communicative interactions are largely influenced by one's cultural and social experiences. . . . [Parents] have a set of expectations, values and beliefs (frameworks) for most social events that is generated by their past experiences in their socio-cultural community. Culturally diverse persons come to interactions with different frameworks—different experiences, expectations, goals, and communication styles. When (librarians) from one communicative framework interact with children and families from different frameworks, there may be a mismatch of communication expectations, styles, values and goals" (Hwa-Froelich and Westby, 2003: 300–301). Cultural orientation may influence how library patrons interact within the library environment as manifested in:

Child-rearing techniques
Language and communication styles
How people seek assistance
Availability of extended family and informal helping networks
Attitude toward bureaucracies and government-sponsored programs and services
Familiarity with American culture

The culture of libraries may differ or conflict with the cultural values and beliefs of the families they are attempting to serve. These cultural or philosophical differences may impact what children's librarians do in communicating with parents. "Understanding the interactional frameworks of the families from diverse cultures and the values and beliefs that underlie these frameworks will facilitate effective communication and meaningful, appropriate interactions" (Hwa-Froelich and Westby, 2003: 303). By becoming aware of their own underlying assumptions and how these may affect their interactions with those children and families who may have different assumptions and expectations, the library staff can take a positive step toward working effectively with parents from a wide variety of backgrounds and cultures. In working with a diverse constituency, librarians should try to scrutinize their own feelings and beliefs about groups other than their own, understand their own frameworks and the frameworks of the families, and acknowledge stereotypes and biases.

In order to effectively communicate with parents, the library staff can become aware of the array of the particular cultures that make up the library's patron base. Having a good collection of materials targeted to specific audiences, displaying posters that depict the diversity of our society, being familiar with community resources for a variety of groups, and developing cooperative programs with agencies that work with diverse cultures are just some ideas for including all families within the library setting (Feinberg, 1999: 68). Other useful strategies can be as simple as hanging a welcome sign that features six to eight of the main languages spoken in the community based on census data; keeping track of the languages other than English spoken by staff members to facilitate conversation and communication with patrons; translating flyers into other languages; or employing a family outreach worker who speaks a language predominant in the community to reach out to parents and families who are not familiar with the library's services and collections. Chapter 14, "Culturally Diverse Families," offers additional information on reaching out to and providing services for culturally diverse families in your community.

Nurturing the Parent as the Child's First Teacher

Parents and caregivers are "the most influential people in a child's life and children model their behavior on the actions of these adults. Most parents want to provide their children with the best opportunities to grow and develop, but many do not know how to maximize opportunities for their child's development. Brain development, language acquisition, emergent literacy, and appropriate materials are often outside the knowledge of a new parent. Parents must learn why and how to read to their children, and to discover the best activities to do with them" (White, Dan R., 2002: 3).

While the parent as teacher role is commonly referred to, community expectations of children's proficiency in print, media, and technological literacy often leave parents feeling inadequate and powerless:

> Many of the parents whom we deal with in the community are parents who can actually read. They read the newspaper and magazines, they read the occasional story to their children, they speak in a way that communicates, and they fill in a form without assistance. These people could never be termed illiterate. Yet in terms of the needs of their children they have a dysfunctional literacy, which prevents them from offering the best of experiences in literature, language and creative, imaginative expression. They are unable to read to a baby, and would never even think of doing so. They do not have the knowledge, or even grasp the importance, of those rhymes and rhythms of early childhood collections that have been long enjoyed by some parents and their children (Fisher, 1999: 2).

"The most important factor is the shared book experience between children and parents or caregivers. No one book is magic on its own; children need someone to make sharing books interactive and fun. Otherwise, books remain unopened. Learning to talk, learning to read, and learning to love books are social experiences" (Arnold, 2002: 24).

Children need parents and caregivers who talk to them, sing to them, and read to them daily. Developmentally appropriate storytimes and Mother Goose programs demonstrate the selection and presentation of books and the use of music, fingerplays, and other activities. Parents "think librarians are doing something magical when they conduct a storytime in the library. In fact what they do is take something, which is freely available, and offer it within a prepared framework with a few embellishments. There is nothing magical about it at all. What we do could be done by many parents if they knew how" (Fisher, 1999: 2).

Helping parents to understand the role of play in learning to read and appreciating the importance of play as child's work is one of the librarian's primary tasks. With knowledge, parents can provide a home environment that is filled with age-appropriate toys, books, and learning games. "The availability of appropriate play materials in the home, throughout infancy and toddlerhood, has a positive effect on achievement in early elementary school, particularly in reading achievement" (Bradley, Caldwell, and Rock, 1988: 864). Showing young children how to play, socially engaging with their play experiences, and interjecting fun with books and literature allow parents to model effective learning strategies for their children and become engaged in their role as primary teacher.

Both the library and the librarian working with families can have an impact on parents and their relationship to a child's attitude toward literacy, language, and learning. They have great potential to inject fun and mutual enjoyment into a family's development along the literacy path with their children. In the process the library is marketed as an endless, free resource for all this activity. This philosophy, with links that offer parents and caregivers strategies and skills for developing a literary environment within the home setting which embodies all the literacies (reading, writing, listening, and speaking) informs parents and caregivers about the different ways in which children learn and involves an exploration of the nature and value of different kinds of formats in the presentation of literature of the creative kind and of the informative kind. It has at its core a lack of timetabling and ritual and the potential for a maximum of fun and shared enjoyment for all the participants. Although it has a serious underlying purpose, the process and the outcomes are unashamedly enjoyable for both parents and their children (Fisher, 1999: 3).

Creating Library Users by Involving Parents

"Librarians have the great advantage of having a relationship with a parent or caregiver that is voluntary and based on mutual trust and respect; a partnership where both are dedicated to achieving the best for a child" (White, Dan R., 2002: 3). Establishing positive one-on-one communication with parents is by far the most important building block in the creation of family-centered services. When working with families, librarians must recognize that the attitudes and beliefs they bring to the partnership as professionals influence the relationship. To be effective, librarians need to acknowledge their personal feelings about parental responsibility, accept parents as individuals and adult learners, and assess their professional beliefs about serving children within the family unit. It is important that librarians uncover their feelings and opinions regarding their role as family support professionals.

Many of the messages librarians give about literacy and learning are subtle and a matter of attitude and perception. Parents who are still developing their own attitudes and philosophies about behaviors and relationships often pick up these subtle messages. Being enthusiastic, appreciative, and informed in our dealings with children and their parents may be a stronger influence for good than we realize. Children also pick up very strongly on the librarian's inner feelings about literacy and learning. A significant part of their entire belief in books and libraries depends on their early experiences with a librarian and the collection to which they are introduced (Fisher, 1999: 73).

Librarians should try to not view the family and the library in isolation from one another. They need to examine connections between these two spheres of influence if they are to integrate how families interact with reading and learning at home and how children learn at the library. How parents feel and act in the library will have an impact on their child's own attitude and behavior in the library. Some parents may be uncomfortable in the library setting or feel that the library is off-putting as an educational institution. They may not have done well in school, never used the library as a child, or are embarrassed because of their own lack of research or computer skills. They may come from another country that has no public libraries. Getting parents comfortable in the library setting, encouraging them to communicate with their child on how the library can enhance their educational and personal lives, and involving parents in their child's work set the model for the child as not only a current but a future library user.

Relationships with librarians, not the collection, services, or buildings, are the most important parts of a child's and family's use of the library. Helping parents recognize the genuine desire of librarians to support them and their children as they grow is critical. Librarians need to convince parents that they are partners in providing children with opportunities to develop to their fullest potential, and they need to demonstrate knowledge and expertise of the many needs of children and the role the library can play in meeting those needs (White, Dan R., 2002: 2).

Linking learning and literature in all their formats with families promotes family literacy and parent involvement in the use of the library. When a librarian works with the young child to locate material on a special topic and involves the parent in the search strategy, the librarian is suggesting a reading relationship between the child and the child's family. Encouraging parent-child listening or viewing a children's story indicates that adults can derive genuine pleasure from this form of literacy and that, even though it is essentially a child's story, it is still acceptable to appreciate it and share it over the generations. When display shelves are filled with materials in diverse formats and stories are enhanced with flannel board and puppetry kits, libraries encourage family sharing and mutual enjoyment.

Providing Information and Referral

The changing needs and status of today's families often mean that parents are turning to professionals, such as the local librarian, to answer their informational needs regarding their child's growth and development, emergent literacy and prereading skills, and special health and medical concerns or to locate local resources for their families. The more libraries open their doors to young children, the more children's librarians will be called upon to access materials and resources to satisfy the parents' information requests (Feinberg et al.,1999: 59–61).

To make the parent feel comfortable when seeking advice and access to information, librarians need to develop a general sensitivity to the needs of the family, practice active and reflective listening skills, and implement strategies to encourage parents to trust and partner with them. Not only are parents their child's first teacher, they are their child's primary advocate as well. Armed with information and resources, parents can better advocate for their child's and families' needs. Becoming involved in a Mothers' Center, a parent support group, and the local chapter of the Parents Teachers Association, parents gain a voice to support a child's growth and development in a proactive way. The roles that adults take on when they become parents are constantly changing and evolving, and children's librarians need to support parents in these roles by connecting them to current and appropriate information and resources.

Parents and caregivers are adult learners who learn at their own pace and in their own styles. They want to incorporate their own knowledge about themselves and their child, preferring a facilitated exchange of ideas rather than a didactic or professional exchange. Being comfortable with a wide array of materials and community resources enhances the exchange of information between librarian and parent and provides the librarian with alternative strategies to satisfy information needs. Some parents may be looking for a support group; others are more comfortable researching information on the Internet; and reading a book or short article may be just what another parent needs. Librarians can ease a parent's anxiety simply by being knowledgeable about alternative learning styles and analyzing what resources a particular parent would most readily utilize to ensure the most "comfortable fit."

Satisfying a parent's request for services, either through referral to other community resources or by providing services within the library itself, is a primary task of children's librarians who wish to create a family-centered library environment. To make the library a connecting link for families, librarians are continuously building skills, competencies, and a knowledge base to assist them in the development of the parent-professional partnership.

Develop Communication Skills

The process of gathering information does not always go smoothly. Parents may be afraid to ask questions, or, when dealing with a special issue, they may have difficulty putting their concerns into words. They may not ask a question directly or ask it so generally that the question could be viewed as a research inquiry, not as the intensely personal request for information and support that it is. Professionals may not take the time to listen or may minimize concerns in an attempt to reassure an anxious parent.

Being prepared for questions and understanding how to appropriately engage parents in the reference interview process help to alleviate discomfort or uneasiness while successfully meeting their needs. It is helpful to keep the following guidelines, adapted from *Including Families of Children with Special Needs* (Feinberg, 1999) in mind:

Anticipate That Parents Will Ask Questions: Be ready for inquiries of a sensitive nature. Knowing how to provide referral information and where such information can be found in the library is essential. Sometimes parents will ask support staff for assistance. Train the support staff on how to assist parents and connect them to the librarian. Having a parent's collection in the children's room, creating special links on the library's Web page, displaying posters and brochures of children and caregivers from a variety of ethnic backgrounds, and offering an array of services for parents and young children demonstrate to families that the library cares about their family.

Give Advice Based on Qualifications and Experience: Though librarians may have degrees and credentials in related fields, it is important to remember that a librarian is not a personal friend, counselor, or social worker. It is a delicate line between being a family-support professional and a personal friend. Learn to say, "I'm not the best person to answer that question or solve that problem. Let's see if we can find some books and Web sites that can provide some information, and I'll be glad to look for someone who is qualified to help you."

Be Approachable, but Draw Boundaries: You cannot solve all problems for all families. Tell parents that the library is pleased to assist them with their request. Listen long enough and ask pertinent questions in order to uncover what the parent actually wants (e.g., a support group, health information, a therapeutic service). There may be a support group that already meets in the library, or you can refer parents to appropriate agencies for help.

Personal boundaries are equally important. Parents sometimes step over the line unintentionally, especially if they are emotionally upset and feel that the librarian is someone who is warm and caring. If the reference interview goes beyond a point that is comfortable, respectfully communicate a limit to the parent.

Become Familiar with Local Resources: Many libraries compile community resource directories on paper, as part of the online public access catalog (OPAC), or on the Internet. It is the responsibility of the children's librarian to ensure that services to families and young children are fully included and that the children's staff is trained in the use of the directory. Parents in need often require information fast. Having brochures or a printed list on hand, as well as personal knowledge of local services, motivates parents to begin the problem-solving process.

Use Active Listening Skills

The most important communication technique when working with families is the ability to listen. Listening improves communication, conveys a caring attitude, and helps the listener to better understand and be in control of a situation. Good listening enables librarians to provide better and more accurate assistance.

Listening is more than hearing. Hearing is a physical act. Listening is an intellectual and emotional act. Hearing acknowledges sounds. Listening requires understanding what is said, getting the whole message, that which is beyond just the words. Active listening is a learned activity.

Effective listening skills do not come naturally. To be an active listener requires practice. Five steps to active listening, adapted from *Listen Up: Hear What's Really Being Said* (Dugger, 1991) include:

Listen to the content. Being prepared and motivated to listen puts you in the right frame of mind. Listen to what the patron is saying in terms of facts and ideas. Reflecting back to the patron the information he or she is trying to impart increases understanding. Strive for accuracy.

Listen to the intent. Use intuition to hear the underlying messages, particularly the emotional meaning of what the patron is saying.

Assess the patron's nonverbal communication. Read and interpret what the patron is saying with body language and other nonverbal signals.

Monitor your nonverbal communication and emotional filters. Be aware of the messages that you may be sending through body language and expressions. Be aware of personal emotional filters that may be affecting your understanding of the message.

Listen to the patron nonjudgmentally and with empathy. Put yourself in the patron's shoes and understand what is shaping the patron's feelings. Do not prejudge the patron.

By applying active listening skills when working with parents, librarians will become better information specialists. By anticipating questions, listening nonjudgmentally, and reflecting back, librarians will more accurately interpret a parent's information needs. This awareness and sensitivity set the stage for librarians to partner with parents from all walks of life.

Speaking with Parents about a Child's Behavior

Often librarians hesitate to confront a problem with a parent because they are afraid that the parent may become angry or defensive. It is important to remember that, even if parents initially deny the librarian's concerns, when the problem recurs in another setting, the parent may be more ready to accept the information. If the problem recurs in the library setting, the librarian can bring the issue up again, reflecting on past experience. Most parents will welcome your interest and involvement with their child. Oftentimes, they have observed the same behaviors at home and do not know where to turn for advice and help.

Before approaching parents, it is important to reflect and make notes on the child's behavior. Try to observe the child on more then one occasion. Asking the following questions, taken from A Family Child Care Provider's Guide to New York's Early Intervention Program: Trainer's Manual (1996: 30), may help to clarify the behaviors that are at issue.

Is the child too active, or not active enough?
Is the child's behavior harmful to himself or others?
Is the social environment frequently disrupted and tense due to the child's behavior?
Does the child seem to have chronic health problems?
Does the child have problems with seeing or hearing?
Is the child talking? Does he talk differently than other children?
Does the child seem excessively fearful?
Does the child consistently withdraw from children, adults, and activities?
Is the child not rolling, walking, or moving like other children the same age?
Has the problem or situation persisted over time, increased in severity or frequency, or become more noticeable, regardless of trying a variety of strategies for coping?
Is the child's behavior significantly unusual compared to typical child behavior?

When speaking with parents about their child, librarians need to talk openly and honestly, focusing on the child's behavior. Consider the approach and setting in which the conversation will occur. Handle the discussion discreetly, with care and sensitivity. The nine tips in the next section may be helpful for a successful intervention.

Nine Tips for a Successful Intervention

Summarize and Write Down Observations of the Child: Use the questions above to guide your observations. If another staff member is in attendance, ask the person for assistance in identifying their observations of the child's behavior. Using written documentation, even in simple note form, makes it easier to clarify specific behaviors and helps keep the conversation on target.

Focus on the Behavior of the Child: Describe what the child is doing or not doing. Never attempt to diagnose problems or make judgments about the child.

Determine in Advance the Major Points: Plan how and what to say to the parent. Speaking confidentially with another staff member before talking with the parent may help to clarify the issues.

Stress the Importance of the Parent as the Child's First and Primary Teacher: Reaffirm that as the child's first and primary teachers, parents have the most knowledge of their child. Listen carefully to the parent's explanation of why a child may be behaving a certain way.

Anticipate a Parent's Range of Reactions: There is a wide range of emotions that parents may have when approached about a problem or issue regarding their child's behavior. Review listening skills before speaking with parents.

Try Not to Get Defensive: It is common for parents to initially deny the problem, resent the intrusion, or blame the staff. This is when written notes summarizing specific behaviors will come in handy.

Listen to the Parents Carefully: Review the guidelines on active listening skills in this chapter. If parents express similar concerns, be prepared to provide information and referral or suggest a possible solution to improve the child's participation within the library program. If a parent feels there is no problem, suggest to the parent that he or she may wish to ask another professional or read an article or book.

Avoid These Discussions When the Child Is Present: It is inappropriate and demeaning to talk about a child with the child present, except to praise. Do not discuss the problems or concerns unless you are alone with the parents. Maybe the child could be taken care of by the support staff for a short period of time while you speak to the parents. Consider phoning the parents at home and asking for a good time to speak with them.

Respect Confidentiality: Confidentiality is a must. Discussing children in front of or with other parents is never appropriate. Being respectful of parents and building trust are primary considerations for the librarian.

Communicating with parents, particularly around sensitive issues regarding their own children, requires flexibility and sensitivity. Being able to communicate effectively is essential. When librarians practice healthy communication skills on a daily basis with parents and adult caregivers, they will be better prepared to constructively handle problems when they arise. They will be more secure in their roles as family support professionals and, in difficult situations, be able to turn to other professionals for advice and help.

Conclusion

Supporting parents as the primary teachers and advocates of their young children is an important task of a family services librarian. In becoming family-centered, libraries and librarians need to reach out to parents, develop a relationship with them, and get them involved in the learning process. Understanding parents' needs and how parents view literacy, learning, and libraries paves the way for librarians to effectively communicate with parents as partners and adult learners. Making parents comfortable with language, literature, play, and social interaction with their children can have a profound impact on how their children develop and learn. By understanding the different parenting styles and how they can affect parents as adult learners, librarians can offer a wider variety of learning opportunities to the families that they serve.

References

Arnold, Renea. "Coming Together for Children: A Guide to Early Childhood Programming." *Journal of Youth Services in Libraries* 15, no. 2 (Winter): 24–30, 2002.

Azar, Sandra T., Robert L. Nix, and Kerry N. Makin-Byrd. "Parenting Schemas and the Process of Change." *Journal of Marital and Family Therapy* 31, no. 1 (January): 45–58, 2005.

Ballantine, Jeanne. "Raising Competent Kids: The Authoritative Parenting Style." *Childhood Education* 78: 46, 2001.

Bradley, R. H., B. M. Caldwell, and S. L. Rock. "Home Environment and School Performance: A Ten Year Follow-up and Examination of Three Models of Environmental Action." *Child Development* 59: 852–67, 1988.

Darling, Nancy. "Parenting Style and Its Correlates." *ERIC Digest* EDO-PS-99-3, 1999.

Dugger, Jim. *Listen Up: Hear What's Really Being Said.* Shawnee Mission, KS: National Press Publications, a division of Rockhurst College Continuing Education Center, 1991.

A Family Child Care Provider's Guide to New York's Early Intervention Program: Trainer's Manual. Albany, NY: Early Intervention Program, New York State Department of Health, 1996.

Feinberg, Sandra, et al. *Including Families of Children with Special Needs.* New York: Neal-Schuman, 1999.

Fisher, Heather. "Family Literacy: The Hidden Need." *Australasian Public Libraries and Information Services* 12, no. 2 (June): 72–82, 1999.

Galinsky, Ellen. *The Six Stages of Parenthood.* Reading, MA: Addison-Wesley, 1987.

Harkey, Nancy J., and Teri L. Jourgensen. *Raising Cuddle Bugs and Bravehearts. Volume II: Adult Temperament and Parenting Styles.* Bloomington, IN: Authorhouse, 2004.

Hwa-Froelich, Deborah H., and Carol E. Wesby. "Frameworks of Education: Perspectives of Southeast Asian Parents and Head Start Staff." *Language, Speech, and Hearing Services in Schools* 34, no. 4 (October): 299–319, 2003.

Jones, Wendy, and Isabella Lorenzo-Hubert. "Culture and Parental Expectations for Child Development: Concerns for Language Development and Early Learning." In *Learning to Read the World: Language and Literacy in the First Three Years*, edited by Sharon E. Rosenkoetter and Joanne Knapp-Philo, p. 188. Washington, DC: Zero to Three Press, 2006.

Rankin, Jane L. *Parenting Experts: Their Advice, the Research, and Getting It Right.* Westport, CT: Praeger, 2005.

White, Burton L. *The First Three Years of Life.* New York: Prentice Hall, 1985.

White, Dan R. "Working Together to Build a Better World: The Importance of Youth Services in the Development and Education of Children and Their Parents." *OLA Quarterly* 8, no. 3 (Fall): 15–19, 2002.

Resources for Parents and Professionals on Parenting

Balter, Lawrence, ed. *Parenthood in America: An Encyclopedia.* Santa Barbara, CA: ABC-CLIO, 2000.

Bavolek, Stephen. *Understanding Cultural Parenting Values, Traditions, and Practices.* Park City, UT: Family Development Resources, 1997.

Beal, Anne. *The Black Parenting Book.* New York: Broadway Books, 1999.

Bigner, Jerry. *Parent-Child Relations: An Introduction to Parenting.* 7th Edition. Upper Saddle River, NJ: Prentice Hall, 2005.

Boehm, Helen. *Fearless Parenting for the New Millennium.* Bloomington, IN: 1st Books, 2004.

Brooks, Jane B. *The Process of Parenting.* 6th Edition. Columbus, OH: McGraw Hill, 2003.

Cline, Foster W., and Jim Fay. *Parenting with Love and Logic.* Updated and Expanded Edition. Colorado Springs, CO: Pinon Press, 2006.

Dunning, Lisa. *Good Parents Bad Parenting: How to Parent Together When Your Parenting Styles Are Worlds Apart.* Lulu.com Publisher, 2004.

Fay, Jim. *Helicopters, Drill Sergeants and Consultants: Parenting Styles and the Messages They Send.* Golden, CO: Love and Logic Press, 1994.

Fay, Jim. *More Ideas about Parenting with Less Stress.* Golden, CO: Love and Logic Press, 2005.

Gordon, Thomas. *Parent Effectiveness Training: The Proven Program for Raising Responsible Children.* Revised and Updated. New York: Three Rivers Press, 2000.

Hamner, Tommie J., and Janine Turner. *Parenting in Contemporary Society.* 4th Edition. Upper Saddle River, NJ: Allyn and Bacon, 2000.

Harkey, Nancy J., and Teri L. Jourgensen. *Raising Cuddle Bugs and Bravehearts. Volume I: Measuring and Understanding Your Child's Temperament.* Bloomington, IN: Authorhouse, 2004.

Harkey, Nancy J., and Teri L. Jourgensen. *Raising Cuddle Bugs and Bravehearts. Volume II: Adult Temperament and Parenting Styles.* Bloomington, IN: Authorhouse, 2004.

Koman, Eleta. *The Parenting Survival Kit*. New York: Penguin Books, 2000.

Nevilee, Helen, and Diane Johnson. *Temperament Tools*. Seattle, WA: Parenting Press, 1997.

Peterson, Gary W., ed. *Parent-Youth Relations: Cultural and Cross-Cultural Perspectives*. New York: Haworth Press, 2005.

Rankin, Jane L. *Parenting Experts: Their Advice, the Research, and Getting It Right*. Westport, CT: Praeger, 2005.

Runkel, Hal Edward. *Scream Free Parenting: Raising Your Kids by Keeping Your Cool*. Duluth, GA: Oakmont Publishing, 2005.

Sclafani, Joseph D. *The Educated Parent: Recent Trends in Raising Children*. Westport, CT: Praeger, 2004.

Siegel, Daniel J. *Parenting from the Inside Out: How a Deeper Self-Understanding Can Help You Raise Children Who Thrive*. New York: Penguin Books, 2004.

Sunderland, Margot, and Jaak Panksepp. *The Science of Parenting: Practical Guidance on Sleep, Crying, Play and Building Emotional Well Being for Life*. New York: Dorling Kindersley, 2006.

Unell, Barbara C., and Jerry Wyckoff. *The 8 Seasons of Parenthood: How the Stages of Parenting Constantly Reshape our Adult Identities*. New York: Crown Publishing Group, 2000.

Vazquez, Carmen Inoa. *Parenting with Pride Latino Style: How to Help Your Child Cherish Your Cultural Values and Succeed in Today's World*. New York: Rayo, 2004.

Westman, Jack C. *Parenthood in America*. Madison: University of Wisconsin Press, 2001.

PART II

Developing Services
for Young Children
and Parents

7

Creating Family Spaces and Places

The first impression one gets upon entering a new environment is influenced by the look and feel of the physical space. Size, location, design, and content communicate messages for and about the target audience, as well as the purpose and type of behavior to expect within the space. In a library, the percentage of space devoted to young children and families reflects the importance the library and community place on early learning and family support. Traditional library settings with their rows of bookstacks, banks of computers, tables, chairs, and reference desks communicate a message that libraries are quiet, orderly places for reading and study. The family-centered library is a purposefully designed public space that welcomes very young children and families, is filled with developmentally appropriate activities and materials, and encourages play, interactive learning, and socialization.

"Learning occurs throughout the myriad of interactions of daily life. This is particularly true for infants and toddlers who, through interactions with their caregivers and their environment, are learning every waking minute. Yet there are few places within the community that recognize and welcome the ways in which infants and toddlers communicate and gather information about their world" (Kuchner, 2001: 11). The public library as a community agency is uniquely suited to facilitate the learning experiences of very young children and their caregivers. To realize this potential, libraries need to go beyond offering programs and collections and create welcoming, developmentally appropriate, learning environments. Such environments "recognize and appreciate the communication and active learning styles of these youngest patrons and respect the learning curve of parents and other accompanying adults as they mature into increasingly complex caregiving roles" (Kuchner, 2001: 12).

By exploring social relationships, manipulating objects, and interacting with people, children are able to formulate ideas, try these ideas out, and accept or reject what they learn. Children understand only what they discover or invent themselves, and this discovery is the vehicle for children's learning. To create an environment that promotes relationships and provides opportunities for exploration, librarians are challenged to rethink the library's social environment and reexamine its physical space.

Whether librarians are designing a new room or renovating an existing area for young children, they need to consider many factors for the space such as health and safety, boundaries, interaction, scale, transitions, age ranges, adult activity, and inclusiveness.

Health and Safety

Protecting the health and safety of infants, toddlers, and preschoolers is paramount when assessing and reshaping the physical environment of the library. Just as programs and materials must be developmentally appropriate, health and safety features of the environment require that librarians recognize how infants and toddlers use places and objects differently than older children and adults. Tasting, touching, and feeling are how infants and toddlers learn about the world around them. They reach for objects from the floor, stroller, or backpack or while in an adult's arms and learn about these new objects by mouthing them. To avoid choking hazards, toys and other materials with small parts might be better suited on higher ground or within program rooms. As defined by the U.S. Product Safety Commission, choking hazards include items that fit into a 1¼-inch cylinder (U.S. Consumer Product Safety Commission).

For toddlers, the sheer joy of independent movement often supersedes attention to obstacles in their path. By sitting on the floor and looking around, an adult can achieve a young child's perspective and become more aware of potentially dangerous situations for crawlers and walkers. Hazards to look for include exposed electrical outlets, cords and wires, furniture, shelving and other equipment with sharp corners, items with small parts, and older heating units that may get hot to the touch. Soft plastic corner guards are an inexpensive safety fix for most furniture and shelving with sharp corners.

Sturdy furniture, shelving, and display units are essential if they are to withstand the tugs and climbing activities of toddlers without falling over. Open staircases require particular attention. Some libraries have installed special gates, because even closely supervised toddlers can quickly dart out of reach. Gates and railings used in multilevel spaces and staircase landings are most effective when they are spaced close enough together to prevent babies and toddlers from slipping through or getting their heads stuck. U.S. government standards for infant cribs require openings be no more than 2⅜ inches apart (National Safety Council).

Family bathrooms located in or near the children's room equipped with changing tables, toddler-height toilets, and sinks with warm, not hot, water provide a safe, healthy, and convenient place for families to attend to the toileting needs of all ages. Including a toddler jump seat with a safety belt helps to keep toddlers safe and in sight while adults are occupied with younger ones at the changing table.

Cleanliness of the space and the furniture and materials within the space are all major health factors. Restrooms including diaper receptacles require disinfecting daily or more frequently. The use of nontoxic cleaning products is a must for restrooms as well as the entire library facility. Plants and other decorations also must be nontoxic. It is vital to ensure the library is free of less obvious hazards such as lead-based paint and asbestos and to assess potential fire hazards. Upholstery, curtains, floor coverings, and wall coverings are required to be nonflammable, and it is preferable to use low flammable materials for decorations and displays. Figure 7-1, adapted from *Learning Environments for Young Children* (Feinberg, Kuchner, and Feldman, 1998: 151), outlines many of the health and safety items librarians need to consider when designing early childhood spaces.

Boundaries

In "Schools to Scale: Learning Environments for Young Children" (Gisolfi, 1999: 39–41), the author describes the importance of creating boundaries—smaller spaces within a larger space—to satisfy the needs of children at various stages of development. Nooks, crannies, and partial enclosures are appealing to very young children who prefer to play in small groups of two to five while keeping significant adults in sight. Organizing space into a variety of large and small, active and quiet areas in which similar materials are grouped together helps define the behaviors that are appropriate in each area and allows children to make choices in their play.

A number of design strategies can be used to create boundaries. Since young children often prefer to play on the floor, colorful carpets or other patterned flooring can be used, or furniture, equipment, and shelving can be arranged to define space: picture book–height shelving can enclose alcoves that serve as a puzzle area, block corner, or cozy nook for book sharing; comfortable adult-size seating arrangements can separate a train or Lego table from a puppet stage; and the back of a large doll house might provide a partial barrier for a writing table. Fish tanks or large terrariums work nicely as natural boundaries between the early childhood area and collections and space for older children.

When creating boundaries, it is important to keep in mind that adults accompany, observe, and interact with children and each other within these spaces. Care needs to be taken to ensure that visual sight lines are not obstructed and some comfortable adult-size seating is integrated throughout the space.

7-1:   Health and Safety Checklist

☐   Emergency phone numbers are clearly posted for staff.

☐   Emergency procedures including clearly marked emergency exits are posted for staff.

☐   Emergency lighting is available in case of power failure.

☐   Rooms are well lighted.

☐   Electrical sockets are covered.

☐   Clearly defined pathways are free from obstruction.

☐   Pathways are wheel chair and stroller accessible.

☐   Heating units are covered or out of reach.

☐   Furniture has rounded corners.

☐   Open staircases are gated and bars on railings are spaced close enough together.

☐   Surfaces are smooth (free of splinters, protruding nails, broken or loose parts and sharp edges).

☐   Equipment and materials in contact with children are clean.

☐   Equipment and materials in contact with children are in working condition (repaired).

☐   Upholstery is made of non-flammable material.

☐   Shelves are stable (and can support the additional weigh of 35 lbs, if necessary).

☐   Trash receptacle openings cannot be reached by a toddler.

☐   Trash is contained within receptacle.

☐   Drinking fountain is accessible to children's room.

☐   Drinking fountain is low enough for a young child to reach on own or a step stool is available.

☐   Bathrooms are accessible to the children's room.

☐   Bathrooms are clean and disinfected daily or more frequently as necessary with a non-toxic substance.

☐   Diaper changing facility is available in the women's room.

☐   Diaper changing facility is available in the men's room.

☐   Step stool is available for use in bathroom and at water fountain, if needed.

☐   Towels or dryer in bathroom is accessible to young children.

Creating Interactive Spaces

Humans are social beings. We need to feel a sense of belonging and connectedness that comes from interactions with one another and our environment. "The design of a children's area must reinforce the function of the space and create the appropriate mood for a range of activities from social interaction, play, reading, computer use, and quiet study. Parents and caregivers are important participants in the child's environment, especially in the public library. While the primary consideration must be the child, the caregivers and the professional staff must also be considered" (Feinberg and Keller, in press). Room designs that offer materials for in-library use as well as circulation for children and their caregivers provide for such interactions and are a major feature of family-centered libraries.

Organization

Young children learn by doing. Access to a variety of appropriate materials encourages children to explore different mediums and interact with parents, other children, and the early learning resources within the environment. Organizing similar materials on low shelves or in baskets or bins on the floor for in-library use helps define and facilitate exploration by young children. A creative dramatic area might include a doll house, kitchen set, train table, puppet stage and puppets, and dress-up clothes. A parent-child literacy corner might have board books, big books, a flannel board with storybook characters, and prepackaged early literacy activities. A building area might have various sizes and types of blocks, floor and table puzzles, and a Lego table. An infant section might include stacking cups, baby mirrors, and cause-and-effect toys.

Computers equipped with preschool software and bookmarked with early childhood Internet sites may comprise a multimedia center along with an audiovisual corner for viewing and listening to stories and songs, and a writing table with large blank paper, crayons, and markers. Room for two seats is preferable because young children often work together or with their parents or caregivers (see Figure 7-2).

Scale

To increase young children's sense of comfort and emotional security, early childhood resources and spaces need to be filled with images and equipment scaled appropriately for their height and adapted to their motor abilities. As in well-designed childcare centers, libraries can provide access to low windows, child-size furniture, child-friendly bathrooms, low shelves, and storage units. Unlike childcare centers, however, libraries need to integrate adult-size comfortable furniture throughout the space or in a closely adjacent area.

It is important that parents recognize that public librarians are not in loco parenti and that children cannot be left unattended. For parents and caregivers, family-centered libraries need to send a message that this is a space for adults and children together—a place for families. A combination of assorted-size seating, the provision of step stools near drinking fountains, sinks, and circulation desks, and a "three bears" early childhood bathroom with toilets scaled for toddlers, elementary age, and adults are additional ways libraries can achieve a balance of scale to meet the needs of adults and little ones.

Placement

Placement of an item within a room may impact how it is used. For example, one library found that placing a cozy book mat adjacent to more active areas (dramatic play, blocks, and Legos) resulted in the item being used as a tumbling mat. When the mat was moved adjacent to the picture book collection, both parents and children used it as it was designed—as a cozy and fun reading space.

Young children often need help with transitions—especially when it involves leaving a welcoming, interactive, fun space. Placing an interesting focal point, such as a fish tank, near the circulation desk, for instance, can entice little ones to leave their play and provides an interesting activity to occupy them while materials are being checked out. Placing a stool or having a lower counter at circulation and reference desks enabling young children to see the activity is yet another way to promote interaction and to ease transitions from one area to another.

Outdoor Environments

In addition to age-appropriate equipment, furniture, and materials, a physical design that provides access to the outdoors further enhances learning environments. Low windows and window seats enable young children to observe the surrounding community, helping them to understand that the library exists within a larger space. Outdoor library areas such as reading gardens allow children to interact with outdoor environments, and outdoor play areas provide opportunities for more physical play and movement that promote gross motor development.

Integrating toys, learning stations, and books sends the message to adults that play and social interaction are essential to children's learning and even the youngest children can have mastery over their environment if that environment is properly designed. Such environments also provide parents with a model of how to

7-2: Materials for In-Library Use

☐ Books of various types (board, cloth, oversized, picture books, easy readers)

☐ Books for infants and toddlers, preschoolers and primary grade students

☐ Books for parents and caregivers

☐ Computer stations with two seats with software and web links to sites appropriate for preschoolers and primary grade children

☐ Computer station with web links for parents and caregivers

☐ Videos and DVDs for preschoolers and primary grade students

☐ Compact discs, for babies, toddlers, preschoolers and primary grade students

☐ Videos and DVDs for parents and caregivers

☐ Listening and viewing stations

☐ Writing center equipped with crayons, washable markers and large sheets of blank paper

☐ Multimedia kits

☐ Toys

☐ Puzzles and pegboards

☐ Art supplies

☐ Blocks and building materials

☐ Active play equipment (e.g. climbing toys, wheel toys, sand/water tables)

☐ Manipulatives to sort, classify and label

☐ Dramatic play equipment and materials (e.g. dress-up items, dollhouse, kitchen set, puppet stage, puppets and dolls, train table, flannel board)

organize space for young children in their own home and what to expect of children within that space.

Establishing a Community Meeting Place

"Creating welcoming environments for infants, toddlers, and their families establishes spaces for both adults and their children to meet and make friends" (Kuchner, 2001: 16). Well-designed environments encourage social interaction between parent and child, casual interaction among children and other adults who may be in the area, and social interaction among adults.

A grouping of comfortable adult seating from which to observe children at play not only introduces adults to the range of behaviors typical for similar ages but also facilitates the development of adult communications and friendships. Likewise integrating some adult furniture and seating into early childhood learning stations and spaces tells adults they are expected to participate. Placing an adult-size seat next to a child's seat at a children's computer station promotes interaction between the two. A train table or Lego table near adult-size seating entices adults, especially fathers, to engage in play with their little ones.

Color and Displays

Color, light, patterns, artwork, and displays all affect the way a child interacts with the space. While library staff members have preferences, it is important to keep in mind the perspective of the child and not to create a space that reflects an adult's perspective of how a child "should be." Areas and spaces need to be cheerful and filled with decorations of interest to children and families. Be careful not to create permanently themed areas that are inflexible and, in time, may become dated or boring.

Painting is a quick and inexpensive way to change a dull space into one that is lively and fun. Infants and young children are attracted by bright primary colors, patterns with strong contrast, and things that move. Paint can add color to endstacks, railings, and furniture. Simple designs such as brightly colored handprints on the inside of white shelving create a childlike whimsy that draws children and adults to the shelves. Framed posters depicting storybook characters stimulate character recognition of popular books. A display of children's artwork is always attractive and often brings families back to view the display.

Young children are attracted to things that move. Hanging mobiles and large wall murals and other decorations that are visible from a distance identify the space and beckon little ones and caregivers. Many libraries have enlisted the artistic talents of staff, community members, and local artists to create beautiful murals, mobiles, and other wall- and ceiling-mounted artwork.

Serving Parents and Caregivers

Young children do not visit the library by themselves. Parents or other caregivers bring them in tandem with strollers, diaper bags, favorite blankets, bottles, and often, siblings and friends. Accessible ramp entrances and electronic doors allow ease of access into the library.

Once adults with children are in the building, the location of the family area can make their visit easy or challenging. The distance it takes to walk or carry a toddler to the appropriate area and the route that must be taken to get there can either encourage or discourage repeat visits. Routes that require stairs or walking through adult or quiet areas to get to an elevator or the final destination can be physically and emotionally challenging for those accompanying young children. Adults who encounter angry stares and concerned looks as they escort an exuberant toddler to the appropriate space or try to calm a fussy baby as they make their way to the exit will sense they are not welcome and perhaps the library really is not a place for babies and toddlers after all. Reconfiguring space and traffic patterns to eliminate or minimize such experiences creates a more welcoming and accepting environment, increasing the likelihood of return visits (Huntington, 2005: 51).

Libraries need to provide support for adults with multiple children of various ages. For instance, a baby activity seat with interactive attachments for prewalkers enables parents to keep little ones safe, engaged, and close at hand while they focus attention on interactions with older toddlers and preschoolers. In-house shopping carts with seats for young children or baskets to carry library items help adults manage selection of materials and their child at the same time.

Family spaces are not just about the development of young children. Adults in children's lives are also growing and developing in their roles as parents, grandparents, educators, childcare providers, and health and human service workers. Integrating parent and family service resources into the family space sends a message that adults play a vital role in the early learning and development of young children. It provides convenient, one-stop access to relevant materials and allows adults to browse while keeping their children in sight.

Having a dedicated computer, collections, and displays for parents either in the children's area or adjacent to it creates a sense of place for parents. Wall space above picture book shelving can be used to house parenting books and DVDs. Parent magazines, brochures, pamphlets, bibliographies, and flyers can be displayed on open shelves, the tops of nearby picture book shelving, or coffee tables near comfortable adult-size seating. An adult computer station featuring parenting, child development, and early literacy software and Web sites further expose adults to the wealth of resources available at the library. Parents will often comment on such an array of materials and information displayed together in one location.

Welcoming All Families

Families come in many configurations and with a wide variety of education and income levels, racial and ethnic backgrounds, literacy levels, English proficiency skills, physical and mental abilities, and familiarity with public libraries. Creating a library environment in which all families can participate and have positive library experiences promotes return visits and is a primary objective of any family-centered space.

Welcoming spaces reflect various cultures and races as well as physical and mental abilities in the posters, pictures, displays, books, and other materials in the room. Multilingual and graphic signage and highly visible, clearly defined learning stations, spaces, and interactive resources help bridge the language and learning barriers that might exist between the parent and the child and between the family and library staff. Families with low literacy and those for whom English is not the primary language can easily utilize well-arranged learning environments, including wordless and multilingual books and multilingual listening, viewing, and computer stations.

When planning for children with developmental delays or learning disabilities, it is important to consider the types of materials that these children may need to successfully use the library, such as adaptive toys, touch screen monitors, and adaptive input devices for computers. Chapters 9, 10, and 16 include many resources specially created for this audience. In the following section, Assessing Current Space, some questions are provided relative to children with disabilities.

Assessing Current Space

An objective assessment of the space often reveals assets not readily apparent that provide a base for further development. No matter the size, it is important to be mindful that the space is suited for infants to kindergartners and caregivers and to ensure a balance of resources for all ages. A first step before embarking on any new development, whether it be collections, programs, or space design, is to evaluate current resources. The following are some items to consider:

Current size of the space
Location of space in relation to other areas of the library
Wall space (both what is currently open and what is currently utilized by shelving, bulletin boards, displays, etc.)
Entries, exits, and current traffic patterns

Content of the space:

Shelving (including dimensions, wall mounted or freestanding)
Reference or circulation desk
Tables and chairs and their sizes
Display units
Equipment
Storage
Content and location of collections
Color, décor, and the ambience of the space

Children with Disabilities

The following questions can be used to further assess the children's space, focusing on how the environment welcomes children with disabilities.

Are all areas of the facility physically accessible to the child?

Are pathways open, clear, and wide enough to accommodate wheelchairs or special strollers?

Are floors covered with tile or wood, perhaps making them slippery to a person using a cane or walker?

Are carpeted floors free of wrinkles, rips, curled or loose corners, or frayed bindings that could present a danger to someone physically or visually challenged?

Does the height of the computer stations, catalogs, activity centers, or tables in the room present any barriers? Keep in mind that a child-size wheelchair is smaller than ones used by adults.

Is the children's room free of clutter, especially near walkways?

Are all areas, including program areas, well lit?

Are signs in clear, large print, with print in distinct contrast from the background color? Are there accompanying picture cues, if possible?

Does the room reflect an inclusionary philosophy? Look at the posters, pictures, book displays, dolls, and other items and materials. Do they reflect diversity and help children learn about disabilities?

Is there a variety of age-appropriate materials to accommodate children of different interests and abilities?

Are there areas for quiet, individual activities as well as other areas for more active, social play so children and parents can select activities most suitable to their needs?

Look at the Space with a Fresh Eye

Determining which items are easily movable and which are more permanently anchored in their current locations provides a realistic starting point for potential redesign. Assessment of collections, equipment, and furniture can result in additional space. A thorough weeding of collections frees up shelving that can either be removed, leaving open space for a learning station, comfortable seating, or other needed furniture or equipment, or be utilized for such items as parent materials, displays, board books, and toys.

Once the assessment, weeding, determination of fixed items, and any discarding of furniture and equipment are completed, it is easier to look at the space and explore what could be added or reconfigured to make it a more visible and welcoming social and learning environment for babies, toddlers, preschoolers, and their caregivers. When doing this it is important to keep all options open, including the relocation of collections, shelving, and furniture. While some of these options may ultimately be deemed unnecessary or impractical, keeping all options open allows the space to be explored from a new perspective.

Keeping an open mind can result in utilizing items for multiple purposes. Manipulative toys such as bead mazes, Lego walls, or touch 'n' see walls can be attached to stack ends if floor, wall, and shelving space are not available. Some items (shape sorters, blocks, and nesting cups) can be placed on open shelves and other items might be housed in clear bins that can be stacked two high, providing maximum use of shelf space while still allowing children to see what is available.

Adapting Small Spaces

While very small spaces can be particularly challenging, weeding and rearranging almost always result in reclaiming a section of shelving near the picture books to house a small collection of appropriate materials. Suggested items for a very small space include:

A shelf or two of parenting materials including books, DVDs, and pamphlets
A shelf (or basket if floor space permits) of board books
Two to three shelves housing some of the following toys:
  Infant nonshatter mirror
  Small bead toy (perhaps attached to end of shelf stack if room permits)
  Nesting cups
  Shape sorter
  Small foam or vinyl blocks
  Cause-and-effect toy (with lids that are easily opened by manipulating various switches)
  Knobbed puzzles
  Lego blocks and base
  Finger puppets
  Small kitchen set (plates, cups, etc.)
  Foldable train mat with magnetic train cars
  Animal figures (farm, jungle)

Assessment Tools

Wisconsin Kid Friendly Spaces: In early 2000, the Wisconsin Library Association's Youth Services Section sponsored a tour of libraries in Wisconsin, Minnesota, and Illinois that were recommended as "kid friendly." Some of the features that were identified as things that libraries can consider to make their physical environments more compatible for infants and toddlers include program rooms, outdoor areas, windows, wall coverings, rocking chairs, portable safety gates, in-house shopping carts, sinks, and artwork. A full checklist is available online at http://dpi.wi.gov/pld/earlylearning.html (Huntington, 2005: 51–53).

Physical Environment and Room Design: Figure 7-3, adapted from *Learning Environments for Young Children* (Feinberg, Kuchner, and Feldman, 1998: 175), provides a good checklist to help librarians with an assessment of their current space.

7-3:   Physical Environment Checklist

Physical Environment/Room Design

Early Childhood Area

☐   Organization of the environment is clear.

☐   Activity and learning centers are easily recognizable (materials with similar use or themes grouped together).

☐   Activity centers contain things that can be touched or manipulated.

☐   Activity areas provide space for children and adults to stand, sit or work next to each other.

☐   Activity areas provide space for young children to move, practice large motor activities and learn with entire body.

☐   Young children can access a portion of collections (book, materials, and manipulative/toys) without adult assistance.

☐   Low shelves, open bins (without lids or covers), and/or low hooks or hangars hold materials for children to access themselves.

☐   Furniture/or seating is available for small groups of 2–4 people to gather in face-to-face interactions.

☐   Quiet and noisy activities are separated.

☐   Activity centers can been seen with unobstructed views from more than one section in the children's area.

☐   A separate room is available for special programs.

☐   Noise levels are minimized by design considerations.

☐   Lighting including windows and natural lighting enhances the environment.

Accommodations for Range of Ages and Families

☐   Strollers and carriages can be accommodated.

☐   If there is a railing, crib or playpen, the railings meet acceptable standards.

☐   An area for infants is available.

☐   Materials with small parts that could be ingested are stored out of reach of infants and toddlers.

☐   Furniture scaled to the needs of young children is adequate to meet demand.

☐   An area with soft furnishing for adults and children to share is available.

☐   Adult size chairs for parents/care givers are available.

☐   Separate places to put equipment and outerwear are available.

Reference Area

☐   Reference desk near young children's area has a lowered section to allow for 4–8 year old to see over top.

☐   Reference desk near young children's area has a space for adults to rest materials out of reach of young children.

☐   Information about programs, services and special collections for young children and their families is visible and accessible.

☐   Information about behavior limits and responsibilities of patrons, both adult and children, is clearly visible.

☐   Activity centers for young children are visible from reference desk.

Displays

☐ Sense of family place and messages of welcome are established through use of design features and/or hanging decorations and displays.

☐ Color, light and design elements are used to create cheerful decorations of interest.

☐ Displays/decorations are free of gender stereotypes.

☐ Displays, exhibits and activity/learning areas are of interest to young children.

☐ Displays, exhibits and informational/learning areas of interest to parents/care givers are located within or adjacent to areas for young children.

☐ Displays, exhibits and interest areas encourage recognition of symbols, letters and numbers.

☐ Pictorial symbols and letters are used to assist in communicating organization of area.

☐ Displays, exhibits and interest areas encourage ethnic pride and the recognition of cultural diversity.

☐ Children's projects and artwork are displayed.

☐ Children's projects and artwork are displayed at eye level for young children.

☐ Displays are made of low flammable material.

Conclusion

Public libraries are places of learning for all ages. Designing welcoming interactive public spaces that support the growth and development of babies, toddlers, and their adults helps to ensure all children will have the opportunities and experiences to optimize early brain development and reach their full potential, but that is not all that good design provides. Through the creation of age-appropriate fun learning environments for very young children and their adults, libraries become so much more than places where one obtains materials, attends a program, and then leaves. Libraries become community destinations for families—community centers that support and empower families through learning, socialization, and community belonging.

References

Feinberg, Sandra, Joan K. Kuchner, and Sari Feldman. *Learning Environments for Young Children: Rethinking Library Spaces and Services.* Chicago: American Library Association, 1998.

Feinberg, Sandra, and James Keller. *Places and Spaces for Children: Partnerships between Librarians and Design Professionals to Create Library Space for Kids and their Families.* ALA Editions (in press).

Gisolfi, Peter A. "Schools to Scale: Learning Environments for Young Children." *American School Board Journal* (October): 39–41, 1999.

Huntington, Barbara. "Early Learning Initiative for Wisconsin Public Libraries. Bulletin No. 0510." Madison: Division for Libraries, Technology, and Community Learning, Wisconsin Department of Public Instruction. Available: http://dpi.wi.gov/pld/early-learning.html, 2005.

Kuchner, Joan. "Creating Welcoming Library Environments for Infants, Toddlers and Their Families." *Zero to Three* 21, no. 3 (January): 11–12, 2001.

National Safety Council. "Crib Safety Tips." Available: www.nsc.org/library/facts/cribtips.htm.

U.S. Consumer Product Safety Commission, Office of Compliance, Small Part Regulations, Toys and Products Intended for Use by Children Under 3 Years Old. Available: www.cpsc.gov.

Resources

Boon, Lesley A. "Designing Library Space for Children and Adolescents." In G. B. McCabe and J. R. Kennedy, *Planning the Modern Library Building.* Westport, CT: Libraries Unlimited, 2003.

Britz, Joan. "Problem Solving in Early Childhood Classrooms." *ERIC Digest* (1993) Available: www.ericdigest.org/1993/early.htm, 1993.

Feinberg, Sandra, Sari Feldman, and Joan K. Kuchner. *Learning Environments for Young Children: Rethinking Library Spaces and Services.* Chicago: American Library Association, 1998.

Feinberg, Sandra, and James Keller. *Places and Spaces for Children: Partnerships between Librarians and Design Professionals to Create Library Space for Kids and Their Families.* ALA Editions (in press).

Huntington, Barbara. "Early Learning Initiative for Wisconsin Public Libraries. Bulletin No. 0510." Madison: Division for Libraries, Technology, and Community Learning, Wisconsin Department of Public Instruction. Available: http://dpi.wi.gov/pld/early-learning.html, 2005.

Kuchner, Joan. "Creating Welcoming Library Environments for Infants, Toddlers and Their Families." *Zero to Three* 21, no. 3 (January): 11–12, 2001.

Meyerhoff, Michael. "Parents Guide to Selecting Toys for Infants and Toddlers." Available: www.williamgladdenfoundation.org, 2005.

Moss, Peter, and Pat Petrie. *From Children's Services to Children's Spaces: Public Policy, Children and Childhood.* New York: Routledge Falmer, 2002.

Catalogs

The following catalogs offer a wide variety of appropriate toys, furniture, and equipment for children starting at birth. (See Chapter 10 for suppliers of adaptive toys.)

ABC School Supply
1156 Four Star Dr.
Mount Joy, PA 17552
(800) 669-4ABC
www.abcschoolsupply.com

All Aboard Toys, LLC
9800 E. Easter Ave., Suite 100
Centennial, CO 80112
(800) 416-7155
www.allaboardtoys.com

Back To Basics Toys—Games and Hobbies
P.O. Box 9300

Pueblo, CO 81008
(800) 356-5360
www.backtobasicstoys.com

BEKA, Inc.
542 Selby Ave.
St. Paul, MN 55102
(888) 999-2352
www.bekainc.com

Big Cozy Books
www.bigcozybooks.com

Child Craft
P.O. Box 3239
Lanchaster, PA 17604
(800) 631-5652
www.childcraftindustries.com

Childswork/Childsplay
45 Executive Dr., Suite 201
P.O. Box 9120
Plainview, NY 11803
(800) 99-YOUTH
www.childswork.com

Community Playthings
Community Products, LLC
359 Gibson Hill Rd.
Chester, NY 10918-2321
(800) 777-4244
www.communityplaythings.com

Constructive Playthings
13201 Arrington Rd.
Grandview, MO 64030
(800) 832-0572
www.constplay.com

Demco Kids and Things
P.O. Box 7488
Madison, WI 53707-7488
(800) 962-4463
www./demco.com

For Kidz Only
P.O. Box 111117
Tacoma, WA 98411
(800) 979-8898
Fax: (253) 983-9840
www.forkidzonly.com

J. L. Hammett Co.
P.O. Box 859057
Braintree, MA 02185-9057
(800) 955-2200
www.hammett.com

HearthSong
(800) 533-4397
www.hearthsong.com

Kaplan Early Learning Company
1310 Lewisville-Clemmons Rd.
Lewisville, NC 27023
(800) 334-2014
www.Kaplanco.com

Lakeshore
2695 E. Dominguez St.
Carson, CA 90749
(800) 421-5354
(800) 778-4456
www.lakeshorelearning.com

Learning Resources
380 N. Fairway Dr.
Vernon Hills, IL 60061
(800) 333-8281
www.learningresources.com

Music in Motion
P.O. Box 869231
Plano, TX 75086-9231
(800) 445-0649
www.musicinmotion.com

Nasco School-Age and Early Childhood
901 Janesville Ave.
P.O. Box 901
Fort Atkinson, WI 53538-0901
(800) 558-9595
www.nascofa.com

One Step Ahead
P.O. Box 517
Lake Bluff, IL 60044
(800) 274-8440
www.onestepahead.com

People Friendly Places, Inc. (a.k.a. Hello Kids)
1954 First St. #301
Highland Park, IL 60035
(800) 369-6331
www.peoplefriendlyplaces.com

Playscapes—Children's Environments
2600 Daniels St.
Madison, WI 53718
(800) 248-7529
www.playscapes.com

Safety First
Dorel Juvenile Group
Consumer Relations Dept.
P.O. Box 2609
Columbus, IN 47202-2609
(800) 544-1108
www.safety1st.com

Sensational Beginnings
P.O. Box 2009
987 Stewart Rd.
Monroe, MI 48162
(800) 444-2147
www.sensationalbeginnings.com

S & S Worldwide
P.O. Box 513
Colchester, CT 06415-0513
(800) 243-9232
Fax: (800) 566-6678
www.ssww.com

Step 2 Educational Sales Company
10010 Auroa-Hudson Rd.
P.O. Box 2412
Streetsboro, OH 44241
(800) 347-8372
www.step2.com

Toys to Grow On
2695 E. Dominquez St.
P.O. Box 17
Long Beach, CA 90801
(800) 987-4454
www/ttgo.com

8

Programs for Young Children and Parents

When offering programs for young children and their parents or caregivers, a family-centered library recognizes that the child and parent or caregiver are a "programming package." Integrating parent education into existing early childhood programs and offering parent education programs that address parental and child-care providers' concerns broaden the reach of the children's department and make the librarian, parents, and caregivers partners in their efforts to educate and expose children to literacy. This chapter focuses on programming examples being offered for young children, birth through age five, and their parents and caregivers within the National Family Place Libraries network.

Family Place Libraries Initiative

The Family Place Libraries initiative transforms libraries into community hubs for healthy child and family development, parent and community involvement, and lifelong literacy beginning at birth. Expanding the traditional role of children's services, a Family Place Library focuses on early childhood information, parent education, emergent literacy, socialization, and family support. Family Place Library staff members, trained in developmentally appropriate and family support prac-

tice, leverage the resources of the library to effectively serve young children (including babies) and their families.

Key features of a Family Place Library include:

Developmentally appropriate programming for young children and their parents or caregivers, including the Parent/Child Workshop

A specially designed space for young children and their parents and caregivers

Collections of books, toys, audiovisuals, and other materials for babies, toddlers, parents, and family service professionals

Access to electronic resources that emphasize emergent literacy, reading readiness, and parent education

The Parent/Child Workshop is the core program at each Family Place Library. This five-week series brings together toddlers and their parents in an informal, interactive setting with professionals from local agencies such as childcare centers, hospitals, speech clinics, universities, public schools, and health departments. The workshop emphasizes and supports the role of parents as first teachers, facilitates early intervention, and teaches strategies that promote healthy child development and literacy through modeling and referral to information and community resources.

The Family Place Library staff is actively involved in:

Building coalitions and networks with family service professionals

Reaching out to families and young children, particularly those most at risk

Assessing the services of the library to address the needs of the community and its families

Acquiring skills and knowledge regarding child development, parent education and support, technology and young children, and family literacy

Ongoing professional development through participation in an electronic listserv and the Family Place Library network

Contact Information

Kathleen Deerr, National Coordinator, Middle Country Public Library, Centereach, NY. Phone: (631) 585-9393 ext. 204. Email: deerrkathleen@mcpl.lib.ny.us.

Additional Resources

Family Place Libraries Initiative. www.familyplacelibraries.org

Feinberg, Sandra, and Diantha Schull. "Family Place Libraries: From One Long Island Library to the Nation." In *Libraries for the Future: Innovation in Action*. New York: Americans for Libraries Council: 6–9, 2005.

Feinberg, S., and Diantha Schull. "Family Place Libraries: Transforming Public Libraries to Serve Very Young Children and Their Families" *Zero to Three* 21 no. 3 (December 2000/January): 4–10, 2001.

Programs for Children and Parents Together

Integrating the concepts of play, child development, infant brain development, early literacy skills, and parenting and family-centered principles within the context of library service provides librarians with the fundamental underpinnings to adapt, develop, and expand their program offerings for families and young children. The library's potential as a key community player in helping children build preliteracy and school readiness skills through age-appropriate, interactive and exploratory, play-based programs that focus on the learning process is a wonderful opportunity for children's staff to reach out and partner with not only caregivers and parents but also other community agencies that focus on serving young children and their families.

Young children need opportunities to engage in various types of play with their parents and caregivers in order to begin building a solid foundation for literacy and learning. Having books, toys, and writing materials available during programs and allowing free time for young children to experiment with these objects allow children to decode and make sense of the concepts of writing and reading—long before they will actually be physically capable of doing both. Today, many libraries are offering play-based programs such as the Parent/Child Workshop as a model of family support.

The Parent/Child Workshop

Twenty-five years ago, it was extremely difficult for parents with very young children, ages birth through three, to find quality play-based, early childhood programs to participate in—and it was virtually unheard of to find them in a library. After becoming a parent herself, one children's librarian vowed to change this, and thus the Parent/Child Workshop was born at Middle Country Public Library (Centereach, NY), eventually transforming itself into the core program for the Family Place Libraries initiative.

Audience: Children ages one through three years and parents and caregivers, with siblings up to age five welcome.

Purpose/Goals: To provide a regularly scheduled, play-based program presented in an informal early childhood setting that encourages parents and caregivers and children to play together, meet other parents in the area, and become familiar with the librarian and library resources, and to bring families into contact with local health and human service professionals from their communities.

Description/Program Overview: This five-week workshop is conducted in the community room or an area in the children's room that is specially arranged with toys, art activities, and a materials resource area containing parenting and early childhood materials for check-out. The librarian facilitates the 1¼-hour program by welcoming the families, interacting with them one on one, and introducing them to the community resource professional of the week. Professionals from local early childhood, parent education, health, and social service agencies move casually about the room and chat with participants about issues pertinent to their children or services that their agency offers for families. The librarian closes the workshop with a simple circle game, song, or fingerplay.

The design of the program (families can come and leave when it is comfortable for them, children self-select the toy or activity, siblings are invited to participate, and the emphasis is on play and verbal interaction between the caregiver and the child) helps parents understand that what toddlers need most are autonomy, flexibility, mobility, and adult-child interactions within an appropriately structured environment.

The workshop makes an immediate impression on how families perceive the resources that the library has to offer. Parents often comment that the workshop provides them with an opportunity to meet other parents in the community or other children around the same age as their own child. For many, it is the first time they have visited the library with their baby or toddler and they will often sign up for other library programs and use the library on a drop-in basis. They may also begin to refer to the librarian as a source of information when they have a problem or issue with their child and need information.

Partnering Organizations: Within the five-week series, most libraries offer three or four resource professionals including a speech therapist or other early language professional, a child development specialist, a nutritionist specializing in early childhood health, and a music or movement/dance person. The following types of organizations often provide or help librarians locate qualified professionals:

Childcare councils or centers
Hospitals
Speech clinics
Universities
Public schools
Cooperative Extension
Public health departments, particularly nurses and social service agencies

Practical Tips/Program in Action: It is important to remember that the librarian's most important role is to get to know each family, promote the many resources that the library has to offer, and link families with community services.

Materials/Supplies: The size of the area or room determines the amount of materials that are needed. Materials may include infant toys, puppets, dress-up items, transportation toys, blocks, musical instruments, a tunnel, kitchen set-ups, and art supplies. A storage area is also needed.

Staff: A children's librarian acts as the facilitator for the series, welcoming parents and caregivers and walking around the room to talk one-on-one with families. Depending on the number of families, another staff member may assist at an art activity station. A resource professional is also available to meet and engage families.

Contact Information: Marci Byrne at Middle Country Public Library, Centereach, NY. Phone: (631) 585-9393 ext. 230. Email: byrnemarcellina@mcpl.lib.ny.us.

Additional Resources:

Feinberg, Sandra, and Kathleen Deerr. *Running a Parent/Child Workshop: A How-To-Do-It Manual.* New York: Neal-Schuman, 1995.

Book Babies

Audience: Infants birth through twelve months and parents or caregivers.

Purpose/Goals: Helps foster early literacy from birth by teaching parents how to book-share with their babies as part of the bonding process, building social and listening skills, and providing information on dialogic reading skills, early literacy development, and how to choose age-appropriate books.

Description/Program Overview: A typical session is thirty minutes in duration, and incorporates book sharing along with some free play time for the participating parents and their babies. Babies are seated on their parent's lap, facing forward so they can easily see the books. Once the group is settled and ready to begin book sharing, the librarian passes out a multitude of board books, making sure that the parent or caregiver and child are both comfortable. The environment is made as inviting and relaxed as possible, with an area rug or cushions for parents and caregivers to relax on while they read and interact with their baby with a wide variety of books being provided, such as durable lift-the-flap books, board books, and simple nursery rhymes.

Many babies will not be able to book-share for the entire thirty minutes. Having some infant toys, soft blocks, and puppets in the room helps parents and models for them that it is okay to take a break from reading if their baby starts to fuss. Using toys and puppets or dolls "stretches" the attention span of the baby and offers parents other ways to engage their baby in early literacy techniques. Often parents will think that they are not "succeeding" with book sharing if their baby is being fussy or inattentive. Reassure parents that any time spent with their baby and a book—opening and shutting the book, looking at pictures, pretending to read, visiting the library—is bonding time that will help foster social and early literacy skills.

Practical Tips/Program in Action: Provide parents with a working definition of early literacy as well as examples of signs of preliteracy in very young children. The Association for Library Services to Children and the Public Library Association have wonderful handouts and resources on early literacy available to libraries through their Every Child Ready to Read initiative. In addition, the Bonding with Baby Web site (see resources below) is geared toward parents, childcare providers, and professionals who work or care for infants and toddlers and includes literacy tips to share.

Materials/Supplies: A variety of board books or sturdy picture books with multiple copies of each title are key to a successful book-sharing program. A few puzzles, infant toys, puppets for imaginative and dramatic play, and a colorful rug make for a welcoming and relaxed environment.

Contact Information: Kristen Todd at Middle Country Public Library, Centereach, NY. Phone: (631) 585-9393 ext. 212. Email: toddkristen@mcpl.lib.ny.us

Additional Resources:

Developing Hearts Systems. www.bondingwithbaby.org.
Public Library Association and Association for Library Services to Children. Every Child Ready to Read. www.ala.org/ala/pla/plaissues/earlyliteracy.htm.

Babygarten

"Read to Them. Sing to Them. Love Them" (see Figure 8-2)

Audience: Children ages birth through two years and parents and caregivers.

Purpose/Goals: To help parents and caregivers understand the complex and exciting nature of infant development while placing a special emphasis on language development and how it contributes to preliteracy skills; provide an environment where parents and caregivers can experience camaraderie and gain support from one another; show the importance of rhythm, rhyme, and repetition; and provide a weekly experience that is enjoyable and enriching for babies.

Program Overview: This forty-five- to fifty-minute program incorporates a research-based curriculum, developed specifically for caregivers and their babies and toddlers, and is rhyme and movement intensive. The five-week series, offered year-round, is centered on the four seasons. Each program features the following timeframe:

20 minutes of action rhymes, movement, and songs
10 minutes of shared book readings
15 minutes of infant toys for children while parents make handmade toys
5 minutes of showcasing books, sharing pamphlets, brochures, flyers, and discussing upcoming programs

Partnering Organizations: The program was started in libraries, but soon expanded to a variety of early childhood settings. Norfolk Public Libraries has brought Babygarten to preschools, daycare centers, mothers' groups, and early childhood centers. Other facilities with which to possibly partner include: recreation facilities (with early childhood programs), hospitals, churches, dance and music classes, or any educational setting where parents, caregivers, and babies come together.

8-2: Babygarten

Baby garten, inc.
"Read to Them, Sing to Them, Love Them."

Practical Tips/Program in Action: Hide any toys or books until the appropriate time so they do not pose a distraction during the circle time. The middle of the room should be kept as open and clear as possible to allow room for everyone to sit on the floor in a circle during the song-and-rhyme portion of the program. Assemble a basket or display of circulating board books, music CDs, and Mother Goose nursery rhyme books for parents to check out, if they wish, to extend the program into the home setting.

Materials/Supplies: Babygarten Curriculum, board books for book sharing, age-appropriate toys (birth to age two), and arts-and-crafts-supplies.

Staff: Libraries need a staff member to serve as a program facilitator who follows the Babygarten curriculum.

Contact Information: Teresa Wanser at Kirn Memorial Library, Norfolk Public Library, VA. Phone: (757) 664-7323 ext. 43747. Email: teresa.wanser@norfolk.gov.

Additional Resources:

Babygarten, Inc. http://www.babygarten.com.

Mother Goose on the Loose

Audience: Children ages birth through two years and parents and caregivers.

Purpose/Goals: To develop early literacy, social, emotional, and language skills (based on brain research) and strengthen bonds between parents or caregivers and their children.

Description/Program Overview: This thirty-minute nursery rhyme program is an interactive program that seamlessly integrates music, movement, and language, using the "Listen, Like, Learn" approach, and helps children strengthen bonds with their caregivers while giving them the chance to learn through play and experience. The librarian leads parents in interacting with their children during the program by using music, rhymes, puppets, and common objects such as colored scarves for

Peek-a-Boo play. The program is structured but allows for the librarian to be creative and adapt to the needs of each individual group.

Practical Tips/Program in Action: There is 80 percent repetition from one session to the next, so once the first session has been planned out, it is very easy to plan subsequent sessions.

Materials/Supplies: Five-in-one teacher's easel, tambourine, bells, maracas, colored scarves, rhythm sticks, farm animal puppets, nursery rhyme books, plastic storage container with cover, stool, CD player, flannel board pieces, assorted books, and CDs.

Contact Information: Betsy Diamant-Cohen at the Enoch Pratt Free Library, Baltimore, MD. Phone: (410) 545-1660.

Additional Resources:

Diamant-Cohen, Betsy. *Mother Goose on the Loose.* New York: Neal-Schuman, 2005.
Diamant-Cohen, Betsy, Ellen Riordan, and Regina Wade. "Make Way for Dendrites: How Brain Research Can Impact Children's Programming." *Children and Libraries* 2, no.1 (Spring): 12–20, 2004.

Mother Goose/Rhyme Time

Audience: Children ages birth through three years and parents or caregivers.

Purpose/Goals: To foster early literacy skills through rhymes, fingerplays, and songs and encourage families with young children to use the library.

Description/Program Overview: This twenty- to thirty-minute program, offered twice a month throughout the year, begins with a warm welcome from the librarian, encouraging parents and caregivers to join along in the singing and repetition of rhymes to make sure that the program is a success and to show parents the need to model interactions for their child. Parents and children sit on the floor in a half circle so everyone can see the librarian in the front of the circle. The librarian uses puppets and flannel board stories as props to keep the children actively engaged. Props and books are spread out on a low table behind and within easy reach of the librarian. By ending with the same goodbye song or rhyme each week, participants get a sense of closure that the program is over.

The program consists of traditional nursery rhymes coupled with songs. Most rhymes and short songs are repeated twice to help the children learn the language and vocabulary of the songs. The length of the program depends on the mood and activity level of the children, though typical sessions last twenty to thirty minutes. A sample curriculum is provided in Appendix B.

Practical Tips/Program in Action: Keep the program at a fast pace. If the pace is too slow, the children may lose interest. Encourage parents to repeat the songs and rhymes at home. A drop-in version called Rhyme Time requires no registration and is offered once a month on Saturday mornings or occasionally in the evenings for working families.

Materials/Supplies: Flannel board props, puppets, and pop-up books to encourage group interaction. One wonderful source for puppets is the company Folkmanis. http://www.folkmanis.com.

Staff: Typically two staff members (librarian, early childhood teacher, program assistant) conduct the program, though it has also been successfully done with just one staff member.

Contact Information: Kristen Todd, Middle Country Public Library, Centereach, NY. Phone: (631) 585-9393 ext. 212. Email: toddkristen@mcpl.lib.ny.us.

Additional Resources:

Butler, Dorothy. *Babies Need Books: Sharing the Joy of Books with Children from Birth to Six.* Portsmouth, NH: Heinemann, 1998.
Marino, Jane. *Babies in the Library!* New York: Scarecrow Press, 2003.
Nespeca, Sue McCleaf. *Library Programming for Families with Young Children.* New York: Neal-Schuman, 1994.

Little Signing Hands: Baby Sign Language Program

Audience: Babies between the ages of eight and eighteen months and parents or caregivers.

Purpose/Goals: To enhance the daily interactions between parents and babies by incorporating the use of sign language into daily communication; based on the concept that pretalkers have much to say and signing provides an easy way for them to tell you things using a few key signs.

Description: This five-week-long series focuses on teaching parents signs for common words that their child might use and assisting parents in exposing their child to those signs through their daily activities. Parents and caregivers sit in a circle on the carpet, with the babies in the middle. In this way, babies can view one another as well as be entertained by watching their parent learn new signs, singing songs together, and participating in other activities. Babies are also free to sit on the parent's lap while signing and singing simple songs.

Practical Tips/Program in Action: A booklet of signs and simple vocabulary is given out during the first week for parents to refer to throughout the series and to keep at home for use with their baby.

Materials/Supplies: Folders are provided for each participant to keep their handouts in. Books on baby sign language, videos, DVDs, and CDs are displayed each week. The library supplies the CD player for the instructor to use.

Staff: A person trained in sign language typically conducts the program, and a children's librarian joins the group each week to interact with the parents and to address additional resource questions.

Contact Information: Anita LaSpina, Rockville Centre Public Library, New York. Phone: (516) 767-6257 ext. 6 Email: alaspina@rvcpl.org.

Additional Resources:

Ault, Kelly. *Let's Sign! Every Baby's Guide to Communicating with Grownups.* Boston: Houghton Mifflin, 2005.
Kubler, Annie. *My First Signs.* Auburn, ME: Child's Play, 2004.
"Sign with Your Baby: How to Communicate with Infants Before They Can Speak." DVD. Seattle, WA: Northlight Communications. 2004.

Toddler Tales

Audience: Babies ages one through two years and parents or caregivers.

Purpose/Goals/Objectives: To develop emergent literacy skills through modeling of the various ways that parents and caregivers can share age-appropriate books, fingerplays, games, and music with toddlers.

Description/Program Overview: A forty-five-minute program that includes a fast-paced, high energy thirty-minute directed program and a fifteen-minute open playtime provided during the last part of the program that allows parents and caregivers to interact with one another while the toddlers play with developmentally appropriate toys. The components of the program are similar each week, but the intensity and duration of each component can be adjusted easily to reflect the short attention spans and changing moods of the children on any particular day. Groups are purposefully kept small (no more than twelve children) to allow for interaction. Parent information materials from the Every Child Ready to Read initiative provide the basis for the talking points used throughout the program. A sample curriculum is provided in Appendix B.

Program Variation: We have added American Sign Language to Toddler Tales. A sign language teacher who works with very young children visits the program occasionally to teach simple signs to parents and toddlers.

Practical Tips/Program in Action: The staff running the program needs to be able to read the atmosphere in the room and the program needs to remain flexible and fluid. It is not necessary to "get through" a story! Be ready to move around the room with the children when sharing a book.

Materials/Supplies: Board books, rhythm instruments, music CDs and a player, age-appropriate toys.

Contact Information: Victoria Thompson-Hess, James V. Brown Library, Williamsport, PA. Phone: (570) 323-7705 ext. 137. Email: vthompson@jvbrown.edu.

Additional Resources:

Every Child Ready to Read @Your Library. Public Library Association and Association for Library Services to Children. www.ala.org/ala/pla/plaissues/earlylit/earlyliteracy.htm.

Booktime/Playtime

Audience: Toddlers ages one to three and parents or caregivers. Siblings may also attend.

Purpose/Goals: To create an early literacy experience for early talkers and parents by modeling replicable early literacy skills and to provide a playgroup environment for child and adult socialization and support.

Description/Program Overview: This one-hour program was created as an outgrowth of the Parent/Child Workshop to meet the wishes of patrons who wanted to continue meeting weekly with their young children. The first twenty minutes of the program is "booktime," which is very much like a lapsit or Mother Goose Rhyme Time program. Each week begins with the same opening song and many of the same songs and rhymes are repeated to help foster early literacy skills. Several books on a single theme, for example, trains or colors, are read out loud by library staff and are interspersed with a few new theme-related songs or rhymes. Ideas are shared about how to extend the books or rhymes through related activities. A handout is available on the week's theme along with an extension activity appropriate for home use. Related children's books and a selection of materials from the Parents Collection are displayed on a table within the room for easy browsing.

The next part of the program is "playtime." Prior to the arrival of the group, toys are brought into the room and placed out of sight or high enough so that they are not a major distraction during booktime. When booktime is over, the toys are uncovered, additional books are displayed, and some of the large motor toys are set up in the room. Items vary each week. Some weeks there is a very simple art experience that is related to the stories shared. The children and parents play and talk until about ten minutes before the ending time, at which point the group cleans up and sings the last song.

Materials/Supplies: Art and craft supplies, picture books and materials gathered from the Parents Collection, and handouts created by staff.

Staff: One staff member is needed to set up and break down the room. A librarian or program staff person prepares the themed books and related activities, selects materials, and facilitates the group each week.

Contact Information: Charlotte Ryan, Upper Darby Township and Sellers Memorial Free Public Library, Upper Darby, PA. Phone: (610) 789-4440. Email: udcsd@delco.lib.pa.us.

Additional Resources:

Mailbox Magazine. The Education Center, Inc., P.O. Box 9753, Greensboro, NC 27429-0753. Phone: (800) 714-7991.

Circle Time

Audience: Children ages 18 months through 36 months and parents or caregivers.

Purpose/Goals: To engage young children in learning activities and in the development of fine and gross motor skills by using movement games, large interactive toys, and a parachute.

Description/Program Overview: This thirty-minute program begins with the parents or caregivers and children sitting in a big circle with the program facilitator. Before introducing the parachute or any other props, warm-up action rhymes and songs are used. The parachute is then introduced very slowly by first spreading it out in the middle of the circle. Children begin doing very simple activities with it, such as having the children walk in a circle holding onto the parachute or lifting the parachute up and down as a group. Once the children are comfortable with the parachute, other props such as beach balls, puppets, and inflatable toys can be introduced. Use a variety of songs and games with the parachute while incorporating other props. At the very end of the program, calm the children down by having them say "goodbye" to the parachute using a song or goodbye game.

Practical Tips/Program in Action: Be prepared for a very active program with a lot of noise and movement. Do not try to get too fancy with the parachute. Keep the games and activities simple until the children feel comfortable. If the children are scared of the parachute and do not want to play with it, do not force the issue; instead, create some movement activities that do not require the parachute. A drop-in version of this program that requires no preregistration is offered once a month on Saturday mornings to accommodate working families. A sample curriculum is provided in Appendix B.

Materials/Supplies: Nylon parachute, parachute props (puppets, balls, and other items that can be bounced around on parachute), CDs with some upbeat children's music, and CD player. Most of these supplies can be ordered from toy catalogs such as Lakeshore Learning (www.lakeshorelearning.com) or Kaplan Early Learning Company (www.kaplanco.com).

Contact Information: Kristen Todd, Middle Country Public Library, Centereach, NY. Phone: (631) 585-9393 ext. 212. Email: toddkristen@mcpl.lib.ny.us.

Additional Resources:
Weikart, Phyllis. *Round the Circle: Key Experiences in Movement for Young Children.* 2nd Edition. Ypsilanti, MI: High/Scope Press, 2000.
Wiertsema, Huberta. *101 Movement Games for Children: Fun and Learning with Playful Moving.* Alameda, CA: Hunter House, 2002.
Wilmes, Liz. *Parachute Play.* Elgin, IL: Building Blocks, 2000.

Four and More

Audience: Children ages four and five years and parents or caregivers.

Purpose/Goals: To support school readiness by focusing on the importance of play in learning, providing developmentally appropriate activities that scaffold on children's prior learning, and engaging children in meaningful, interactive experiences and quality parent-child interactions. Helps parents recognize their role as their child's first and forever teacher by providing information about and modeling of techniques that will help develop their child's early literacy skills.

Description/Program Overview: A ten-week workshop that starts with a story time, which allows the staff to model best practices for parents. During this section of the workshop, parents learn how to have meaningful interactions with their child as they read together. Parents are encouraged to ask their children open-ended questions, teach unfamiliar vocabulary or concepts encountered in the story, make children aware of various concepts of print, and discover how to develop phonological awareness. During the second part of the workshop, parents and their children explore activities at various developmentally appropriate stations set up throughout the room. Activity stations are devised to be open ended so that children of all abilities can participate, learn, and explore through a variety of fun and developmentally appropriate activities that embrace various learning modalities. A sample curriculum is provided in Appendix B.

Practical Tips/Program in Action: In designing the program, workshops were based on the six emerging literacy skills as defined under Every Child Ready to Read (a national research-based program sponsored by Public Library Association and the Association for Library Services to Children), input from area school districts, and the Head Start program. Allow at least one hour for the program.

Because of the heavy interaction between the parent and the participating child, siblings do not attend. This program originally began as a five-week program and was extended to ten weeks because of patron demand.

Materials/Supplies: Books, games, and materials for different stations, for example, rhyming games, alphabet puzzles, items for counting and sorting, magnetic letters, lacing cards, a "make it take it" art activity for each week, and handouts on the topic for that week.

Contact Information: Kathy Hagenbaugh, J. V. Brown Library, Williamsport, PA. Phone: (570) 323-7705. Email: khagenbaugh@jvbrown.edu.

Additional Resources:

Every Child Ready to Read @Your Library. Public Library Association and Association for Library Services to Children. www.ala.org/ala/pla/plaissues/earlylit/earlyliteracy.htm.

Off to a Good Start

Audience: Children ages three through five years (not yet in kindergarten) and parents or caregivers.

Purpose/Goals: To provide early learning games and activities that help promote reading readiness skills and support the parent as first teacher.

Description/Program Overview: This three- or four-week program provides activity stations set up within a meeting room that are filled with manipulatives, puzzles, creative play materials, books, and other resources. Parents and children move freely from table to table as they complete different games and activities. An art activity and a story are also included in each session. The staff interacts with each family throughout the program. Parent handouts are included each week to extend the activities and games to the home setting.

Practical Tips/Program in Action: Let the parents and children take as much time as necessary at each table. The goal is to enhance the child's creativity and reading readiness. Do not make either parent or child feel rushed. Provide activities, toys, and games for varying ages and abilities.

Materials/Supplies: Manipulative toys for ages three through five, puzzles, picture books, art supplies.

Staff: Facilitated by two early childhood teachers.

Contact Information: Lisa G. Kropp, Middle Country Public Library, Centereach, NY. Phone: (631) 585-9393 ext. 230. Email: kropplisa@mcpl.lib.ny.us.

Child Health and Safety Fair

Audience: Children ages preschool through early elementary and parents or caregivers.

Purpose/Goals: To provide access to a wide range of information in the areas of child health and safety and an opportunity to interact with representatives from local organizations and become familiar with their services.

Description/Program Overview: A "one-stop-shopping" annual fall event, this fair provides resource tables and children's activities on health and safety. The program takes place on Saturday morning and, depending on the number of participating agencies, is held in the community room and children's area. Some services may require outdoor space, in which case the parking lot is utilized.

Each agency provides a station (one or two tables) at which flyers, brochures, information packets, and posters are displayed. In most instances, organizations bring along an activity to engage children. Chairs are provided at each station. In addition to local agencies, the library provides several activity stations, including the library's Catastrophe Readiness Clearinghouse and a Teddy Bear Clinic as well as book displays and bibliographies on health and safety topics.

Upon entering the library, parents and children register in a sign-in book (which helps to keep track of attendance) and are given a "Passport to Health and Safety," which lists the different stations that are participating in the fair and includes agency contact information. As children and parents move throughout the fair, children are given a sticker to place next to the name of each station they visit. Upon leaving the fair, parents and children who have visited a certain number of stations are handed a certificate of completion that acknowledges their participation.

Partnering Organizations: This program originally began through a partnership with Middle Country Public Library (Centereach, NY), Kiwanis, and the Suffolk County Department of Health. Other local partners include: health clinics, hospitals, the American Red Cross, dentists and doctors who specialize in children's health, the department of parks and recreation, police department (Ident-a-Kid), fire department, ambulance or emergency management team, veterinarians, physical therapists, speech and language pathologists, and Child/Family Health Plus representatives.

Practical Tips/Program in Action: Research the local area thoroughly to see what types of services are available and may want to be represented. Develop a contact list and mail letters with an RSVP to determine the number of tables and the size of the space required, including the possibility of parking lot usage. To avoid confusion, a sign with the name of each agency is placed on their respective tables. Be sure to ask if anyone requires special equipment (i.e., TV or VCR, access to an outlet). Follow up with phone calls prior to the fair, and send thank-you letters after the event.

A Child Health and Safety Fair will vary from community to community depending on the size of the library and the local resources. Assess what you want to achieve, what is available, and what the library deems manageable. If hesitant, start small, get feedback, and make adjustments or additions.

Materials/Supplies: Tables, signage, Passport to Safety flyers, stickers, certificates of completion, stationery, registration book, small bags to carry pamphlets and materials.

Contact Information: Marci Byrne, Middle Country Public Library, Centereach, NY. Phone: (631) 585-9393 ext. 230. Email: byrnemarcellina@mcpl.lib.ny.us.

Parent-to-Parent Interaction and Parent Education Programs

Some of the best information parents obtain is acquired through interactions with other parents, such as sharing stories and discussing similar experiences. Opportunities for parents to network and take time for themselves is extremely important, as well as having access to professionals specializing in early childhood development and parenting. Libraries can provide both informal spaces and opportunities and more formal parent education programs, enhancing their role as a family support institution. This section highlights some examples of programs that focus on parents and caregivers and work well in a library setting. Many of them can be provided only in partnership with other organizations or family support professionals who provide the necessary expertise.

Create and Learn

Audience: Parents or caregivers of preschool children. Family home childcare providers are also welcome.

Purpose/Goals: To create games and educational tools to use with young children while networking with other parents and caregivers. In a low-key nondidactic manner, the program facilitator (librarian, early childhood teacher) provides tips and advice on the purpose of the game or educational tool and highlights skills that would be developed with their use.

Description/Program Overview: Create and Learn provides an opportunity for participants to make learning games and educational tools such as flannel boards and accompanying activities, concentration or memory-type board and card games, and sequential scrapbooks. These are inexpensive materials to be used at home with children. Parents and caregivers are encouraged to network and exchange ideas within each program session. The program is conducted four times per season and each session runs for approximately two hours during the evening hours. Held in a meeting room, the program is facilitated by a librarian or early childhood educator. Some games or tools that are easy to create include:

Memory match games
ABC books
Flannel boards and accompanying stories
Number match games
Library book tote bags
Homemade puzzles
File folder games

Materials/Supplies: Materials and supplies for each session of the program will vary depending on the activity or game to be created. The library generally provides most supplies. A small fee may be charged depending on the tool or game created.

Additional Information: It is important that all the games and tools are developmentally appropriate for young children and as inexpensive as possible so that parents and caregivers will be comfortable using them at home or, if necessary, they can be easily replicated.

Contact Information: Lisa G. Kropp, Middle Country Public Library, Centereach, NY. Phone: (631) 585-9393 ext. 230. Email: kropplisa@mcpl.lib.ny.us.

Nursery School Fair

Audience: Parents of Toddlers and Preschoolers

Purpose/Goals: To provide an opportunity for parents of preschool children to meet local nursery school and preschool staff, learn about various school philosophies and approaches to learning and education, and have questions answered. This exercise also decreases parents' need to make appointments and meet with every school in the area. Moreover, school staff are provided exposure and an opportunity to speak to parents one-on-one.

Description/Program Overview: Conducted annually, this popular "one-stop-shopping" fair is traditionally held on a Saturday morning during the winter months when parents are often making decisions for the upcoming school year. Organized by a children's librarian in cooperation with local nursery school and preschool programs, the fair is held in the community room. Room setup requires one table for each school represented and chairs for staff. To avoid confusion, a sign with the name of each school is placed on their respective tables. Schools display handouts, registration forms, flyers, and posters. Parents register in a sign-in book (which helps to keep track of attendance), visit tables of interest, and speak with school representatives.

Practical Tips/Program in Action: Research your area thoroughly and invite all nursery schools and preschools. Mail letters with an RSVP. This helps determine the number of tables and the size of the space required and also serves as a confirmation of attendance. Follow up with phone calls prior to the fair. Send thank-you letters after the event. Retain contact information on all schools that attend for next year's fair and use the information to create a "Local Nursery School and Preschool" bibliography for inquiring parents.

Partnering Organizations: Local childcare, school district, nursery school, and preschool programs and the Child Care Resource and Referral Agency.

Materials/Supplies: Tables, stationery, flyers, identification materials for tables, registration book.

Contact Information: Nancy Handy, Middle Country Public Library, Centereach, NY. Phone: (631) 585-9393 ext.143. Email: handynancy@mcpl.lib.ny.us.

Infant CPR/First Aid

Audience: Parents, caregivers, and adults working with children.

Purpose/Program Goals: To learn proper methods and techniques of executing infant CPR or first aid in the event of an emergency.

Description/Program Overview: Infant CPR and first aid courses will vary in their teaching methods, depending on the instructor and organization. Infant CPR courses normally consist of a combination of lecture, hands-on, and questions and answers with respect to awareness of breathing and signs of cardiac emergency as well as how to act quickly and effectively. Similarly, first aid courses provide proper techniques for caring for scrapes and bruises as well as more serious injuries such as accidental poisoning or ingestion of toxic cleansers.

Partnering Organizations: Nationally, the American Red Cross offers a variety of health and safety programs, including both infant CPR and first aid. Local hospitals, fire departments, and ambulance companies are trained as well and are often eager to educate parents and adults caring for children.

Practical Tips/Program in Action: Although many libraries do not charge for youth programs, infant CPR and first aid programs may require a small fee based on the needs of the agency or organization providing the service. To help defray the costs for individual families, libraries may choose to pay the fee or a portion of the fee and decrease the cost to the patron.

Materials/Supplies: Programs like infant CPR and first aid more often than not simply require a space or room. Instructors typically provide handouts and bring along mannequins for hands-on experience. However, libraries may want to consider having a resource table available consisting of parenting and picture books, articles, videos, and bibliographies on emergencies, safety, and first aid in conjunction with emergency phone numbers.

Staff: Infant CPR and first aid programs need to be facilitated by a trained professional. These professionals may include an EMT, public health nurse, or firefighter.

Contact Information: Marci Byrne, Middle Country Public Library, Centereach, NY. Phone: (631) 585-9393 ext. 263. Email: byrnemarcellina@mcpl.lib.ny.us.

Discipline Is Not a Dirty Word

Audience: Parents and caregivers.

Purpose/Program Goals: To learn techniques for applying positive and effective discipline with children without feelings of guilt.

Description/Program Overview: A three-session, six-hour course, Discipline Is Not a Dirty Word focuses on building parenting skills relative to disciplining in a positive and effective manner. The program focuses on helping children exercise self-control while sustaining self-esteem; emphasizes the idea of guiding children's behavior; and promotes the philosophies of rewards, punishments, and bribes. Parents learn to feel confident in their role as disciplinarian without feeling guilty.

Partnering Organizations: The Family and Consumer Services Division of Cornell Cooperative Extension of Suffolk County, New York, offers this program on an ongoing basis in many public libraries as well as county agencies and other community-based organizations.

Materials/Supplies: Parents and caregivers receive informational handouts as well as in-class exercises. These materials are supplied by the partnering organization.

Staff: Discipline Is Not a Dirty Word is facilitated by a human development specialist from Cornell Cooperative Extension.

Contact Information: Marci Byrne, Middle Country Public Library, Centereach, NY. Phone: (631) 585-9393 ext. 263. Email: byrnemarcellina@mcpl.lib.ny.us.

Apple of My Eye Childhood Sexual Prevention Program

Audience: Parents, caregivers, and professionals working with children

Purpose/Program Goals: To learn techniques and tips to help prevent sexual child abuse, recognize warning signs, and know where to turn for assistance. The program provides an overview of legislation including Megan's Law, statistics, and the mission of the Parents for Megan's Law organization.

Description/Program Overview: Apple of My Eye is a single-session public education program presented by Parents for Megan's Law that teaches practical and effective methods to help parents, caregivers, and professionals keep children safe. The program promotes teaching children the boundaries and responsibilities of the adults in their lives and the reassurance of speaking out when feeling uncomfortable. Likewise, it presents a series of questions parents can ask themselves when evaluating a situation.

Partnering Organizations: Parents for Megan's Law is a national organization whose mission is to prevent and treat childhood sexual abuse through public education, advocacy, counseling, policy development, and legislative support services. In addition to the Apple of My Eye program, the organization also maintains a hotline, provides information and referral, keeps communities abreast of registered sex offenders, and works with the court systems.

Materials/Supplies: Materials are supplied by the facilitator. Libraries may choose to have other resources available, including parenting and picture books, articles, videos and DVDs, and bibliographies on the topic of keeping children safe from predators.

Staff: Apple of My Eye is facilitated by a trained representative of Parent's for Megan's Law.

Contact Information: Marci Byrne, Middle Country Public Library, Centereach, NY. Phone: (631) 585-9393 ext. 263. Email: byrnemarcellina@mcpl.lib.ny.us.

Additional Resources:

Parents for Megan's law. www.parentsformeganslaw.com.

Mothers' Centers

Audience: Mothers of very young children.

Purpose/Program Goals: To provide mothers the opportunity to network, share experiences and concerns, lessen feelings of isolation, discuss parenting issues, and gain insights into positive parenting.

Description/Program Overview: This parent-driven peer-to-peer program provides an opportunity for mothers to discuss parenting topics, share concerns, and support one another in their multiple roles as a parent, mother, and child's first teacher. A trained facilitator conducts each session, which renews every eight weeks, and members of the group select session topics. A group member may provide childcare, or the group may decide to pay someone, so that rather than overseeing their children, mothers can engage in open conversation with ease. The program generally meets weekly for ninety minutes each week.

Partnering Organizations: Located in Levittown, New York, the National Association of Mothers' Centers presently consists of thirty-seven centers in the United States and two sites outside the United States. A national staff provides peer facilitator training and assists in the development and sustainability of centers.

Practical Tips/Program in Action: Mothers' Centers are facilitated in a variety of environments, including churches, parent resource centers, or even the home of a participating member. In some instances, members may need or choose to charge member dues in order to pay for a location to conduct meetings, for childcare, or for a speaker brought in to discuss a particular topic. Each center varies and is managed in the manner each particular group agrees upon.

Materials/Supplies: Mothers' Centers require a space or room on a weekly basis in which mothers can converse openly. Children participating in childcare should be in a cordoned-off area or separate room in close proximity to the mothers in order to have an environment conducive to play and active behavior which is developmentally appropriate.

Staff: A volunteer mother, trained by the National Association of Mothers' Centers, facilitates weekly Mothers' Center meetings. A librarian, identified to act as a liaison, is available to provide information on library resources.

Contact Information: Nancy Handy, Middle Country Public Library, Centereach, NY. Phone: (631) 585-9393 ext. 143. Email: handynancy@mcpl.lib.ny.us.

Additional Resources:
National Association of Mothers' Centers: http://www.motherscenter.org.

Marketing to Parents

Reaching parents and caregivers of very young children and establishing the library as a family-centered institution are challenging for many libraries that are concerned about their role within the local community. To effectively engage this audience, libraries need to examine their marketing and outreach efforts. Ideas for marketing early childhood programs and programs for parents and caregivers include:

Advertising through the library newsletter, local newspapers, and public service radio and television spots.

Creating flyers describing the program, often multilingual, depending on the needs of the community, and distributing them around the neighborhood to Head Start and other nursery school and childcare centers, churches, laundromats, health centers, local Mothers' Centers and clubs, family-serving community agency offices, pediatricians' offices, and supermarkets.

Handing out flyers in other early childhood programs at the library.

Distributing flyers at senior programs in which grandparents may be active.

Grandparents are increasingly serving as childcare providers and have the time to bring young children to the library.

Speaking with patrons and asking them to tell neighbors and friends. Word of mouth is one of the most effective public relations tools.

Visiting local family service agencies and talking about the program. Many professionals have a limited view of the public library from their own childhood. Introducing them to the programs, collections, and other resources will entice them to bring their own clients to the library. Chapter 4 discusses mutual advertising as a benefit of coalition building.

Conclusion

Family-centered library programs address early childhood and parenting concerns and provide librarians with enjoyable and effective ways to share books, toys, language, movement, and music. Through these programs, parents and caregivers gain the skills, support, and validation they need to take on the role of their child's nurturer, first teacher, and partner in learning. Providing this broad scope of programs enables libraries to fulfill their mission as lifelong learning institutions that help build healthy, literate families and strong communities.

9

Early Childhood Collections

Libraries looking to develop into family-centered institutions need to enhance and expand their collection offerings for young children. Traditional collections might include picture books, easy readers, and beginning nonfiction titles for preschool readers, whereas a family-centered library expands the targeted age of the young children's collection to include very young children (babies, infants, and toddlers) and all types of families. These collections provide resources that are multisensory, interactive, and available in a variety of formats and that highlight play, creativity, and individual development.

Collection Development Guidelines

Policies and procedures related to collection development and the circulation of materials from the children's collection also need to be addressed. The following guidelines from *Learning Environments for Young Children: Rethinking Library Spaces and Services* (Feinberg, Kuchner, and Feldman, 1998: 156) provide a solid starting point for children's departments looking to assess both their collections and their family friendliness in terms of circulation policies and procedures.

The children's collection reflects a balanced proportion of circulating items for children from birth through age eight, based on the number of potential and actual users and in relationship to the total collection and acquisition budget for children's materials.

General selection and acquisition policies ensure availability of pertinent materials for parents and children.

Children are allowed to reserve and interloan materials.

Materials are ordered on a planned, regularly scheduled basis using a variety of journals, catalogs, and reference sources.

Materials are diversified to meet the needs of children who represent different populations and cultures, languages, gender, and abilities.

Collections and displays promote awareness of different cultures.

Materials are included that address the needs of children with disabilities, for example, Braille books, large print books, talking books, adaptive toys, assistive technology, and access to a CCTV (closed-circuit television).

Special kits provide an array of materials on specific topics including infancy and prenatal care, siblings, going to the hospital, death and dying, reading readiness skills, and children with special needs.

Computers are available with appropriate software for preschool and primary grade children.

Computers are available for parents to access electronic resources relevant to parenting and child rearing.

Web sites are bookmarked for use by children and parents.

Listening stations and appropriate audio materials are available for young children.

Equipment and materials are organized to attract the interest of young children and promote independence.

An ample amount of art supplies is available for programs, and, if applicable, for use in the children's room.

Manipulative materials, including items that focus on sort and order, fit together and take apart, decode, and pretend play, are available.

Multiple copies of popular books and toys are available.

Bibliographies related to parenting and child-rearing issues are regularly published and displayed.

Bibliographies on materials available for young children are regularly published and displayed.

Displays addressing parenting and child-rearing issues are available.

Books

The best books for very young library users are brief and straightforward, with colorful, eye-catching illustrations. The texts should be simple and use a clear and natural language that captures the child's interest and attention. The formats and titles listed here represent some of the best literature available for the birth to six-year-old child, but should in no way be interpreted as a comprehensive listing. It is merely a starting point for the library that is moving in the direction of family-centered collections.

Board Books

While it is relatively easy today to find a wide variety of board books, not all are suitable for very young children. Care must be taken when purchasing board books to make sure that the story is suited to the format; not all picture books, for example, make a quality board book. Look for titles with colorful illustrations, bold graphics for babies, and simple texts. Too many words on the smaller pages of board books can be a distraction to young readers. Think about where the board books in your library are housed. Placing them on higher shelving makes them inaccessible to the right audience. Try looking for a low browsing shelf to display titles, or consider purchasing large baskets to put by seating areas, making it that much easier for an adult and a baby balanced on his or her lap to reach down and share a book together.

Aliki. *One Little Spoonful.* New York: HarperCollins Children's Books, 2001.
Baby Faces. New York: DK Publishing, 1998.
Barton, Byron. *Machines at Work.* New York: Harper Festival, 1987.
Barton, Byron. *Trucks.* New York: Harper Festival, 1986.
Brown, Margaret Wise. *Good Night Moon.* New York: Campbell Books, 2001.
Christian, Cheryl. *Where Does It Go?* New York: Star Bright Books, 2004.
Christian, Cheryl. *Where's the Baby?* New York: Star Bright Books, 2004.
Crews, Donald. *Freight Train.* New York: Greenwillow, 1996.
Degan, Bruce. *Jamberry.* New York: Harper Festival, 1995.
Emberley, Rebecca. *My Animals/Mis Animales.* Boston: Little, Brown and Company, 2002.
Emberley, Rebecca. *My Food/Mi Comida.* Boston: Little, Brown and Company, 2002.
Hoban, Tana. *Black on White.* New York: Greenwillow, 1993.
Hoban, Tana. *White on Black.* New York: Greenwillow, 1993.
Intrater, Roberta Grobel. *Splash!* New York: Cartwheel Books, 2002.
Katz, Karen. *Counting Kisses: A Kiss and Read Book.* New York: Little, Brown and Company, 2001.
Kubler, Annie. *Row Row Row Your Boat.* Auburn, ME: Child's Play International, 2003.
Kubler, Annie. *Ten Little Fingers.* Auburn, ME: Child's Play International, 2003.
Laden, Nina. *Peek-a-Who?* San Francisco: Chronicle Books, 2000.
Martin, Bill Jr. *Brown Bear, Brown Bear, What Do You See?* New York: Henry Holt and Company, 1996.
Miller, Margaret. *Baby Faces.* New York: Little Simon, 1998.
Oxenbury, Helen. *Clap Hands.* New York: Macmillan, 1987.
Oxenbury, Helen. *I See.* New York: Greenwillow Books, 1985.
Stanley, Mandy. *What Do You Say?* New York: Little Simon, 2003.
Stanley, Mandy. *What Do You Do?* New York: Little Simon, 2005.
Trapani, Ida. *Itsy Bitsy Spider.* Watertown, MA: Charlesbridge Publishers, 1998.

Cloth and Lift-the-Flap Books

Just as important as board books, cloth and lift-the-flap books incorporate different textures, materials, and surfaces for young babies and toddlers to explore and touch. They are also very useful for children with special needs, as they might be easier for them to hold and manipulate. Some libraries circulate these materials, while others keep a collection on hand as "in-house only" materials to use within the early childhood area. Since some of these books come with removable pieces, cataloging them and storing them in plastic hanging bags might make shelving the collection easier.

Bailer, Darice. *Pet for Josh.* New York: Little Simon, 2002.

Boynton, Sandra. *Fuzzy, Fuzzy, Fuzzy: A Touch, Skritch, and Tickle Book.* New York: Little Simon, 2003.

Campbell, Rod. *Dear Zoo.* Pop-up edition. New York: Little Simon, 2005.

Carter, David A. *Little Mouse Plays Peek-a-boo.* Santa Monica, CA: Intervisual Books, 2003.

Cimarusti, Marie Torres. *Peek-A-Moo!* New York: Dutton's Children's Books, 1998.

Cousins, Lucy. *Maisy's Twinkly Crinkly Fun Book.* Cambridge, MA: Candlewick Publishing, 2004.

Deprisco, Dorothea. *Back in My Arms.* Santa Monica, CA: Intervisual Books, 2006.

Elliot, Rachel. *Old MacDonald Had a Farm! A Touch and Feel Book.* Worthington, OH: Brighter Minds Children's Publishing, 2005.

Emberley, Ed. *Go Away, Big Green Monster!* Boston: LB Kids, 1993.

Hill, Eric. *Where's Spot?* New York: Putnam, 1980.

MacDonald, Suse. *Here a Chick, Where a Chick?* New York: Cartwheel Books, 2004.

Page, Josephine. *Bye Bye Bear.* New York: Cartwheel Books, 2005.

Park, Linda Sue. *Mung-Mung: A Fold Out Book of Animal Sounds.* Watertown, MA: Charlesbridge Publishing, 2004.

Park, Linda Sue, and Julia Durango. *Yum! Yuck! A Foldout Book of People Sounds.* Watertown, MA: Charlesbridge Publishing, 2005.

Priddy, Roger. *Fuzzy Bee and Friends.* Gordonsville, VA: Priddy Books, 2003.

Priddy, Roger. *Quack Quack: Touch and Feel Baby Animals.* Gordonsville, VA: Priddy Books, 2004.

Priddy, Roger. *Squishy Turtle and Friends.* Gordonsville, VA: Priddy Books, 2003.

Radar, Laura. *These Little Piggies.* New York: Little Simon, 2001.

Rowe, Jeannette. *Whose Ears?* Boston: Little, Brown and Company, 2000.

Saltzberg, Barney. *Animal Kisses.* New York: Harcourt Publishing, 2000.

Simmons, Jane. *Daisy's Hide and Seek.* Boston: Little, Brown and Company, 2001.

Sleepy Bunny (Pat the Bunny Cloth Book). New York: Random House, 2003.

Steptoe, Janaka. *Sweet, Sweet, Baby.* New York: Cartwheel Books, 2005.

Touch and Feel Farm. New York: DK Publishing, 1998.

Van Fleet, Matthew. *Fuzzy Yellow Ducklings.* New York: Dial Publishing, 1995.

Weeks, Sarah. *Who's Under That Hat?* New York: Harcourt, 2005.

Wells, Rosemary. *Bunny Mail.* New York: Penguin Group, 2004.

Yaccarino, Dan. *Baby Face.* New York: HarperCollins, 2001.

Zelinsky, Paul D. *The Wheels on the Bus.* New York: Dutton Books, 2000.

Picture Books

The "backbone" of an early childhood collection, picture books entice users with their crisp lines, magical illustrations, and, of course, their stories—told with or without words. Today, more than ever, picture books expose us as readers to the corners of the world. Care should be taken when selecting books to make sure that the families living in your community can find themselves pictured in the pages "living" on your library's shelves. In addition to titles that are listed in this section, Chapter 14 provides information on multicultural sources.

Ada, Alma Flor. *Gathering the Sun: An Alphabet Book in Spanish and English*. New York: Morrow, 1997.

Adoff, Arnold. *Black Is Brown Is Tan*. New York: Amistad Publishers, 2002.

Agard, John. *Wriggle Piggy Toes*. London: Frances Lincoln Children's Books, 2005.

Appelt, Kathi. *Oh My Baby, Little One*. New York: Harcourt Children's Books, 2000.

Asch, Frank. *Good Night, Baby Bear*. San Diego, CA: Voyager Books, 2001.

Ashman, Linda. *Babies on the Go*. New York: Harcourt Children's Books, 2003.

Baker, Keith. *Big Fat Hen*. New York: Harcourt Children's Books, 1994.

Balian, Lorna. *Aminal*. New York: Star Bright Books, 2005.

Bang, Molly. *Ten, Nine, Eight*. New York: Greenwillow, 1983.

Barry, Frances. *Duckie's Rainbow*. Cambridge, MA: Candlewick, 2004.

Barton, Byron. *My Car*. New York: Greenwillow, 2001.

Beaumont, Karen. *Baby Danced the Polka*. New York: Dial Books for Young Readers, 2004.

Beaumont, Karen. *I Ain't Gonna Paint No More!* New York: Harcourt Children's Books, 2005.

Bonning, Tony. *Fox Tale Soup*. New York: Simon and Schuster, 2001.

Brett, Jan. *Honey, Honey, Lion! A Story from Africa*. New York: G. P. Putnam's Sons, 2005.

Brett, Jan. *The Mitten*. New York: Putnam Juvenile, 1989.

Brown, Margaret Wise. *Goodnight Moon*. New York: HarperCollins, 1947.

Bunting, Eve. *I Love You Too!* New York: Cartwheel Books, 2004.

Carle, Eric. *My First Book of Numbers*. New York: Penguin Young Readers, 2006.

Carle, Eric. *My First Book of Words*. New York: Penguin Young Readers, 2006.

Carle, Eric. *The Very Busy Spider*. New York: Penguin Young Readers, 1989.

Carle, Eric. *The Very Hungry Caterpillar*. New York: Putnam Publishing Group, 1983.

Chamberlin, Mary. *Mama Panya's Pancakes*. Cambridge, MA: Barefoot Books, 2005.

Chen, Chih-Yuan. *Guji Guji*. La Jolla, CA: Kane/Miller Book Publishers, 2004.

Christelow, Eileen. *Five Little Monkeys Jumping on the Bed*. Wilmington, MA: Houghton Mifflin, 1999.

Crews, Donald. *Inside Freight Train*. Topeka, KS: BT Bound, 2003.

Crews, Nina. *One Hot Summer Day*. New York: Greenwillow Books, 1995.

Cronin, Doreen. *Click, Clack, Moo: Cows That Type*. New York: Simon and Schuster, 2000.

Cronin, Doreen. *Click, Clack, Splish Splash: A Counting Adventure*. New York: Simon & Schuster, 2006.

Cronin, Doreen. *Giggle, Giggle, Quack*. New York: Simon and Schuster, 2002.

Curtis, Jamie Lee. *Today I Feel Silly and Other Moods That Make My Day*. Scranton, PA: Joanna Cotler, 1998.

Dann, Penny. *The Wheels on the Bus*. New York: Barron's Educational Series, 2002.

Dunrea, Olivier. *Gossie*. Boston, MA: Houghton Mifflin, 2002.

Ehlert, Lois. *Leaf Man!* New York: Harcourt Children's Books, 2005.

Ehlert, Lois. *Snowballs!* New York: Harcourt Children's Books, 1995.

Egielski, Richard. *The Gingerbread Boy.* New York: Laura Geringer, 1997.

Falconer, Ian. *Olivia.* New York: Atheneum Books for Young Readers, 2000.

Falconer, Ian. *Olivia Forms a Band.* New York: Atheneum Books for Young Readers, 2006.

Fisher, Valorie. *My Big Brother.* New York: Atheneum Books for Young Readers, 2002.

Fleming, Candace. *Muncha! Muncha! Muncha!* New York: Atheneum Books for Young Readers, 2002.

Fleming, Denise. *Alphabet Under Construction.* New York: Henry Holt and Company, 2002.

Fleming, Denise. *The Everything Book.* New York: Henry Holt and Company, 2000.

Fleming, Denise. *Lunch.* New York: Henry Holt and Company, 1992.

Fox, Mem. *Time for Bed.* New York: Harcourt, 1993.

Freeman, Don. *Corduroy.* New York: Viking Juvenile, 1968.

Gritz, Ona. *Tangerines and Tea: My Grandparents and Me.* New York: Harry N. Abrams, 2005.

Guy, Ginger Fogleson. *Siesta.* New York: Greenwillow, 2005.

Hamanaka, Sheila. *Grandparent's Song.* New York: HarperCollins, 2003.

Harrell, Beatrice Orcutt. *How Thunder and Lightning Came To Be.* New York: Dial, 1995.

Heide, Florence Parry, and Judith Heide Gilliland. *The Day of Ahmed's Secret.* New York: Lothrop, Lee and Shepard, 1990.

Henkes, Kevin. *Julius, Baby of the World.* New York: Greenwillow, 1990.

Henkes, Kevin. *Kitten's First Full Moon.* New York: Greenwillow, 2004.

Henkes, Kevin. *Owen.* New York: Greenwillow, 1993.

Hills, Tad. *Duck and Goose.* New York: Schwartz and Wade Books, 2006.

Hindley, Judy. *Baby Talk: A Book of First Words and Phrases.* Cambridge, MA: Candlewick Press, 2006.

Hindley, Judy. *Eyes, Nose, Fingers and Toes: A First Book About You.* Cambridge, MA: Candlewick Press, 1999.

Ho, Minfong. *Hush: A Thai Lullaby.* Burbank, CA: Orchard Books, 1996.

Hobbie, Holly. *Toot and Puddle: The New Friend.* New York: Little, Brown and Company, 2004.

Horacek, Peter. *A New House for Mouse.* Cambridge, MA: Candlewick Press, 2004.

Horacek, Peter. *Silly Suzy Goose.* Cambridge, MA: Candlewick Press, 2006.

Horacek, Peter. *Strawberries Are Red.* Cambridge, MA: Candlewick Press, 2001.

Horacek, Peter. *What Is Black and White?* Cambridge, MA: Candlewick Press, 2001.

Hudson, Cheryl Willis. *Bright Eyes, Brown Skin.* Orange, NJ: Just Us Books, 1990.

Intrater, Roberta Grobel. *Peek-a-Boo, You.* New York: Scholastic, 2002.

Isadora, Rachel. *Caribbean Dream.* New York: Putnam, 1998.

Isadora, Rachel. *Peekaboo Morning.* New York: Putnam, 2002.

Jocelyn, Marthe. *ABC x 3: English, Espanol, Francais.* Plattsburgh, NY: Tundra Books, 2005.

Johnson, Crockett. *Harold and the Purple Crayon.* New York: HarperCollins, 1981.

Johnston, Tony. *The Tale of Rabbit and Coyote.* New York: G. P. Putnam's Sons, 1994.

Juster, Norton. *The Hello, Goodbye Window.* New York: Hyperion, 2005.

Kanevsky, Polly. *Sleepy Boy.* New York: Simon and Schuster, 2006.

Lacome, Julie. *Walking Through the Jungle.* Cambridge, MA: Candlewick Press, 2003.

LaRochelle, David. *The Best Pet of All.* New York: Dutton Children's Books, 2004.

Lee, Spike. *Please, Baby, Please.* New York: Simon and Schuster, 2002.

Markes, Julie. *Shhh! Everybody's Sleeping.* New York: HarperCollins, 2005.

Martin, Bill Jr. *Brown Bear, Brown Bear, What Do You See?* New York: Henry Holt and Company, 1992.

Martin, Bill Jr. *Chicka Chicka Boom Boom.* New York: Simon and Schuster, 2001.

Martin, Bill Jr. *Panda Bear, Panda Bear, What Do You See?* New York: Henry Holt and Company, 2003.

McBratney, Sam. *Guess How Much I Love You.* Cambridge, MA: Candlewick Press, 2002.

McDonnell, Flora. *I Love Animals.* Cambridge, MA: Candlewick Press, 1994.

McDonnell, Flora. *Splash!* Cambridge, MA: Candlewick Press, 1999.

McKissack, Patricia. *Flossie and the Fox.* New York: Dial Books for Young Readers, 1986.

Medearis, Angela. *Rum-a-Tum-Tum.* New York: Holiday House, 1997.

Medearis, Angela. *The Singing Man.* New York. Holiday House, 1994.

Meyers, Susan. *This Is the Way a Baby Rides.* New York: Harry N. Abrams, 2005.

Morgan, Pierr. *The Turnip: An Old Russian Folktale.* New York: Philomel, 1990.

Most, Bernard. *If the Dinosaurs Came Back.* San Diego, CA: Voyager Books, 1984.

Murphy, Mary. *I Kissed the Baby.* Cambridge, MA: Candlewick Press, 2003.

Muth, Jon J. *Zen Shorts.* New York: Scholastic, 2005.

Nakamura, Katherine Riley. *Song of Night: It's Time to Go to Bed.* Scranton, PA: Blue Sky Press, 2002.

Nolen, Jerdine. *Harvey Potter's Balloon Farm.* New York: Lothrop, Lee and Shepard Books, 1994.

Numeroff, Laura. *If You Give a Pig a Pancake.* New York: HarperCollins, 1998.

Nye, Naomi Shihab. *Baby Radar.* New York: Greenwillow, 2003.

Oughton, Jerrie. *How the Stars Fell into the Sky.* Boston: Houghton Mifflin, 1992.

Oxenbury, Helen. *Pig Tale.* New York: Simon and Schuster, 2005.

Pinkney, Andrea. *Watch Me Dance.* San Diego, CA: Harcourt Brace, 1997.

Pinkney, Brian. *Hush Little Baby.* New York: Greenwillow Books, 2006.

Pinkney, Brian. *Max Found Two Sticks.* New York: Simon and Schuster, 1995.

Piper, Watty. *The Little Engine That Could.* Reillustrated Edition. New York: Penguin Young Readers Group, 2005.

Polacco, Patricia. *Mrs. Katz and Tush.* New York: Dell, 1994.

Rathmann, Peggy. *Good Night Gorilla.* New York: Putnam Juvenile, 1994.

Rathmann, Peggy. *Ten Minutes Till Bedtime.* New York: Putnam Juvenile, 1998.

Robbins, Maria Polushkin. *Mother, Mother, I Want Another.* New York: Knopf Books for Young Readers, 2005.

Root, Phyllis. *Quack!* New York: Walker Books Ltd., 2005.

Root, Phyllis. *What Baby Wants.* Cambridge, MA: Candlewick Press, 2001.

Sanfield, Steve. *Bit by Bit.* New York: Philomel Books, 1995.

Sayre, April Pulley. *Stars Beneath Your Bed: The Surprising Story of Dust.* New York: Greenwillow, 2005.

Scarry, Richard. *Cars and Trucks and Things That Go.* Westminster, MD: Golden Books, 1998.

Sendak, Maurice. *Where the Wild Things Are.* New York: HarperCollins, 1963.

Shannon, David. *A Bad Case of Stripes.* Scranton, PA: Blue Sky Press, 1998.

Shannon, David. *Duck on a Bike.* Scranton, PA: Blue Sky Press, 2002.

Shannon, David. *No David!* Scranton, PA: Blue Sky Press, 1998.

Shaw, Charles. *It Looked Like Spilt Milk.* New York: HarperCollins, 1947.

Sierra, Judy. *Wild about Books.* New York: Knopf Books for Young Readers, 2004.

Simmons, Jane. *Daisy and the Beastie*. Burbank, CA: Orchard Books, 2000.

Siomades, Laura. *The Itsy Bitsy Spider*. Honesdale, PA: Boyds Mill Press, 1999.

Slobodkina, Esphyr. *Caps for Sale*. New York: HarperCollins, 1947.

Steptoe, John. *Baby Says*. New York: Lothrop, Lee and Shepard, 1988.

Stevens, Janet, and Susan Steven Crummel. *The Great Fuzz Frenzy*. New York: Harcourt, 2005.

Stickland, Paul. *Dinosaur Roar!* New York: Dutton, 1997.

Stuve-Bodeen, Stephanie. *Elizabeti's Doll*. New York: Lee and Low Books, 2002.

Tafuri, Nancy. *Goodnight My Duckling*. New York: Scholastic, 2005.

Tafuri, Nancy. *Spots, Feathers and Curly Tails*. New York: Greenwillow, 1988.

Thompson, Lauren. *Little Quack's Bedtime*. New York: Simon and Schuster, 2005.

Walsh, Melanie. *Do Donkeys Dance?* New York: Houghton Mifflin, 2000.

Walsh, Melanie. *Do Pigs Have Stripes?* Boston, MA: Houghton Mifflin, 1996.

Weeks, Sarah. *Mrs. McNosh Hangs Up Her Wash*. New York: Harper Trophy, 2002.

Wells, Rosemary. *Bunny Cakes*. New York: Viking Juvenile, 1999.

Wells, Rosemary. *Bunny Money*. New York: Viking Juvenile, 2000.

Willems, Mo. *Don't Let the Pigeon Drive the Bus*. New York: Hyperion, 2003.

Willems, Mo. *The Pigeon Finds a Hotdog!* New York: Hyperion, 2004.

Williams, Sue. *I Went Walking*. San Diego, CA: Gulliver Books, 1990.

Williams, Vera. *A Chair for My Mother*. New York: Greenwillow, 1982.

Williams, Vera. *More, More, More, Said the Baby*. New York: Greenwillow, 1990.

Winthrop, Elizabeth. *Squashed in the Middle*. New York: Henry Holt, 2005.

Wood, Audrey. *The Deep Blue Sea*. New York: Scholastic, 2005.

Wood, Audrey. *The Napping House*. New York: Harcourt, 1984.

Wood, Audrey. *Piggies*. New York: Harcourt, 1991.

Wood, Don. *The Little Mouse, the Red Ripe Strawberry, and the Big Hungry Bear*. Auburn, ME: Child's Play International, 1987.

Yolen, Jane. *How Do Dinosaurs Say Goodnight?* Scranton, PA: Blue Sky Press, 2000.

Young, Ed. *My Mei Mei*. NY: Philomel Books, 2006.

Nursery Rhyme Collections

Research has shown that children who know at least eight nursery rhymes by heart are more likely to do well in school than their peers who are less familiar with Mother Goose rhymes. The repetition found in many rhymes is a wonderful way for children to engage in literacy activities.

Ada, Alma Flor. *Pio Peep! Traditional Spanish Nursery Rhymes*. New York: HarperCollins, 2003.

Beaton, Clare. *Playtime Rhymes for Little People*. Cambridge, MA: Barefoot Books, 2001.

Brown, Marc. *Finger Rhymes*. New York: Dutton, 1980.

Brown, Marc. *Play Rhymes*. New York: Dutton, 1987.

Calmenson, Stephanie. *Good for You! Toddler Rhymes for Toddler Times*. New York: Harper-Collins, 2001.

Collins, Beverly. *Pat-A-Cake and Other Play Rhymes*. New York: Morrow Junior Books, 1992.

Cousins, Lucy. *The Little Dog Laughed*. New York: Dutton Publishing, 1990.

Crews, Nina. *The Neighborhood Mother Goose*. New York: Greenwillow Books, 2004.

Delacre, LuLu. *Arroz Con Leche: Popular Songs and Rhymes from Latin America.* New York: Scholastic, 1989.

DePaola, Tomie. *Tomie DePaola's Mother Goose Favorites.* New York: Grosset and Dunlap, 2000.

Halpern, Shari. *Little Robin Redbreast: A Mother Goose Rhyme.* New York: North-South Books, 1994.

Hoberman, Mary Ann. *You Read to Me, I'll Read to You: Very Short Mother Goose Tales to Read Together.* New York: Little, Brown and Company, 2005.

McMullen, Kate. *Baby Goose.* New York: Hyperion, 2004.

Opie, Iona. *Here Comes Mother Goose.* Cambridge, MA: Candlewick Press, 1999.

Opie, Iona. *My Very First Mother Goose Rhymes.* Cambridge, MA: Candlewick Press, 2001.

Prelutsky, Jack. *Read Aloud Rhymes for the Very Young.* New York: Alfred Knopf, 1986.

Roffey, Maureen. *Grand Old Duke of York.* New York: Whispering Coyote Press, 1993.

Sabuda, Robert. *The Movable Mother Goose.* New York: Little Simon, 1999.

Thomas, Joyce Carol. *Hush Songs: African American Lullabies.* Collingdale, PA: Diane Publishing Company, 2000.

Whatley, B. *My First Nursery Rhymes.* New York: Harper Festival, 1999.

Wyndham, Robert. *Chinese Mother Goose Rhymes.* New York: PaperStar Books, 1998.

Yaccarino, Dan. *Dan Yaccarino's Mother Goose.* Westminster, MD: Golden Books, 2004.

Yolen, Jane. *This Little Piggy: And Other Rhymes to Sing and Play.* Cambridge, MA: Candlewick Press, 2006.

Young, Ed. *Seven Blind Mice.* New York: Philomel, 1992.

Big Books

For young children in groups, big books can help focus a child's attention and make it easier to see details. Though many children enjoy seeing their favorite books enlarged, big books are also extremely useful for children with visual disabilities or other cognitive and attention disorders. Some libraries circulate big books to teachers and other early childhood professionals, while others have them in the library for "in-house use" only.

Sources:

ABC School Supply, Inc.
3312 North Berkeley Lake Rd.
P.O. Box 100019
Duluth, GA 30136
(800) 669-4222
www.abcschoolsupply.com

Demco
P.O. Box 7488
Madison, WI 53707
(800) 279-1586
www.demco.com

Lakeshore Learning Materials
2695 East Dominguez St.

P.O. Box 6261
Carson, CA 90749
(800) 421-5354
www.lakeshorelearning.com

Scholastic
557 Broadway
New York, NY 10012
(800) 724-6527
www.scholastic.com

Audio Books

Audio books, both on cassette and CD, provide another strategy for integrating literature within the daily lives of young children. They are wonderful companions for families who are traveling and are especially useful to those who have physical difficulties holding a print book or seeing pictures or print or who have certain types of learning disabilities. Using audio books, parents with limited literacy skills can still "read" to their children. In today's computer-savvy world, libraries are also incorporating audio downloads as an online service.

Sources:

Audible
65 Willowbrook Blvd.
Wayne, NJ 07470
(888) 283-5051
www.audible.com

Educational Record Center
(888) 372-4543
www.erckids.com

OverDrive, Inc.
Valley Tech Center, Suite N
8555 Sweet Valley Dr.
Cleveland, OH 44125
(216) 573-6886
www.overdrive.com

Random House/Listening Library
1745 Broadway
10th Floor
New York, NY 10019
www.randomhouse.com/audio/listeninglibrary

Recorded Books, LLC
270 Skipjack Rd.
Prince Frederick, MD 20678
(800) 638-1304
www.recordedbooks.com

Spoken Arts
195 South White Rock Rd.
Holmes, NY 12531
(800) 326-4090
www.spokenartsmedia.com

Videos/DVDs

Many parents and caregivers look for videos and DVDs that are educational and appropriate for young children. The American Academy of Pediatrics recently recommended that children watch no television from the age of birth to two and then limited amounts thereafter. Videos and DVDs (unlike unsupervised and controlled TV viewing) provide a certain amount of control for the parent or caregiver, are selected with particular tastes and ages in mind, are watched for a limited amount of time, and often are viewed in tandem with parents or caregivers. Many videos and DVDs are animations of popular books and book characters. This increases their educational and recreational value and can provide a little bit of respite for the weary mom or dad.

Sources:

Children's Circle
CC Studios Inc.
Weston, CT 06883

Library Video Company
P.O. Box 580
Wynnewood, PA 19096
(800) 843-3620

Random House
400 Hahn Rd.
Westminster, MD 21157

Midwest Tape
P.O. Box 820
Holland, OH 43528
(800) 875-2785

Weston Woods
143 Main St.
Norwalk, CT 06851
(800) 243-5020
(203) 845-0197
Fax: (203) 845-0498

Music

Young children love listening and dancing to a wide variety of music. Activity songs, lullabies, nursery rhymes, classical music, and folk songs can be a source of joy and wonder to most children, beginning at birth. Listening to music and danc-ing together provides a fun outlet for parents and caregivers as well as children. While selecting music geared for children, parents and caregivers need to keep in mind children will enjoy many of their favorites also.

Suggested Titles:

All You Need Is Love: Beatles Songs for Kids. Music for Little People, 1998.
Baby Einstein: Lullaby Classics, 2004.
Baby Games. Kimbo, 1987.
Berkner, Laurie, Buzz Buzz. Music for Little People, 2001.
A Child's Celebration of Music. Music for Little People, 1996.
Hamett, Carol. It's Toddler Time. Kimbo, 1982.
Nursery Rhyme Time. Kimbo, 2000.
Palmer, Hap. Babysongs. New York: Educational Activities, 1991.
Palmer, Hap. More Babysongs. New York: Educational Activities, 1984.
Putumayo Kids Present: Folk Playground. Putumayo, 2006.
Raffi. The Singable Songs Collection. MA: Rounder Records, 1997.
Sharon, Lois, and Bram. Mostly Mother Goose. A&M, 2004.
Sharon, Lois, and Bram. Sing A to Z. A&M, 1990.
Toddler Favorites. Music for Little People, 1998.
Zanes, Dan. Catch That Train! Music for Little People, 2006.

Sources:

Educational Activities
P.O. Box 87
Baldwin, NY 11510
(800) 645-3739
Fax: (516) 623-9282
www.edact.com

Kimbo
P.O. Box 477
Long Branch, NJ 07740
(800) 631-2187
Fax: (732) 870-3340
www.kimboed.com

Music for Little People
P.O. Box 1460
Redway, CA 95560
(800) 409-2457
www.musicforlittlepeople.com

Putomayo World Music
411 Lafayette Ave.
Fourth Floor
New York, NY 10003
(212) 625-1400

Fax: (212) 460-0095
www.putomayo.com

Software

Children at younger and younger ages are becoming aware of and using computers. While librarians and parents may have mixed feelings about computer use, our changing world is affecting the way our society integrates computers into daily lives. For those families of young children who want to explore and discover math and reading readiness through computer programs, libraries can provide a selection of those materials that are of high quality.

Suggested Titles:

Reader Rabbit Toddler
Jumpstart Kindergarten
Just Grandma and Me
Dr. Seuss ABC
Curious George Preschool Learning Games
Mercer Mayer's Just Me and My Dad
Stanley's Sticker Stories

Sources:

Academic Software USA
141 Ayers Ct.
Teaneck, NJ 07666
(201) 837-8174
(800) 227-5816
www.academicsoftwareusa.com

Children's Technology Review
120 Main St.
Flemington, NJ 08822
(800) 993-9499
www.childrenssoftware.com

Kids Click Software
1285 Park Forest
San Antonio, TX 78230
(888) 219-9030
Fax: (210) 408-8054
www.kidsclick.com

Riverdeep, Inc.
222 Third Ave. SE, 4th Floor
Cedar Rapids, IA 52401
(319) 395-9626
Fax: (319) 395-0217

Smart Kids Software
P.O. Box 590464
Houston, TX 77259
(888) 881-6001
www.smartkidssoftware.com

Materials for Children with Special Needs

In addition to the early childhood materials already mentioned in this chapter, the following materials are designed specifically to meet the needs of differently abled children. For additional information on serving children with special needs and their families, see Chapter 16.

Tactile Materials

Recreational reading material for visually impaired children, in Braille, recorded, and print or Braille format, as well as tactile children's books can be accessed through the National Library Service for the Blind and Physically Handicapped Network of cooperating libraries. Produced with raised pictures and textures, tactile books can be felt by a child with a visual impairment or any child who could benefit from the tactile learning mode. The American Printing House for the Blind is the official source for textbooks in Braille, recorded, and large-type format for blind students from preschool through high school. Twin Vision books combine Braille and traditional text. This combination allows sighted and visually impaired children or adults to share the same book.

Sources:

American Printing House for the Blind
P.O. Box 6085
Louisville, KY 40206-0085
(502) 895-2405 or (800) 223-1839
Fax: (502) 899-2274
www.aph.org

National Braille Press, Inc.
88 Saint Stephen St.
Boston, MA 02115
(617) 266-6160

National Library Service for the Blind and Physically Handicapped
Library of Congress
Washington, DC 20540
(202) 707-5100 or (888) NLS-READ
Fax: (202) 707-0712
TDD: (202) 707-0744
www.loc.gov/nls.html

Seedlings Braille Books for Children
P.O. Box 51924
Livonia, MI 48151
 (744) 427-8552 or (800) 777-8552
www.seedlings.org

Captioned and Voice-over-Narration Videos and DVDs

For children with learning disabilities or low literacy, videos and DVDs are often a preferred format for information and entertainment. For those children with hearing impairments, there are both closed-captioned (requiring a decoder) and open-captioned (sign or text appears on the screen) videos and DVDs. In addition to captioning, voice-over-narration videos and DVDs describe in detail what is visually happening on the screen, besides having a regular soundtrack.

Sources:

Gallaudet University Book Store
Gallaudet University
800 Florida Ave., NE
Washington, DC 20002
(800) 621-2736
(888) 630-9347 (TTY)
www.gupress.gallaudet.edu

Sign Media, Inc.
4020 Blackburn Lane
Burtonsville, MD 20866
(800) 475-4756
Fax: (301) 421-0270
www.signmedia.com

Adaptive and Specialized Software and Equipment

Many children with special needs require software or communication devices that are very simple to operate. Switch software is a type of software program that is operated by only a few defined keystrokes or a mouse click. For a comprehensive list of accessibility tools and sources, go to the vendor section of Alliance for Technology Access at: www.tasc.ataccess.org.

Sources:

Judy Lynn Software
P.O. Box 373
East Brunswick, NJ 08816
Phone/Fax: (732) 390-8845
www.judylynn.com

Slater Software, Inc.
351 Badger Lane
Guffey, CO 80820
(719) 479-2255 or (877) 306-6968
Fax: (719) 479-2254
www.slatersoftware.com

Kid/TECH/SoftTouch
3204 Perry Pl.
Bakersfield, CA 93306
(805) 873-8744

Books about Children with Special Needs

Sharing books depicting children with special needs introduces typically developing young children to others with diverse abilities, increasing their knowledge about, comfort with, and acceptance of their differently abled peers. This is particularly helpful when explaining a child's disability to a sibling or young friend. When children with special needs see children like themselves in books, it helps lessen their feelings of isolation and being different.

Books about Children with Special Needs

Amenta, Charles A. *Russell Is Extra Special: A Book about Autism for Children*. Washington, DC: Magination Press, 1992.

Brown, Katrin, and Fran Ortiz. *Someone Special, Just Like You*. New York: Dulet, 1995.

Carter, Alden R. *Stretching Ourselves: Kids with Cerebral Palsy*. Morton Grove, IL: Albert Whitman and Company, 2000.

Caseley, Judith. *Harry and Willy and Carrothead*. New York: Greenwillow Books, 1991.

Davis, Patricia. *Brian's Bird*. Morton Grove, IL: Albert Whitman and Company, 2000.

Gagnon, Elisa, and Brenda S. Myles. *This Is Asperger Syndrome*. Shawnee Mission, KS: Autism Asperger Publishing Company, 1999.

Galvin, Matthew. *Otto Learns about His Medicine: A Story about Medication for Children with ADHD*. Washington, DC: Magination Press, 2001.

Glatzer, Jenna. *Taking Down Syndrome to School*. Plainview, NY: JayJo Books, 2002.

Hames, Annette, and Monica McCaffrey, eds. *Special Brothers and Sisters: Stories for Siblings of Children with Special Needs, Disability or Serious Illness*. Dulles, VA: Jessica Kingsley Publishers, 2005.

Heelan, Jamee R. *Can You Hear a Rainbow?: The Story of a Deaf Boy Named Chris*. Atlanta, GA: Peachtree Publishers, 2002.

Kraus, Robert. *Leo the Late Bloomer*. Saint Paul: Minnesota Humanities Commission, 2000.

Lears, Laurie. *Ian's Walk: A Story about Autism*. Morton Grove, IL: Albert Whitman and Company, 1998.

Litchfield, Ada B. *A Button in Her Ear*. Chicago: Albert Whitman and Company, 1976.

Meyers, Cindy. *Rolling Along with Goldilocks and the Three Bears*. Bethesda, MD: Woodbine House, 1999.

Millman, Isaac. *Moses Goes to School*. New York: Farrar, Straus and Giroux, 2000.

Moss, Deborah Lee. *Shelley, the Hyperactive Turtle*. 2nd Edition. Bethesda, MD: Woodbine House, 2006.

Murrell, Diane. *Tobin Learns to Make Friends*. Arlington, TX: Future Horizons, 2001.

Nemiroff, Marc. *Help Is on the Way: A Child's Book about A.D.D.* Washington, DC: Magination Press, 1998.

Niner, Holly. *I Can't Stop! A Story about Tourette Syndrome*. Morton Grove, IL: Albert Whitman and Company, 2005.

Rickert, Janet. *Russ and the Firehouse*. Bethesda, MD: Woodbine House, 2000.

Robb, Diane B. *The Alphabet War: A Story about Dyslexia*. Morton Grove, IL: Albert Whitman and Company, 2004.

Rogers, Fred. *Extraordinary Friends*. New York: G. P. Putnam, 2000.

Shriver, Maria. *What's Wrong with Timmy?* Boston: Little, Brown and Company, 2001.

Stuve-Bodeen, Stephanie. *We'll Paint the Octopus Red*. Bethesda, MD: Woodbine House, 1998.

Thompson, Mary. *Andy and His Yellow Frisbee*. Bethesda, MD: Woodbine House, 1996.

Thompson, Mary. *My Brother Matthew*. Bethesda, MD: Woodbine House, 1992.

Woloson, Eliza. *My Friend Isabelle*. Bethesda, MD: Woodbine House, 2003.

Conclusion

By offering patrons materials in a wide access of formats and languages, early childhood collections will help parents and caregivers in their role as first teacher to their child; professionals working within the field of early childhood will be able to find materials to use with their families; and libraries will truly be family-centered, serving their youngest patrons with quality resources to help them grow and learn.

Reference

Feinberg, Sandra, Joan F. Kuchner, and Sari Feldman. *Learning Environments for Young Children: Rethinking Library Spaces and Services*. Chicago: American Library Association, 1998.

10

Toy Collection

"Play is the 'work' of children. Toys, as the tools of play, can help any child learn" (Breen and Fazio, 2001: 21). When librarians create space and develop resources for an early childhood learning environment in a public library, toys serve as a critical element in the overall setting. In-house toy collections include not only toys that are available on the public floor but also those that are regularly used in programs. Establishing a circulating toy collection stretches the library's mission of resource sharing and offers a valuable resource for families with young children and, more important, can be used to attract children with special needs—a hard-to-reach audience. A circulating toy collection provides an opportunity for parents and caregivers to try new and different toys, encourages parents and caregivers to learn about the skills that toys help to develop, and promotes the central importance of toys and play in a young child's literacy and social development. As with any form of materials, toys require selection, ordering, and processing procedures that are conducive to circulation and public use.

Selection Guidelines

Just as a library's reading collection contains copies of classics, there are certain toys that compose a core collection. While many families already have basic items

155

in their home collections, certain toys are so important to children's play—and therefore to their development—that no toy collection is complete without them. A selection of commercial toys that fall into the following categories should be considered for a core circulating toy collection:

> Building blocks (alphabet blocks, magnetic blocks, bristle blocks, etc.)
> Nesting and stacking toys (stacking cups, stacking rings, nesting dolls, etc.)
> Balls of various sizes and textures
> Dolls and hand puppets
> Easy-grip puzzles
> Imaginary play toys (animal sets, dolls, dishes, doctor kits, toy cars and trucks)
> Shape/sorting toys
> Push-pull toys
> Musical instruments
> Science-related toys (magnets, magnifying glasses, etc.)

Versatility

In general, circulating toys need to exhibit a high degree of "functional versatility" (the ability of a toy to be used in a number of different ways to fit a child's moods, personality, and capabilities). Examples of such toys include balls, dolls, blocks, puppets, musical instruments, and stacking or nesting toys. This is in contrast to a toy that can be used only in rigidly defined ways, such as a jack-in-the-box. Toys that have a high level of functional versatility allow children to use their imagination to fill in the details and expand their use. Toys that have open-ended play potential will create a positive learning play experience for children and will assist in further development.

Choose well-designed toys that are easy to manipulate, have multisensory appeal, have potential for interaction, show cause and effect, are safe and durable, are adjustable (for height, sound volume, speed, and level of difficulty), and can be used by children of a wide range of ages and abilities.

While it is not necessary to select only toys that have a limited number of pieces, it is important to choose toys that are versatile enough to function even if a few pieces are damaged or lost, such as Duplo blocks or a set of dishes. If each piece of a multiple-item toy is essential to the operation of that toy, then it is not an advisable purchase.

Quality and Safety

Certain toy companies have established reputations as providers of quality products for children. Be cautious of discount toy catalogs that offer "clones" of popular toys at reduced prices. Products made with inferior materials may not be as durable or safe as their better-known counterparts. For example, one toy discount supplier offers low-priced "easy grip" puzzles, from which the "grip" is easily dislodged from the puzzle piece. This creates a potential choking hazard.

Limit selections to toys that are durable and safe. Better toys are constructed of materials such as shatter-proof, durable plastic, safety mirrors, and solid wood rather than flimsy wood laminates. There should be no small pieces that could easily break or fall off.

Bypass toys with hard-to-clean surfaces. Circulating toys require a cleaning procedure that is outlined later in this chapter. Select toys that have surfaces that can be easily cleaned.

The Toy Manufacturers of America give specific guidelines when choosing toys for children under three years old:

Avoid small parts that can be swallowed, aspirated, or inserted in the nose or ears.

Check that the eyes and nose of stuffed animals and dolls are sewn or fastened securely.

Avoid latex balloons, which present a choking hazard.

Select unbreakable toys that are lightweight, washable, and free of sharp corners, rough edges, or strings.

Avoid dangerous entanglement: toys should not be hung or attached to a crib, playpen, stroller, or infant seat or around a child's neck with elastic, string, or ribbon.

Check toys regularly, at least every three months, for tears, breaks, or rips that expose stuffing, sharp edges, or small parts.

Age Appropriateness

At the outset, establish the age level to which the collection is geared. Early childhood includes children from birth to six years. While it is essential that the age appropriateness of a toy be considered, do not be bound by suggested age levels printed on the package. Many conventional toys geared for younger children may be ideal for older children who need to work on a skill or for children with special needs.

Cost

Parents are less likely to buy some toys because of their cost. When a library purchases and circulates toys, as with other materials, the cost is a shared expense. The library's toy collection, especially one that includes adaptive toys for children with special needs, gives all children a wider range of choices than any individual family's budget may allow. In addition to allowing expensive resources to be shared, the library's toy collection offers an opportunity for parents and children to experience playing with a toy prior to purchasing it. A circulating toy collection is often a treasured resource for grandparents who may have visiting grandchildren or who may provide childcare on a sporadic basis.

Cost is of particular importance for families who need to purchase adaptive toys. Adaptive toys are often expensive, and the library offers a way to share that expense, particularly because children generally use toys for a limited period of time.

If the collection includes battery-operated toys, a library must determine whether it can afford to provide batteries on an ongoing basis. Providing batteries can be costly. One option is to have the families borrowing the toys responsible for providing batteries for their own use. When selecting toys (if the library opts to provide batteries), it is a good idea to keep track of the number and size of batteries each requires, estimate how many times the toy can circulate on one set of batteries, and purchase batteries in bulk. This is a particularly important cost consideration when purchasing adaptive toys and switches, many of which are battery operated.

The initial costs for developing a circulating toy collection includes toy purchases, cleaning and storage supplies, publicity materials, and possibly replacement batteries. How and where the toys are housed can also add to the initial budget, depending upon the type of storage units used. Once the toy collection is in place, it becomes less expensive and can be maintained on a smaller budget.

Toys and Children with Special Needs

Toys are of particular importance for children with special needs. To promote inclusion, libraries that circulate toys often include toys for children with and without disabilities. The National Lekotek Center, a leader in the development of toy-lending libraries, was founded on the principle of play and the use of toys to promote literacy in children with disabilities. Roughly translated from Swedish, Lekotek means "play library." The Lekotek concept originated in Sweden in 1963 when two mothers of children with disabilities sought ways to help their children during their early formative years. They believed that the first years of life significantly determined later development and that intervention strategies must be a part of a child's earliest experiences. Both women were intimately aware of the loneliness and isolation felt by the family of a child with disabilities. It was important to them to have their children with special needs enjoy as natural a childhood as possible and become part of the mainstream of society. Since the most natural activity of young children is play, a play-based approach to the inclusion of children with disabilities became the guiding philosophy of the Lekotek movement.

This approach to learning holds great promise for children with disabilities because it expands the definition of literacy to encompass a broader range of behaviors. It stresses the importance of a supportive environment, rather than the individual's particular abilities, for learning to read and write. When children with cognitive, physical, communication, or sensory challenges are given access to adapted toys, books, computer equipment, and communication devices, they often have surprised their caregivers and teachers by participating in learning activities—including literacy-building play—that would have been impossible without these accommodations (National Lekotek Center, 2000).

If children with disabilities are to develop into readers and writers, they must have the same opportunities to participate in literacy-building play experiences during their early childhood years as their peers without disabilities. Providing these opportunities is the responsibility of libraries dedicated to the development and promotion of literacy. Reaching out in nontraditional ways to children with special needs and providing access to adapted play materials, equipment, and books assure that these children can reach their potential as readers and writers.

A collection that integrates commercial toys and ideas for adapting them with specially designed adaptive toys and switches entices families and children with a wide range of abilities and disabilities to come to the library and utilize its resources. For a child with a disability that limits his or her ability to move, communicate, or manipulate a toy, the availability of toys is more than delightful. It can make the difference between whether or not the child can independently experience the pleasure and learning afforded by play.

Selection of Adaptive Toys

Many librarians working with children may not feel they have the education or experience to select toys for children with special needs. The Toy Resource Helpline, operated by the National Lekotek Center, provides free, personalized consultation on how to select appropriate play materials and activities for children with special needs. Lekotek experts have at their fingertips hundreds of resources on where specialized information, equipment, toys, software, and books are available to help families find the resources they need to promote their children's development and learning. Experts can help parents identify toys that will bring success rather than frustration to their child. The toll-free help line can be reached by dialing (800) 366-PLAY.

As a project of Parents Educating Parents and Professionals, the United Parents Syndicate on Disabilities and Toys "R" Us have teamed up to provide the *Toys "R" Us Toy Guide for Differently Abled Kids!* (United Parents Syndicate on Disabilities and Toys "R" Us, 2005), which focuses on commercially produced toys that have been recommended for use with children with disabilities. In this annually published guide, each toy is described and assigned a symbol that alerts adults to the specific play benefits associated with the toy. *Let's Play: A Guide to Toys for Children with Special Needs* (Citrin et al., 2006) is another valuable guide that is available free from the Toy Industry Foundation.

Local professionals working in the early intervention or special education field can play an important role in toy selection. Many will be happy to share their expertise, especially if their families can use the library's collection. Contact them through the local school district, state and local government agencies working in early intervention and special education, or private schools serving children with disabilities. In addition to working with these providers when selecting toys, librarians need to consider the following guidelines.

Adaptability

A toy collection targeted to children with disabilities needs to include capability switches, specially designed adaptive toys, and generic commercial toys that can be used by children with a range of abilities. These toys and materials promote physical and cognitive growth and empower the child to control his or her environment. Consider simple adaptations such as adding foam tubing to grips on objects like spoons or adding dowels or spools to puzzle pieces for an easier grip.

Capability Switches: Capability switches permit children to activate toys with minimal pressure, sound, or movement. Having a variety of switches available anticipates the needs of individual children and enables them to play with adapted toys. Plate switches of various sizes utilize the slightest pressure from individual body parts, whereas other switches may rely on a puff of air or tilt of the head to power the toy. Capability switches include a lighted sensory plate switch, grip switch, vibrating plate switch, joystick, pillow switch, or signal switch.

Adaptive Toys: Adaptive toys are modified battery-operated toys that can accommodate any capability switch. There are also adaptive toys, such as multisensory activity boxes, bead chains, and stacking towers that do not require an external switch to be operational. Adaptive toys include:

Toys for sensory play (texture boards, rhythm instruments, balls with different tactile sensations, etc.)
Manipulation toys (tracking boards, lacing sets, etc.)
Toys that emphasize sensorimotor exploration (multisensory activity boxes, somatosensory bead chains, etc.)
Toys that stimulate cause-effect or visual tracking (switch-activated toys, toys with levers to press or turn for an immediate response)
Infant sensory stimulation toys (crib mobiles, music box or mirror, floor rollers, plastic rattles with bumps or grooves, etc.)

Commercial Toys: Toys need not be specially designed with adaptive devices in order to be appropriate for children with special needs. Many traditional toys are appropriate to use with all types of disabilities. The manufacturer-assigned age range for a toy should be interpreted flexibly. A toy geared for a nondisabled three-year-old may be appropriate for a six-year-old with special needs. The most effective way to find the perfect toy is to base your decision on the child's interest and skill level (Citrin et al., 2006). Some features, such as easy-grip puzzle pieces or blocks that connect with magnets or bristles, may help make toys more suitable for children with physical disabilities. Adding Velcro can adapt standard building blocks for use with children who lack fine muscle control. Purchasing soft foam instead of hard plastic blocks is safer for all young children. Awareness of safety issues and ways of making toys more accessible is critical. Lists of resources and catalogs to assist in building a toy collection can be found at the conclusion of this chapter.

Cataloging and Processing

Toy circulation works best when toys are processed like other collections in the library. When properly cataloged and included in the computerized catalog, staff

10-1:   Toy Cataloging Form

WFMG   **PUZZLE OR TOY WORKFORM**

TYPE: r	ELVL: k	SRCE: d	LANG: _ _ _
BLVL: m	TMAT: w	GPUB: _	CTRY: _ _ _
DESC: a	TIME: nnn	DTST: _ DATES: _ _ _ _, _ _ _ _

PHYSICAL
DESCRIPTION   ØØ7   k ≠ b z   ≠ d _ ≠ e_

STOCK
CALL #   Ø37 ♭ ♭

CALL NO.   Ø99 ♭ 9

MAIN ENTRY   1_ _♭

TITLE   245_ _   ≠ h toy

                              ≠ b
                              ≠ c
                                             ≠ b
IMPRINT   26Ø ♭ ♭
                              ≠ c

PHYSICAL   3ØØ ♭ ♭
DESC.

NOTES   5Ø_ _ _

SUBHEADING   65Ø ♭ Ø   Puzzles
      OR: 65Ø ♭ Ø   Toys
                 6_   _ _
                 6_   _ _

ADDED ENTRY   7_

                              CATALOGED BY _____ DATE _____
                              KEYED BY _____ DATE _____

and patrons can easily access them (see Figure 10-1). Guidelines for cataloging toys and other realia can be found in Chapter 10 of *Anglo-American Cataloging Rules* (American Library Association, 2005). The Toy Work Form can help librarians to catalog toys in machine readable format.

Many MARC (Machine-Readable Cataloging) records for toys are available on OCLC (the Online Computer Library Center). If a specific toy does not yet have a record, librarians can search OCLC for the record of another toy manufactured by the same company. This record provides a template for the toy being cataloged.

Checking existing records ensures consistency in the catalog and streamlines accessibility for the user.

Processing

After a toy has been cataloged, additional processing tips include:

Mark each piece of the toy with indelible, nontoxic ink, using an identifying name and/or number specific to that toy, such as a bar code number.

Package the toys in bags for storage and circulation. Mesh bags are preferred because they are flexible for use with toys of varying shapes, can be ordered in an assortment of sizes, and are durable and washable. Sources for mesh bags include JanWay Company, 11 Academy Rd., Cogan Station, PA 17728, (800) 877-5242 and Safety 1st, Inc., 210 Boylston St., Chestnut Hill, MA 02167, (800) 962-7233 (Wash & Dry mesh bags for small toys).

Attach a laminated identification tag to the mesh bag using either a nylon or plastic tie. This tag should include the following information: toy title, Dewey decimal number, bar code (or other identifying number), number of pieces, and recommended age range as stated by the manufacturer. Including the recommended age range is helpful in identifying the developmental level for which the toy was designed. If the toy has many pieces, and the loss of a few of them will not keep it from circulating, do *not* include the exact number of pieces on the tag. Instead, substitute a generic description such as "multiple pieces." This will prevent the necessity of producing a new tag each time a piece is lost or destroyed (see Figure 10-2).

Storage

Housing the circulating toy collection out of the public area or in locked display cases is advised. Maintaining the collection for circulation purposes is difficult if the toys are left open for public use. Establishing a separate collection of toys, as part of the early childhood area, specifically for children to use in the library setting that includes items such as floor puzzles, puppets, and blocks is recommended.

Retrieving toys takes time. The toy storage space needs to be easily accessible to staff members responsible for retrieving them. Placing the toy storage space near the children's room yet out of the patron's reach is the ideal location.

An efficient and flexible storage system for a toy collection is a wall grid system, complete with detachable baskets and hooks of various sizes and shapes. Hooks may be used for smaller toys, while larger or heavier toys require the extra support of a basket. This type of storage system provides for collection expansion, because additional grid pieces and accessories may be purchased at a later date. Since this is a wall-mounted system, it can make use of otherwise unusable space, often at a premium in library buildings. Examples of such a space include a basement wall adjacent to an elevator, for easy access by library staff, or the walls of a stairwell directly off the public floor.

10-2:   **Tag for Toys**

CALL NO: TOY COLLECTION J793.7 DOME

TITLE: DOME ALONE WITH SWITCH

CONTENT: 1 SELF-CONTAINED DOME,
                   4 C BATTERIES

> Place Library Barcode Here

O

THIS ITEM IS NOT RENEWABLE

DO NOT REMOVE THIS TAG

PLEASE CHECK CONTENTS FOR MISSING PIECES.
IF THE TOY IS RETURNED WITH MISSING PIECES,
YOU WILL BE CHARGED FULL PRICE OF TOY.

O

Toys may be arranged on the grid by call number, similar to the shelving of traditional library materials. Another option is to arrange the toys according to type, for example, mazes, puppets, puzzles, manipulative toys, imaginary play, adaptive switches, and so on. A portion of the grid system can be designated for each type, with a color assigned to each section. The same colored label is then affixed to the laminated tag on each toy's mesh bag. A source for wall grid systems is:

Library Display Design Systems
P.O. Box 8143
Berlin, CT 06037
(860) 828-6089

Policies and Procedures

Each toy collection is unique in scope, organization, policies, and procedures. If possible, visit an established toy lending or play library to observe and learn what works best for them. The USA Toy Library Association, located at 1326 Wilmette Ave., Wilmette, IL 60091, (847) 920-9030 has a complete list of over 300 toy libraries, including those for children with special needs.

Policies

Some of the issues to consider when establishing policies include:

> Who can borrow the toys—parents only, each child in the family, grandparents, or others?
>
> How many toys can be borrowed—per family, per child, early intervention specialists, and so forth?
>
> What is the length of the loan period?
>
> Can toys be reserved or renewed?
>
> What is a patron's responsibility and liability regarding damaged toys or missing pieces?
>
> Can out-of-district early intervention professionals borrow items to use in working with in-district children?
>
> Will you use donated toys?

The size of the collection will be a determining factor in many of these policies. If patrons are limited to one toy per cardholder, remember that certain adaptive toys require the loan of a capability switch in order to be activated. Since the toy collection is part of a public library, many lending policies would exclude out-of-district residents from borrowing these items. However, if the size of the collection permits, consideration may be given to early intervention professionals working with families within the library district. Consideration may also be given to local early childhood centers or agencies that would like to borrow toys for use at their site. By expanding the loan of toys to early intervention specialists and agencies, the library reaches children and families that may not be regular library users. Early intervention specialists can assist families in deriving the maximum benefit in the utilization of the toy collection.

Procedures

Necessary to any well-maintained toy collection are clearly stated guidelines regarding access to the toy collection and circulation procedures. Maximizing access with minimal inconvenience to staff and patrons should be of primary importance.

Accessing the Collection: For patrons to use the toy collection, there must be sensible, easy ways for them to discover what toys are in the collection and if a particular toy is available for circulation. Alternatives include a record in the library card or online catalog and a special toy collection notebook. A record in the computer or card catalog integrates the collection into the library's other holdings. It allows patrons to search for specific toys using standard access points, for example, subject, toy name, or manufacturer.

A specially designed binder, kept at the children's reference desk, is an alternative method for recording toys. A visual record helps the patron determine if the toy is appropriate for the child's needs, interests, and abilities. Some libraries keep both the catalog record and a binder. The binder contains a one-sheet description of each toy with a picture copied (in color if possible) from the toy catalog or from the box which housed the toy. The description needs to include whether a switch and/or batteries are required. For durability, this toy record can be laminated or placed in plastic sleeves.

If space allows, toys can be housed in glass display cases. This is a great way to advertise the collection and boost circulation.

Check-out Procedures: When a patron has chosen a particular toy from the toy notebook, public access catalog, or display case, the staff needs to check the item for availability. Libraries with online catalogs generally have a status entry for each item. If this is not available, other methods may be devised. For example, placing a "checked out" card in a pocket attached to the plastic sleeves in the toy notebook alerts the patron that the item is circulating. If the toy is available, a staff member can retrieve the toy for the patron.

Check-in Procedures: When a toy is returned to the library, it is placed in a special bin and not reshelved until a staff member:

Checks the toy for damage or missing pieces.

Cleans hard plastic surfaces with a bleach and water solution using a ratio of 1 tablespoon bleach to 1 quart of water or ¼ cup of bleach to 1 gallon of water. This solution must be prepared daily to maintain its effectiveness. A spray bottle is a convenient way to apply the solution. If batteries are stored in the toys, the cleaning should be done without the batteries inserted to prevent corrosion.

Replaces weak or dead batteries. Keep in mind that batteries stored outside the toy will have a prolonged life.

Checks the identification number or bar code on the toy and rewrites the information if necessary with an indelible marker.

Checks that the number matches the bar code on the laminated tag.

Checks the laminated tag to ensure it is still firmly attached to the bag.

Examines the mesh bag and replaces it if necessary.

Reshelves the toy on the wall grid system.

Removes the check-out card from the notebook, if necessary.

If there are any problems when a toy is returned, an explanatory note or form may be used to describe the problem, for example, a missing tag, ripped bag, or lost pieces, and placed in the bag before it is brought to the designated staff for repairs. Most toy manufacturers have replacement parts free of charge or for a nominal fee. An alternative idea is to purchase extra copies of toys to keep for replacement parts.

Marketing and Promotion

"If you build it, they will come!" is not necessarily true in the case of a new circulating toy collection. Patrons, community agencies, professionals working with families, and the entire library staff must be made aware of this special collection. Remember, circulating toy collections are not typical. The public rarely thinks of accessing toys through the library. In order to promote the toy lending collection, librarians may adopt specific strategies including publicity, collaboration, and programming.

Publicity

Publicity needs to begin even before the toys are ready to circulate and needs to continue after the collection is developed. Since the toy collection can be beneficial to a wide variety of people (grandparents and others appreciate being able to borrow toys when young children come to visit), publicity needs to target the entire community. Types of publicity include:

In-house flyers and brochures
Posters
Press releases in local newspapers
Personal promotion by library staff
Displaying toys during library programs
Displaying toys in glass display cases

Distribution and Programming through Collaboration

Each community has early intervention agencies that work directly with families and children with special needs. Identifying and working cooperatively with these agencies maximizes the benefits of the toy collection. Flyers publicizing the toy collection can be distributed to early intervention agencies so staff members can utilize the collection and inform their families of its availability. The librarian can visit these agencies to demonstrate some of the toys to the teachers and explain policies and procedures governing the collection. Special arrangements can be made to circulate these toys to staff members, or a copy of the toy notebook can be kept at the agency for the teachers to refer to. Parent organizations affiliated with the early intervention agencies can be invited to the library for an orientation program.

Special programs can be developed in collaboration with these agencies to promote awareness and demonstrate appropriate ways of using the toys in the collection. Occupational and physical therapists, special education teachers, and other professionals are invaluable facilitators for such programs. Evening programs for parents might be offered to give parents an opportunity to learn how to use the toys or even how to make commercially produced toys adaptable to their child's needs. Special parent-child programs held in the library also give families an opportunity to become familiar with the toys from the collection. The inclusion of early intervention and preschool education providers in such programs provides a personal resource to answer specific questions parents may have on how best to utilize certain toys with their child.

Conclusion

Toys foster emergent literacy in young children. As family-supportive institutions, libraries can give children and their families play opportunities that are social, recreational, and educational. Developing a circulating toy collection provides parents and caregivers with tools that help develop literacy with young children and is invaluable for children with special needs. "Building a toy lending collection for young children with a wide range of developmental capacities is itself a developmental process. Growth is a matter of being flexible and listening to the needs of the community" (Breen and Fazio, 2001: 21). The library with a toy lending library tells *all* families that libraries welcome *all* children.

References

"Anglo-American Cataloguing Rules." Chicago: American Library Association, 1988.

Breen, Sharon, and Nancy Fazio. "The Tools of Play: Toy Lending in a Public Library." *Zero to Three* 21, no. 3 (January): 21, 2001.

Citrin, Adrienne, et al. *Let's Play: A Guide to Toys for Children with Special Needs.* New York: Toy Industry Foundation, 2006.

Feinberg, Sandra, et al. *Including Families and Children with Special Needs.* New York: Neal-Schuman, 1999.

National Lekotek Center. "Why Is Play Important?" www.lekotek.org, 2000.

United Parents Syndicate on Disabilities and Toys "R" Us. *Toy Guide for Differently Abled Kids: 12th Edition.* Alexandria, VA, 2005.

Resources for Building a Toy Collection

Ordering Sources

Discovery Toys
(800) 341-TOYS

Environments Inc.
P.O. Box 1348
Beaufort, SC 29901
(843) 846-8155

Lakeshore Learning Materials
2695 E. Dominguez St.
Carson, CA 90895
(800) 428-4414

Sensational Beginnings
987 Stewart Rd.
Monroe, MI 48162
(800) 444-2147

Toys "R" Us
One Geoffrey Way
Wayne, NJ 07470
(800) TOYSRUS

Ordering Sources for Adaptive Toys and Switches

Abilitations
P.O. Box 922668
Norcross, GA 30010
(800) 850-8602
www.abilitations.com

Able Net, Inc.
2808 Fairview Ave. North
Roseville, MN 55113-1308
(800) 322-0956

Achievement Products for Children
P.O. Box 9033
Canton, OH 44711
www.specialkidszone.com
(800) 373-4699

A.D.D. Warehouse
300 Northwest 70th Ave., Suite 102
Plantation, FL 33317
(800) 233-9273
www.addwarehouse.com

Crestwood Communication Aids, Inc.
P.O. Box 090107
Milwaukee, WI 53209
(414) 352-5678
www.communicationaids.com

Dragonfly Toy Company, Inc.
291 Yale Ave.
Winnipeg, MB, Canada R3M 0L4
(800) 308-2208
www.dragonflytoys.com

Enabling Devices
385 Warburton Ave.
Hastings-On-Hudson, NY 10706
(914) 478-0960
(800) 832-8697

Flaghouse
601 Flaghouse Dr.
Hasbrouck Heights, NJ 07604-3116
(800) 793-7900

Integrations
P.O. Box 922668
Norcross, GA 30010-2668
(800) 622-0638

Jesana Ltd.
P.O. Box 17
Irvington, NY 10533
(800) 443-4728

Southpaw Enterprises
P.O. Box 1047
Dayton, OH 45401
(800) 228-1698
www.southpawenterprises.com

S & S Worldwide
P.O. Box 513
75 Mill St.
Colchester, CT 06415
(860) 537-3451
www.ssww.com

Switch Kids
8507 Rupp Farm Dr.
West Chester, OH 45069-4526
(513) 860-5475

TFH (USA) Ltd.
4537 Gibsonia Rd.
Gibsonia, PA 15044
(800) 467-6222
www.tfhuse.com

TherAdapt Products, Inc.
11431 N. Port Washington Rd., Suite 103-B
Mequon, WI 53092
(800) 261-4919
www.theradapt.com

Toys for Special Children-Enabling Devices
385 Warburton Ave.

Hastings-On-Hudson, NY 10706
(800) 832-8697
www.enablingdevices.com

Informational Sources for Adaptive Toys and Switches

Access-Able. "Quality of Life: Daily Living—Toys." www.access-able.com, 2005.

Jackson, Sara. "A Puff of Breath, a Tilt of the Head and . . . Presto! . . . It's a Toy Library for Children with Disabilities." *Mississippi Libraries* 56, no. 3 (Fall): 76–78, 1992.

Jackson, Sara. "Toys, Not Books: A Special Youth Services Program." *Youth Services in Libraries* 9 (Winter): 199–201, 1996.

Klauber, Julie. "Toy Story: How to Select and Buy Adaptive Toys." *School Library Journal* 42, no. 7 (July): 22–25, 1996.

National Lekotek Center. Lekotek Play Guide for Children with Special Needs. Play Is a Child's World: A Lekotek Resource Guide on Play for Children with Disabilities for Families, Friends and Professionals. Come Play with Me! A Developmental Play Curriculum Guide for Teen Parents of Children from Birth to Three Years Old. Lekotek Plan Book of Adaptive Toys: Volume I, Volume II, Volume III. Evanston, IL.

Oppenheim Toy Portfolio. An independent guide to children's media featuring the best in toys, books, videos, and software. Each quarterly issue features a section entitled "Using Ordinary Toys for Kids with Special Needs." New York.

Schwartz, Sue, and Joan Heller Miller. *The New Language of Toys: Teaching Communications Skills to Children with Special Needs.* Bethesda, MD: Woodbine Press, 1996.

Sinker, Mary. *Toys for Growing: A Guide to Toys That Develop Skills.* Chicago: Year Book Medical Publishers, 1996.

Talcott, Anne E. "The Early Intervention Resources/Toy Lending Library: Helping At Risk Toddlers and Their Parents." *Ohio Libraries* 4 (July–August): 8–10, 1991.

Walling, Linda Lucas, and Marilyn H. Karrenbrock. *Disabilities, Children, and Libraries: Mainstreaming Services in Public Libraries and School Library Media Centers.* Englewood, CO: Libraries Unlimited, 1993.

Zigler, Edward F., Dorothy G. Singer, and Sandra J. Bishop-Josef, eds. *Children's Play: The Roots of Reading.* Washington, DC: Zero to Three Press, 2004.

11

Parents' Collection

In tracking the national movement toward integrating services for children and families, Sharon Lynn Kagan looked at the growth of family support programs, which "are committed to serving the entire family, to preventing social problems and intervening before problems escalate, and to broad-based community engagement" (Kagan, 1993: 61). Establishing a parents' collection is a first and foremost objective for those libraries that aim to provide family-centered services. As public libraries begin to focus more on the family unit, the argument can strongly be stated for providing a collection that supports parents and caregivers as a child's primary nurturers and first teachers. To establish the collection, librarians need to identify the specific clientele that will be targeted, the collection's location within the library, the scope and size of the collection, and the types of materials and selection criteria for materials that will be included. For each of these issues, guiding questions and checklists may help with the initial implementation in the establishment of a parents' collection.

Clientele

Will the collection be designed for parents only, or will it include materials for professionals working with families? See Chapter 12 for guidelines for developing collections for family support professionals.

Should the collection target only parents of young children or expand to parents of a school-age child or teenager?

How will the collection reflect the cultural community it serves with sensitivity to the diversity within our society?

Do the staff and clientele support the concept that children's librarians are capable and natural information providers to parents and professionals?

Location and Management

Where will the collection be housed? Will it be housed in the children's or adult department?

Will the collection be placed in or in close proximity to an area designed for young children in an effort to support the parent-child dyad?

Which department will oversee the collection regarding selection of materials, weeding, marketing, staff training, evaluation, and general collection procedures?

Is the library prepared to answer the question as to why such a collection is housed in the children's department?

Will certain materials be duplicated in the adult collection within the library?

Will libraries with branches have individual collections, or will there be only a central collection at the main library building?

Scope of Information

Will professionals be utilizing the collection?

Will there be a means by which professionals can provide input into the selection of materials?

Will consideration be given to the school district curriculum and teacher support?

Will materials include popular titles only?

Will the collection include various literacy levels, for example, basic parenting and child rearing, low literacy materials, research, and academic studies?

Will children's books dealing with difficult issues, determined most effective when read to the child with a parent or adult, be placed in this collection or within the regular picture book or easy reader collection?

Size

What is the size of the room that will house the collection?
What is the room's maximum capacity?

Will other collections or areas within the room need to be moved or reorganized in order to accommodate space for this collection?

What relationships exist with other library departments, neighboring libraries, or outside agencies with regard to resource sharing?

Will Internet resources be available? (Accessibility to downloadable documents may decrease costs and space requirements.)

What financial accommodations have been allocated for this collection?

Will a library with multiple branches have a centralized collection at one building location? (This may require more, rather than less, space in the main building in order to accommodate all of the branches' needs.)

Materials Selection

Determining the types of materials to include in the collection depends on a variety of factors. These factors may include budget limitations, space restrictions, internal policies and procedures (which may prohibit certain purchases), and patron requests. In order to be most effective, the collection should reflect not only the topics most requested by the community but also the formats most appropriate to satisfy individual needs and skills.

Variety of Formats

Circulating Books
Parents Collection Reference
Periodicals
Pamphlets and Flyers
Videos/DVDs
Audiocassettes/CDs
Manuals
Curriculums
Kits
Vertical File
Internet Resources/Access to Parenting/Professional Links and Databases
Computer Software

Range of Topics

What range of topics will be represented within the collection? Will limits be placed on the topics covered and, if so, what might they be? Topics to consider include:

General Parenting
Child Development and Infant Care
Parenting Children with Special Needs
Child Care

Health and Disability Issues
Education and School
Divorce, Single-Parent Families, and Stepfamilies
Nutrition and Fitness
Sibling, Family Relationships, and Grandparenting
Adoption and Foster Care
Children's Toys, Equipment, Parties, and Furniture
Literacy and Reading
Language, Speech, and Hearing
Play and Activities for Children
Pregnancy, Prenatal Care, and Childbirth
Children's Fears and Anxieties
Toilet Learning
Sleep Issues
Sexual Education
Children and the Media
Music and Movement
Family Travel and Recreation
Death and Bereavement
Safety and Health

Selection Criteria

What are the author's reputation, credentials, and affiliations?

What is the publisher's and/or distributor's reputation?

Has the item been reviewed or recommended?

Is the item current?

What is the cost of the item?

Has the community demonstrated a demand for the item or has the library anticipated a demand?

Will the item fill a gap and therefore strengthen a subject area within the collection?

Will materials be purchased as a direct result of feedback from surveys, focus groups, an advisory council, or internal collection assessment?

Special Materials

Kits

While there are numerous formats by which to provide information, kits are a unique medium worth exploring in further detail. There are various ways of packaging, presenting, and guiding people to family support information in order to increase access, awareness, and utilization of materials. Kits provide an opportunity to gather an assortment of materials with a specific focus and package them together so they are easy to distribute. Kits can be developed to welcome new babies, provide pregnant mothers with prenatal and early infant care information, provide information to children on what to expect at their visit to the hospital, introduce a young child to the concept of having a new sibling, or assist grandparents living with grandchildren. The possibilities are endless.

Libraries can design kits that circulate in packaged plastic containers or in cloth or mesh bags. Kits can also be intended as giveaways, to be kept by the patron, packaged in large paper envelopes, and printed with colorful logos and illustrations for eye-catching appeal. Kits of all types can be developed to meet the needs of parents of children with disabilities.

Hospital Kit: Hospital kits target children of all ages and are designed to entertain the child while in the hospital. This type of kit can be packaged in a backpack, making it easy to bring along for an overnight hospital stay. This kit works best if developed for two separate audiences or by the age of the child (for example, primary and intermediate) and may include the following materials:

Books with a "going to the hospital" theme for children to read themselves or for parents to read aloud to very young children.

Pamphlets for parents and children to prepare for and cope with the hospital experience available from the Association for the Care of Children's Health (ACCH), 7910 Woodmont Ave., Suite 300, Bethesda, MD 20814; (800) 808-2224, and the American Academy of Pediatrics, P.O. Box 747, Elk Grove Village, IL 60009-0747; (847) 434-4000.

A bibliography of materials available from the library on preparing children for the hospital experience.

Videos, DVDs, and CD-ROMs for children on coping with illness and the hospital experience available from Starlight Starbright Children's Foundation, 1850 Sawtelle Blvd., Suite 450, Los Angeles, CA 90025; (310) 479-1212.

Activities to do in the hospital, such as puzzles, games, felt boards, activity sheets, and coloring books. To keep with the hospital theme, try incorporating a children's medical kit, available from Fisher Price, P.O. Box 620978, Middleton, WI 53562-0978; (800) 747-8697.

Infant Kits: Infant kits may take the form of free information packages for expectant and new parents. Two types of Infant Kits—one geared toward prenatal care and one focusing on newborn care—may be created. These kits work best if they are giveaways that parents can keep and use at their leisure. If you want to provide more than just an information packet, infant kits can include a gift such as a board book to promote early literacy. The following are examples of materials worth considering:

Brochures on child development, behavior, safety, and health issues relating to infants

Local agencies that provide classes, workshops, or support groups for new or expectant parents and their infants

Information about the library and services that are offered to parents and infants, including the library's policy on library card eligibility

Brain Boxes

Created by the New Directions Institute for Infant and Brain Development in Phoenix, Arizona (www.newdirectionsinstitute.org), Brain Boxes are designed for parents and caregivers to use with children ages birth through five and a half years. Each of the twelve Brain Boxes includes activities that encourage healthy brain development at a designated age level. Boxes include a card for each activity, which provides specific directions, material lists, extension activities, and research-based information on how the activities relate to brain development. All activities incorporate the "ABC's of Brain Development," otherwise known as Attention, Bonding, and Communication. The activities encourage positive interaction between the caregiver and child, while emphasizing quality time.

Bibliographies

Current and readily available lists of materials are a quick source of information for parents who, more often than not, feel overwhelmed by the quantity of information surrounding them. Bibliographies offer professionally selected books, periodicals, videos or DVDs, Web sites, and pamphlets that parents may be looking for and are more likely to consider because of the preselection process. Topics can range from one as broad as Child Development to as specific as Dealing with the Loss of a Parent or a New Sibling.

Parents need information they can trust, especially when dealing with difficult subject matter. The simple act of offering a bibliography provides an opportunity for an interaction between the librarian and parent. Such an interaction carries the potential to share a variety of other programs and services the library may have to offer or perhaps a referral to a local agency that might be helpful in meeting the needs of that parent and family.

Recommended Materials for a Parents' Collection

Librarians who have decided to build a parents' collection may want to use the following lists to begin their collection. The materials included are targeted to parents and caregivers of very young children and include books, audiovisual materials, Web sites, and catalogs that can help with locating additional resources.

Books

Acredolo, Linda P. *Baby Minds: Brain-Building Games Your Baby Will Love.* New York: Bantam Books, 2000.

Agin, Marilyn C., Lisa F. Geng, and Malcolm J. Nicholl. *The Late Talker: What to Do If Your Child Isn't Talking Yet.* New York: St. Martin's Press, 2003.

Ames, Louise Bates, and Frances Ilg. *Your One Year Old: The Fun-Loving, Fussy 12 to 24 Month Old.* New York: Doubleday, 1995.

Ames, Louise Bates, and Frances Ilg. *Your Three Year Old: Friend or Enemy*. New York: Delacorte Press, 1993.

Ames, Louise Bates, and Frances Ilg. *Your Two Year Old: Terrible or Tender*. New York: Delacorte Press, 1993.

Apel, Kenn, and Julie Masterson. *Beyond Baby Talk: From Sounds to Sentences: A Parent's Complete Guide to Language Development*. Roseville, CA: Prima Publishers, 2001.

Bardige, Betty Lynn Segal. *At a Loss for Words: How America Is Failing Our Children and What We Can Do About It*. Philadelphia: Temple University Press, 2005.

Bardige, Betty Lynn Segal. *Building Literacy with Love*. Washington, DC: Zero to Three Press, 2005.

Bennett, Howard J. *Waking Up Dry: A Guide to Help Children Overcome Bedwetting*. Elk Grove Village, IL: American Academy of Pediatrics, 2005.

Berk, Laura. *Child Development*, 7th Edition. Boston: Allyn and Bacon, 2005.

Berman, Christine, and Jacki Fromer. *Meals without Squeals: Childcare Feeding Guide and Cookbook*. Palo Alto, CA: Bull Publishers, 1997.

Bilingual Language Development and Disorders in Spanish-English Speakers. Baltimore, MD: Brookes Publishing, 2004.

Boehm, Helen F. *The Official Guide to the Right Toys*. Bloomington: Authorhouse, 2005.

Brazelton, T. Berry. *Feeding Your Child: The Brazelton Way*. Cambridge, MA: Da Capo Press, 2004.

Brazelton, T. Berry. *Infants and Mothers: Differences in Development*. Revised Edition. New York: Delacorte Press, 1989.

Brazelton, T. Berry. *Sleep: The Brazelton Way*. Reading, MA: Perseus, 2003.

Brazelton, T. Berry. *The Irreducible Needs of Children: What Every Child Must Have to Grow, Learn, and Flourish*. Cambridge, MA: Perseus, 2000.

Brazelton, T. Berry. *To Listen to a Child: Understanding the Normal Problems of Growing Up*. Cambridge, MA: Perseus, 1992.

Brazelton, T. Berry. *Toddlers and Parents: A Declaration of Independence*. Revised Edition. New York: Delta/Seymour Lawrence, 1989.

Brazelton, T. Berry. *Toilet Training: The Brazelton Way*. Cambridge, MA: Da Capo Press, 2004.

Brazelton, T. Berry. *Touchpoints: Both Volumes of the Nation's Most Trusted Guide to the First Six Years of Life*. Cambridge, MA: Perseus, 2002.

Brazelton, T. Berry. *Understanding Sibling Rivalry: The Brazelton Way*. New York: Da Capo Lifelong Books, 2005.

Brill, Marlene Targ. *Raising Smart Kids for Dummies*. New York: J. Wiley, 2003.

Caplan, Frank, and Theresa Caplan. *The First Twelve Months of Life: Your Baby's Growth Month by Month*. New York: Bantam Books, 1995.

Chamberlain, Mark D. *Kids Are from Jupiter: A Guide for Puzzled Parents*. Salt Lake City, UT: Shadow Mountain, 2000.

Cheatum, Billye Ann. *Physical Activities for Improving Children's Learning and Behavior: A Guide to Sensory Motor Development*. Champaign, IL: Human Kinetics, 2000.

Cherry, Clare. *Creative Movement for the Developing Child: An Early Childhood Handbook for Non-Musicians*. Belmont, CA: Fearon Teacher Aids, 2001.

Cohen, Lawrence J. *Playful Parenting: A Bold New Way to Nurture Close Connections, Solve Behavior Problems, and Encourage Children's Confidence*. New York: Ballantine Books, 2002.

The Complete Book of Rhymes, Songs, Poems, Fingerplays, and Chants. Compiled by Jackie Silberg and Pam Schiller. Beltsville, MD: Gryphon House, 2002.

Crain, William C. *Reclaiming Childhood: Letting Children Be Children in Our Achievement-Oriented Society.* New York: Times Books, 2003.

The Early Childhood Consortium. *Play in Practice: Case Studies in Young Children's Play.* St. Paul, MN: Redleaf Press, 2002.

Edgelow, Dorothy. *Apple a Day: Nutritional Reference and Cook Book for Children's Health and Well Being.* Toronto, Ontario: Warwick Publishing, 2006.

Eisenberg, Arlene. *What to Expect the First Year.* New York: Workman Publishing, 1996.

Ellison, Sheila. *365 Games Babies Play: Playing, Growing and Exploring with Babies from Birth to 15 Months.* Naperville, IL: Sourcebooks, 2003.

Ellison, Sheila, and Susan Ferdinandi. *365 Smart Babies Play.* Naperville, IL: Sourcebooks, 2005.

Ellison, Sheila, and Judith Anne Gray. *365 Days of Creative Play.* Naperville, IL: Sourcebooks, 2005.

Endres, Jeannette, and Robert E. Rockwell. *Food, Nutrition, and the Young Child.* New York: Prentice Hall, 2003.

Feeding Your Child. Minneapolis, MN: MELD, 2002.

Fish, Donna. *Take the Fight Out of Food: How to Prevent and Solve Your Child's Eating Problems.* New York: Atria, 2005.

Foxman, Paul. *The Worried Child: Recognizing Anxiety in Children and Helping Them Heal.* Alameda, CA: Hunter House Publishers, 2004.

Fraiberg, Selma H. *The Magic Years: Understanding and Handling the Problems of Early Childhood.* New York: Simon and Schuster, 1996.

Fraser, Diane L. *Danceplay: Creative Movement for Very Young Children.* Lincoln, NE: Iuniverse Press, 2000.

Frost, Joe L. *The Developmental Benefits of Playgrounds.* Olney, MD: Association for Childhood Education International, 2004.

Frost, Joe L., Sue C. Wortham, et al. *Play and Child Development.* Upper Saddle River, NJ: Prentice Hall, 2005.

Gavin, Mary L., Steven A. Dowshen, and Neil Isenberg. *Fit Kids: A Practical Guide to Raising Active and Healthy Children—From Birth to Teens.* New York: DK Publishing, 2004.

Gessell, Arnold. *Infant and Child in the Culture of Today: The Guidance of Development in Home and Nursery School.* Northvale, NJ: J. Aronson, 1995.

Goldstein, Brian A., ed. *Bilingual Language Development and Disorders in Spanish-English Speakers.* Baltimore, MD: Brookes Publishing, 2004.

Golinkoff, Roberta M. *How Babies Talk: The Magic and Mystery of Language in the First Three Years of Life.* New York: Dutton, 1999.

Gordon, Dr. Thomas. *Parent Effectiveness Training: The Proven Program for Raising Responsible Children.* New York: Three Rivers Press, 2000.

Greenspan, Stanley. *First Feelings.* New York: Penguin USA, 1994.

Greenspan, Stanley. *Building Healthy Minds: The Six Experiences that Create Intelligence and Emotional Growth in Babies and Young Children.* Perseus Publishing, 2000.

Hamaguchi, Patricia McAleer. *Childhood Speech, Language and Listening Problems.* New York: J. Wiley, 2001.

Herr, Judith. *Making Sounds, Making Music, and Many Other Activities for Infants: 7 to 12 Months.* Clifton Park, NY: Delmar Learning, 2003.

Herr, Judith. *Rattle Time, Face to Face, and Many Other Activities for Infants: Birth to 6 Months*. Clifton Park, NY: Thomson/Delmar Learning, 2003.

Herr, Judith. *Rhyming Books, Marble Painting, and Many Other Activities for Toddlers: 25 to 36 Months*. Clifton Park, NY: Thomson/Delmar Learning, 2003.

Herr, Judith. *Sorting Shapes, Show Me, and Many Other Activities for Toddlers: 13 to 24 Months*. Clifton Park, NY: Delmar Learning, 2003.

Ilg, Frances, et al. *Child Behavior*. Revised Edition. New York: Harper Perennial, 1992.

Julien, Ronni Litz. *What Should I Feed My Kids? How to Keep Your Children Healthy by Teaching Them to Eat Right*. Franklin Lakes, NJ: New Page Books, 2006.

Kohn, Alfie. *Unconditional Parenting: Moving from Rewards and Punishments to Love and Reason*. New York: Atria, 2005.

Kuffner, Trish. *The Toddler's Busy Book: 365 Creative Games and Activities to Keep Your 1½ to 3-Year Old Busy*. Minnetonka, MN: Meadowbrook; Poole: Chris Lloyd, 2000.

Lang, Jennifer Harvey. *Jennifer Lang Cooks for Kids: 153 Recipes and Ideas for Good Food That Kids Love to Eat*. New York: Crown, 1993.

Lansky, Vicki. *Feed Me! I'm Yours*. Revised Edition. Deephaven, MN: Meadowbrook Press, 2003.

Larimore, Walt, Sherri Flynt, and Steve Halliday. *Super-sized Kids: How to Rescue Your Child from the Obesity Threat*. New York: Center Street, 2005.

Leach, Penelope. *The First Six Months: Getting Together with Your Baby*. New York: Knopf, 1987.

Leach, Penelope. *Terrific Toddlers: (Whoever Said That Two-Year-Olds Were Terrible?)*. Chicago: Prevent Child Abuse America, 2000.

Leach, Penelope. *Your Baby and Child: From Birth to Age Five*. New York: Knopf, 1997.

LeComer, Laurie. *A Parent's Guide to Developmental Delays: Recognizing and Coping with Missed Milestones in Speech, Movement, Learning, and Other Areas*. New York: Perigee, 2006.

Lerner, Claire. *Bringing Up Baby: Three Steps to Making Good Decisions in Your Child's First Years*. Washington, DC: Zero to Three Press, 2005.

Leshan, Eda. *When Your Child Drives You Crazy*. New York: St. Martin's, 1993.

Levine, Melvin. *A Mind at a Time*. New York: Simon and Schuster, 2002.

Levy, Ray. *Try and Make Me! Simple Strategies That Turn Off the Tantrums and Create Cooperation*. New York: St. Martin's, 2001.

Lipson, Eden Ross. *The New York Times Parent's Guide to the Best Books for Children*. New York: Three Rivers Press, 2000.

Losquadro-Liddle, Tara. *Why Motor Skills Matter: Improve Your Child's Physical Development to Enhance Learning and Self-Esteem*. Chicago: Contemporary Books, 2004.

Lunden, Joan, and Myron Winick, M.D. *Growing Up Healthy: A Complete Guide to Childhood Nutrition, Birth Through Adolescence*. New York: Atria, 2005.

McCartney, Kathleen, and Deborah Phillips, eds. *Blackwell Handbook of Early Childhood Development*. Malden, MA: Blackwell Publishing Professional, 2006.

McGuinness, Diane. *Growing a Reader from Birth: Your Child's Path from Language to Literacy*. New York: W. W. Norton, 2004.

MacKenzie, Robert J. *Setting Limits with Your Strong-Willed Child: Eliminating Conflict by Establishing Clear, Firm, and Respectful Boundaries*. Roseville, CA: Prima, 2001.

Marotz, Lynn. *Health, Safety, and Nutrition for the Young Child*. Clifton Park, NY: Thomson Delmar Learning, 2005.

Mayes, Linda C., and Donald J. Cohen. *The Yale Child Study Center Guide to Understanding Your Child: Healthy Development from Birth to Adolescence.* Boston: Little, Brown, 2002.

Miller, Karen. *Things to Do with Toddlers and Twos.* Marshfield, MA: Teleshare, 2000.

Mitchell, Grace L. *A Very Practical Guide to Discipline with Young Children.* Beltsville, MD: Gryphon House, 1998.

Moxley, Cathy. *The Busy Mom's Ultimate Fitness Guide.* Germantown, MD: Fitness InSight, 2006.

Newman, Susan. *Parenting an Only Child: The Joys and Challenges of Raising Your One and Only.* New York: Random House, 2001.

Nordahl, Karen, Carl Petersen, et al. *Fit to Deliver: An Innovative Prenatal and Postpartum Fitness Program: Safe and Fun Exercises Tailored By Professionals to Benefit Both You and Your Baby.* Vancouver, BC: Hartley and Marks Publishers, 2005.

Oppenheim, Joanne. *Read It! Play It!* New York: Oppenheim Toy Portfolio, 2006.

Owens, Judith. *Take Charge of Your Child's Sleep: The All-In-One Resource for Solving Sleep Problems in Kids and Teens.* New York: Marlowe and Company, 2005.

Paley, Vivian Gussin. *A Child's Work: The Importance of Fantasy Play.* Chicago: University of Chicago Press, 2005.

Piaget, Jean. *Language and Thought of the Child.* New York: Routledge, 2001.

Pica, Rae. *Experience in Movement: Birth to Age Eight.* 3rd Edition. Clifton Park, NY: Thomson Delmar Learning, 2003.

Pica, Rae. *Your Active Child: How to Boost Physical, Emotional, and Cognitive Development through Age-Appropriate Activity.* New York: McGraw-Hill, 2003.

Proactive Parenting: Guiding Your Child from Two to Six. Tufts University's Eliot-Pearson Department of Child Development. New York: Berkley Books, 2004.

Puckett, Margaret B., and Janet K. Black. *The Young Child: Development from Prebirth through Age Eight.* Upper Saddle River, NJ: Pearson/Merrill Prentice Hall, 2005.

Reitzes, Fretta. *Wonder Play: Interactive and Developmental Games, Crafts, and Creative Activities for Infants, Toddlers, & Preschoolers: From the 92nd St. Y Parenting Center.* Philadelphia: Running Press, 1995.

Rogers, Fred. *Mister Rogers' Play Time: Encourage Your Child to Create, Explore, and Pretend with Dozens of Easy-To-Do Activities.* Philadelphia: Running Press, 2001.

Rooyackers, Paul. *101 More Dance Games for Children: New Fun and Creativity with Movement.* Alameda, CA: Hunter House Publishers, 2003.

Runkel, Hal Edward. *ScreamFree Parenting: Raising Your Kids by Keeping Your Cool.* Duluth, GA: Oakmont Publishing, 2005.

Sanders-Butler, Yvonne, and Barbara Alpert. *Healthy Kids, Smart Kids: The Principal-Created, Parent-Tested, Kid-Approved Nutrition Plan for Sound Bodies and Strong Minds.* New York: Perigee Trade, 2005.

Saphir, Richard L., M.D., Lucy Burney, and Noelle Sheehan. *Boost Your Child's Immune System: A Program and Recipes for Raising Strong, Healthy Kids.* New York: Newmarket Press, 2005.

Satter, Ellyn. *Child of Mine: Feeding with Love and Good Sense.* Palo Alto, CA: Bull Publishers, 2000.

Satter, Ellyn. *Your Child's Weight: Helping without Harming.* Madison, WI: Kelcy Press, 2005.

Sax, Leonard. *Why Gender Matters: What Parents and Teachers Need to Know About the Emerging Science of Sex Differences.* New York: Doubleday, 2005.

Schaefer, Charles E. *Ages and Stages: A Parent's Guide to Normal Childhood Development*. New York: J. Wiley, 2000.

Schaefer, Charles E., and Theresa Foy Digeronimo. *Toilet Training without Tears*. New York: Signet, 1997.

Sclafani, Joseph D. *The Educated Parent: Recent Trends in Raising Children*. Westport, CT: Praeger Publishers, 2004.

Sears, William, M.D. *Dr. Sears' L.E.A.N. Kids: A Total Health Program for Children Ages 6–11*. New York: New American Library, 2003.

Sears, William, M.D. *Feeding the Picky Eater: America's Foremost Baby and Childcare Experts Answer the Most Frequently Asked Questions*. Boston: Little, Brown and Company, 2001.

Seefeldt, Carol. *Playing to Learn: Activities and Experiences That Build Learning Connections*. Beltsville, MD: Gryphon House, 2001.

Segal, Marilyn M. *Your Child at Play—Five to Eight Years: Building Friendships, Expanding Interests and Resolving Conflicts*. New York: Newmarket Press, 2000.

Segal, Marilyn, and Wendy Masi. *Your Child at Play—One to Two Years: Exploring, Daily Living, Learning and Making Friends*. New York: Newmarket Press, 1998.

Segal, Marilyn, and Wendy Masi. *Your Child at Play—Two to Three Years: Growing Up, Language, and the Imagination*. New York: Newmarket Press, 1998.

Sen, Pika, and Radika Vasudeva. *No More Baby Talk: A Parent's Guide to Speech and Language Development*. Pearson Malaysia Sdn Bhd 4, 2002.

Shelov, Steven P., et al. *Caring for Your Baby and Young Child: Birth to Age 5*. New York: Bantam Books, 2004.

Shore, Rima. *What Kids Need: Today's Best Ideas for Nurturing, Teaching, and Protecting Young Children*. Boston: Beacon Press, 2002.

Siegel, Daniel, and Mary Hartzel. *Parenting from the Inside Out*. New York: Putnam Publishing Group, 2003.

Silberg, Jackie. *Games to Play with Babies*. Mt. Rainier, MD: Gryphon House, 2001.

Silberg, Jackie. *Games to Play with Toddlers*. Mt. Rainier, MD: Gryphon House, 2002.

Silberg, Jackie. *Go Anywhere Games for Babies: The Packable, Portable Book of Infant Development and Bonding*. Beltsville, MD: Robins Lane Press, 2000.

Silberg, Jackie. *125 Brain Games for Babies*. Translation and adaptation by Leonora Saavedral. Barcelona: Oniro, 2000.

Silberg, Jackie. *125 Brain Games for Toddlers and Twos: Simple Games to Promote Early Brain Development*. Beltsville, MD: Gryphon House, 2000.

Singer, Dorothy G. *Make-Believe: Games and Activities for Imaginative Play*. Glenview: IL: Magination, 2000.

Solter, Aletha Jauch. *Helping Young Children Flourish*. Goleta, CA: Shining Star Press, 1998.

Sowell, Thomas. *The Einstein Syndrome: Bright Children Who Talk Late*. New York: Basic Books, 2001.

Stearns, Peter N. *Anxious Parents: A History of Modern Childrearing in America*. New York: New York University Press, 2003.

Stoppard, Miriam. *Complete Baby and Child Care*. New York: Dorling Kindersley, 2001.

Stoppard, Miriam. *Conception, Pregnancy and Birth*. New York: DK Publishing, 2005.

Tartamella, Lisa, and Elaine Hersher. *Generation Extra Large: Rescuing Our Children from the Epidemic of Obesity*. New York: Atria, 2006.

Trelease, Jim. *The Read-Aloud Handbook*, 5th Edition. New York: Penguin USA, 2001.

Van Pelt, Katie. *Potty Training Your Baby.* Garden City Park, NY: Signet, 2002.

Virgilio, Stephen J. *Active Start for Healthy Kids: Activities, Exercises, and Nutritional Tips.* Champaign, IL: Human Kinetics, 2006.

Ward, Sally, Dr. *Baby Talk: Strengthen Your Child's Ability to Listen, Understand, and Communicate.* New York: Ballantine Books, 2001.

White, Burton L. *The New First Three Years of Life.* New York: Fireside, 1995.

Wiertsema, Huberta. *101 Movement Games for Children: Fun and Learning with Playful Moving.* Illustrated by Cecilia Bowman. Alameda, CA: Hunter House Publishers, 2001.

Videos/DVDs

Age-Appropriate Play: The First 12 Months. Boulder, CO: Injoy Videos, 2002.

Age-Appropriate Play, Volume 2: 12 to 24 Months. Boulder, CO: Injoy Videos, 2002.

Age-Appropriate Play, Volume 3: 2 and 3 Year Olds. Boulder, CO: Injoy Videos, 2002.

Baby Babble by Talking Child. Maple Groove, MN: Talking Child LLC, 2004.

Baby Gourmet: The First Course. United States: Baby Gourmet, 2002.

Child's Play: How Having Fun Turns Kids into Adults. Lake Zurich, IL: Learning Seed, 2004.

Fisher-Price. Baby Moves. Santa Monica, CA: Artisan Home Entertainment, 2004

How Boys and Girls Differ: The First Six Years. Lake Zurich, IL: Learning Seed, 2002.

Make Baby Laugh. Evanston, IL: Make Baby Laugh! Company LLC, 2004.

Steps and Stages: A Caregiver's Guide to Child Development. Monmouth Junction, NJ: Cambridge Educational, 2002.

Journals and Magazines

Adoptive Families
39 West 37th St.
New York, NY 10018
(800) 372-3300
www.adoptivefamilies.com

American Baby
125 Park Ave.
New York, NY 10017
www.americanbaby.com

Child
125 Park Ave.
New York, NY 10017
(800) 777-0222
www.child.com

Early Childhood Today
Scholastic Inc.
555 Broadway
New York, NY 10012
(800) 724-6527
http://teacher.scholastic.com/products/ect.htm

Exceptional Children
Council for Exceptional Children
1110 North Glebe Rd., Suite 300
Arlington, VA 22201
www.cec.sped.org

Exceptional Parent
EP Global Communications
551 Main St.
Johnstown, PA 15901
www.eparent.com

Family Fun
47 Pleasant St.
Northampton, MA 01060
(800) 289-4849
http://familyfun.go.com/

Gifted Child Today
Prufrock Press
5926 Balcones Dr., Suite 220
Austin, TX 78731
(800) 998-2208
www.prufrock.com

Home Education Magazine
P.O. Box 1083
Tonasket, WA 98855-1083
(800) 236-3278
www.homeedmag.com

Infants and Young Children
Lippincott Williams and Wilkins
P.O. Box 1600
Hagerstown, MD 21740-1600
(800) 638-3030
www.iycjournal.com

Instructor
Scholastic Inc.
555 Broadway
New York, NY 10012-3999
(866) 436-2455
http://teacher.scholastic.com/products/instructor.htm

Mothering
Mothering Publishing Inc.
P.O. Box 1690
Santa Fe, NM 87504
(505) 984-8116
www.mothering.com

Parenting
Time Inc.
1271 Ave. of the Americas, Room 307
New York, NY 10020
http://parenting.com/parenting

Parents
Gruner & Jahr USA Publishing
375 Lexington Ave.
New York, NY 10017
(212) 499-2130
www.parentsmagazine.com

Scholastic Parent and Child
Scholastic Inc.
555 Broadway
New York, NY 10012
(866) 436-2464
www.scholastic.com/parentandchild/index.htm

Teaching PreK–8
Early Years Inc.
40 Richards Ave.
Norwalk, CT 06854
(800) 678-8793
www.teachingk-8.com

Twins Magazine
11211 E. Arapahoe Rd., Suite 101
Centennial, CO 80112-3851
(888) 558-9467
www.twinsmagazine.com

Understanding Our Gifted
Open Space Communications
P.O. Box 18268
Boulder, CO 80308
(800) 494-6178
www.our-gifted.com

Working Mother
Working Mother Media
135 West 50th St., 16th Floor
New York, NY 10020
www.workingmother.com

Young Children
Journal of the National Association for the Education of Young Children
1313 L St. NW, Suite 500
Washington, DC 20005
(800) 424-2460
www.journal.naeyc.org

Zero to Three
National Center for Infants, Toddlers and Families
2000 M St. NW, Suite 200
Washington, DC 20036
(800) 899-4301
www.zerotothree.org

Catalogs

Active Parenting Pubs.
1955 Vaughn Rd. NW, Suite 108
Kennesaw, GA 30144
(800) 825-0060
www.activeparenting.com

ADD Warehouse
300 Northwest 70th St., Suite 102
Plantation, FL 33317
(800) 233-9273
www.addwarehouse.com

American Academy of Pediatrics
141 Northwest Point Blvd.
Elk Grove Village, IL 60007
(847) 434-4000
www.aap.org

Boys Town Press
14100 Crawford St.
Boys Town, NE 68010
(800) 282-6657
www.girlsandboystown.org

Center for the Improvement of Child Caring (CICC)
11331 Ventura Blvd., Suite 103
Studio City, CA 91604
(800) 325-CICC
www.ciccparenting.org

Child Development Media, Inc.
5632 Van Nuys Blvd., Suite 286
Van Nuys, CA 91401
(800) 405-8942
www.childdevelopmentmedia.com

ETC Associates
4 Carbonero Way
Scotts Valley, CA 95066
(831) 438-4060
www.etr.org

Gryphon House, Inc
P.O. Box 207
Beltsville, MD 20704
(800) 638-0928
www.gryphonhouse.com

Learning Seed
330 Telser Rd.
Lake Zurich, IL 60047
(800) 634-4941
www.learningseed.com

National Association for the Education of Young Children
P.O. Box 96261
Washington, DC 20090
(202) 328-2649
www.naeyc.org

New Readers Press
Dept. FS02
P.O. Box 35888
Syracuse, NY 13235-5888
(800) 448-8878
www.newreaderspress.com

NICHCY
P.O. Box 1492
Washington, DC 20013
(800) 695-0285 (Voice/TTY)
www.nichcy.org

Nurturing Parenting Programs
3070 Rasmussen Rd., Suite 109
Park City, UT 84098
(800) 688-5822
www.nurturingparenting.com

Parenting Press
P.O. Box 75267
Seattle, WA 98125
(800) 992-6657
www.ParentingPress.com

Parents' Action
1875 Connecticut Ave. NW, Suite 650
Washington, DC 20009
(202) 238-4878
www.parentsaction.org

Paul H. Brookes Publishing
P.O. Box 10624
Baltimore, MD 21285-0624

(800) 638-3775
www.brookespublishing.com

Prevent Child Abuse America
500 N. Michigan Ave., Suite 200
Chicago, IL 60611
(312) 663-3520
www.preventchildabuse.org

Redleaf Press
10 Yorkton Ct.
St. Paul, MN 55117
(800) 423-8309
www.redleafpress.org

United Learning
1560 Sherman Ave., Suite 100
Evanston, IL 60201
(888) 892-3484
www.unitedlearning.com

Woodbine House
6510 Bells Mill Rd.
Bethesda, MD 20817
(800) 843-7323
www.woodbinehouse.com

Zero to Three
National Center for Infants, Toddlers and Families
2000 M St. NW, Suite 200
Washington, DC 20036
(800) 899-4301
www.zerotothree.org

Web Sites

American Academy of Pediatrics
www.aap.org

American Speech-Language-Hearing Association
www.asha.org/default.htm

Association for the Help of Retarded Children
www.ahrcnyc.org

Autism Society of America
www.autism-society.org/site/PageServer

Birth to Six
www.multcolib.org/birthtosix/index.html

Born Learning
www.bornlearning.org

Childbirth Organization
www.childbirth.org

Child Health Plus
www.health.state.ny.us/nysdoh/chplus/index.htm

Children Now
www.childrennow.org

Children, Youth and Families Education and Research Network
www.cyfernet.org

Children's Defense Fund
www.childrensdefense.org

Cornell University Cooperative Extension
www.cce.cornell.edu

Council for Exceptional Children
www.cec.sped.org//AM/Template.cfm?Section=Home

Dr. Toy's Guide to the Internet
www.drtoy.com

Every Child Ready to Read
www.ala.org/ala/pla/plaissues/earlylit/earlyliteracy.htm

Family Place Libraries™ Network
www.familyplacelibraries.org

Get Ready to Read!
www.getreadytoread.org

Home Schooler Legal Defense Association
www.hslda.org/Default.asp?bhcp=1

Home School World
www.home-school.com

Household Products Database
http://householdproducts.nlm.nih.gov

Insure Kids Now!
www.insurekidsnow.gov

Internet Resources for Special Children
www.irsc.org

KidsHealth.org
www.kidshealth.org/index2.html

KIDSNET
www.kidsnet.org

KidSource Online
www.kidsource.com

National Association for the Education of Young Children
www.naeyc.org

National Association of Child Care Resource and Referral Agencies
www.naccrra.org

National Center for Learning Disabilities
www.ncld.org

National Center for Learning Disabilities/Get Ready To Read!
www.getreadytoread.org

National Dissemination Center for Children with Disabilities
www.nichcy.org

National Down Syndrome Society
www.ndss.org

National Health Information Center
www.health.gov/NHIC/

National Network for Child Care
www.nncc.org/homepage.html

Parents Action for Children
www.parentsaction.org

Parents for Megan's law
www.parentsformeganslaw.com

Pathways Awareness Foundation
www.pathwaysawareness.org

Ready at Five Partnership
www.readyatfive.org/index.html

Speechville
www.speechville.com

United Cerebral Palsy
http://www.ucp.org/

U.S. Consumer Product Safety Commission
http://www.cpsc.gov/

U.S. Department of Education
www.naeyc.org

U.S. Department of Health and Human Services/Administration for Children and Families—Office of Head Start
www.acf.hhs.gov/programs/hsb/

Vaccine Education Center
www.chop.edu/consumer/jsp/microsite/microsite.jsp?id=75918

Zero to Three
www.zerotothree.org

Zero to Three's Brain Wonder
www.zerotothree.org/brainwonders/EarlyLiteracy.html

Conclusion

In order to serve parents effectively, librarians need to take a proactive stance by providing collections, programs, and other services. Establishing a parents' collection in the children's room greatly enhances the role of children's services and encourages parents to seek out parenting information from the local librarian. Having a parents' collection helps link the librarian to parent needs and changes the way parents perceive the public library in their everyday lives.

References

Jordan, Barbara. 1996. "Building a Family Support Collection." In *Serving Families and Children Through Partnerships* by Sandra Feinberg and Sari Feldman. New York: Neal-Schuman.

Kagan, Sharon Lynn. 1993. *Integrating Services for Children and Families.* New Haven, CT: Yale University Press.

PART III

Reaching Out to Special Audiences

12

Family Support Providers

Libraries and librarians committed to their role as the hub of family support in their communities have much to offer the network of providers working with children and families with whom they are creating connections. Local social service agencies, childcare providers, youth workers, public health nurses, and school personnel all have needs that present opportunities for libraries to demonstrate the many practical ways they can assist them in their work with families, including local resource and referral information; professional collections and family literacy resources; access to families; meeting space; training, education, and networking; and offsite program delivery.

Local Resource and Referral Information

The identification of community resources is a natural fit for the information role of the public librarian who is skilled at both locating and organizing information. The gathering of local information about services that address the needs of families and children is a critical service and one which family support providers may look to the local library to provide. Questions and issues that family support providers may need assistance with include:

What childcare centers are located in our community?

What Head Start or Even Start programs serve our area?

Where is the local health clinic or WIC (Women Infant and Child) site?

Where can I refer families for counseling, substance abuse treatment, food pantry, or early intervention screening?

Is there a parent support group in our area?

Where is the nearest women's domestic violence shelter?

Libraries committed to family support find ways to fulfill this need. For some it may be as basic as a Rolodex file or printed listing which can be disseminated to providers and parents alike. Creating a display of brochures of local resources in the library's children's room makes referral information easily accessible and reminds providers and families that the library can be a source of this type of information. Some libraries have gone on to take the leadership in developing resource and referral directories for their communities, and, with the increased reliance on the Internet for information, some create and maintain online databases of health and social service referral information. These can be critical supports for local family support providers and great service opportunities for libraries.

Community Resource Database of Long Island (CRD)

When the Suffolk Coalition for Parents and Children identified a computerized database of local health and human services as a major need for the Long Island, New York, region, the Middle Country Public Library responded (see Figure 12-1). Working in partnership for over fifteen years with representatives of dozens of public and private community organizations, the Community Resource Database (CRD) of Long Island (www.crdli.org) has developed into an online database with detailed information on 12,000 Long Island agencies and programs. Although initially focused on services for children, youth, and families, the database has evolved into a comprehensive information source, relied upon by family support professionals serving an area of more than 2.6 million people as their primary source of health and human service referral information. Now all libraries, community agencies, government offices, schools, faith organizations, and civic groups in the region have access to this information and referral resource to support their work with families.

Middle Country Public Library has managed the CRD since its inception, expanding and maintaining its extensive information and fundraising for support from local county governments, the United Way, private foundations, and corporations. Recent (and probably the most critical) steps in the CRD evolution were the transformation of the look of its front page, the addition of a new quick-search feature, and the opening up of the database on the Web (formerly by subscription only) as a result of the integration of sponsorship opportunities on the site.

Contact Information: Barbara Jordan, Middle Country Public Library, Centereach, NY. Phone: (631) 585-9393 ext. 224. Email: jordanbarbara@mcpl.lib.ny.us.

12-1:   Community Resource Database Flyer

At the Detroit Public Library (TIP Database), Berkeley Public Library (Berkeley Information Network), Queens Borough Public Library (Queens Community Resources Database), and libraries across the country, similar solutions to community information needs have put libraries at the forefront of library-community partnerships that bring together the information management skills of libraries and the practical end-user insights of practitioners. Family-centered libraries can look to the providers' need for information and referral as a good starting point when reaching out to the providers in their community.

Professional Collections

Most family-centered libraries will develop some sort of special collections or resources for parents and caregivers. These materials will, of course, be of interest to family support providers. They can refer families to the collection and recommend titles and tapes that address specific family issues, and they may find the resources personally useful to help them stay abreast of the latest reading for parents. It is very important when developing a family support collection to consider either incorporating materials or establishing a separate collection for professionals who work with children and families as a complement to the parents' collection. Family practitioners and childcare and youth workers typically have limited agency resources and no budget line for resource materials to support their professional development or their work with families. This can be a wonderful opportunity for libraries to provide collections of resources that especially address their needs.

Planning and Decision Making

Planning and decision making require some careful consideration. Answering the following questions helps to guide the scope and direction of the collection.

1. What types of professionals will the collection be aimed at?

    early childhood educators
    childcare providers
    school-based professionals: teachers, guidance, and health staff
    social service and health workers
    youth workers
    early intervention specialists
    academics or students in related fields

2. What types of materials will be included?

    books
    professional journals
    videotapes and DVDs
    workshop curricula and multimedia program packages
    games, toys, adaptive toys, and equipment
    software
    posters
    themed kits
    school curriculum and teaching materials

3. What topics will be covered in the professional collection?

    early childhood education and curricula
    childcare management, health, and safety

working with culturally diverse audiences
working with diverse family structures
working with pregnant and parenting teens
child abuse, neglect, and family dysfunction
parent education programs, curricula, and group work activities
art, music, and recreational activities for children
parent-teacher communication
classroom management and discipline techniques
developmentally appropriate environments and activities
family-centered care and practice
conflict resolution and anger management techniques

Careful reflection on the intended audience, the scope of the collection, and types of materials to be included is necessary before launching a professional collection and will help to guide its development. A collection aimed at teachers or childcare providers and early childhood educators will be quite different from a broad-based collection aimed at the full scope of family support professionals. Once you have determined the target audience for the special collection you are developing for family support professionals, as well as the location and scope of the collection, there are some useful and recommended catalogs to know about. Often the best way to learn about new resources is to regularly review catalogs of subject-specific sources that publish for family-serving professionals. Some of the best sources are included at the end of this chapter.

The Suffolk Family Education Clearinghouse

An example of a comprehensive professional collection targeted to family support professionals is the Suffolk Family Education Clearinghouse: A One-Stop Information Center for Professionals Serving Children and Families. The clearinghouse is a countywide resource center that has been housed and administered by the Children's Services Department of the Middle Country Public Library for nearly 20 years.

Audience: Professionals working directly with children, youth, and families in school and community settings: health professionals, social workers, teachers, guidance counselors, youth workers, childcare providers, clergymen, psychologists, and substance abuse counselors.

Purpose/Goals: The clearinghouse is both a collection and a service. It is designed to support families by assisting the professionals working to assist them by providing access to the resources and tools they need in their individual and group family support activities: print and audiovisual material, including books, video and audiocassettes, professional and research periodicals, multimedia kits, curricula, posters, and therapeutic games.

12-2:   Suffolk Family Education Clearinghouse Logo

Middle Country Public Library

Description/Program Overview: The clearinghouse collection is located within the children's room, adjacent to the parents' collection. The reference and program planning assistance is provided by telephone request or by appointment only. A current public library card from any Suffolk County library is required to borrow materials. A computer with Internet access and links to Web sites of particular interest to family support providers is available for use on a drop-in basis and a VCR and monitor are available for previewing video materials prior to selection and check-out.

Partnering Organizations: The clearinghouse was developed as an outgrowth of the Suffolk Coalition for Parents and Children, in response to their requests for materials to assist them in conducting programs for parents and children in various community settings. Their feedback—that their agencies had no budgets for the kind of videos, journals, curriculums, and other materials that could help them in their work with families—gave rise to the development of the clearinghouse. Items from the clearinghouse collection are displayed at each coalition meeting, highlighting materials related to the subject area of the coalition program. Professors in the local university's School of Social Work and child study departments regularly inform students of the existence of the clearinghouse, encouraging them to utilize the resources in their school assignments and field placement activities.

Practical Tips/Program in Action: Items circulate for twenty-one days, but this time limit can be extended based on need. Specially labeled, zippered bags are utilized to facilitate interlibrary transfer of clearinghouse materials. Online and other specialized database searches are conducted at the discretion of the librarian as time permits. Clearinghouse items are designated by a clearinghouse spine label and housed separately from but adjacent to the parents' collection. Parents are permitted to borrow clearinghouse items as well as parents' collection items, and items in the parents' collection may be utilized in responding to a clearinghouse reference request.

Marketing/Outreach: A brochure advertising the Suffolk Family Education Clearinghouse was developed and is distributed at every meeting of the Suffolk Coalition for Parents and Children as well as at conferences that reach the appropriate audiences (guidance and school counselor conferences, etc.).

Staff: Designated children's librarians handle clearinghouse reference questions as part of their regular responsibilities on the reference desk. A log of questions is maintained by the department.

Contact Information: Marci Byrne at Middle Country Public Library, Centereach, NY. Phone: (631) 585-9393 ext. 230. Email: byrnemarcellina@mcpl.lib.ny.us.

Kits and Early Literacy Collections

Childcare providers and early childhood educators in a variety of settings are in a position to play a vital role in promoting and nurturing early literacy. They have proximity, close and trusted relationships, and long periods of intimate contact with families and young children. Supporting their literacy efforts is often a priority for public libraries in their ultimate goal of reaching children in care who may not visit the library on a regular basis. Creating and circulating prepackaged, themed kits targeted to childcare providers and early childhood educators is a comfortable role which capitalizes on the special expertise of children's librarians who are skilled at identifying and selecting quality, age-appropriate books and literacy materials and creating learning activities to extend their usefulness. Cleverly packaged literacy kits or storytime kits (they go by a variety of names across the country) are a popular and effective way to reach out to this important audience.

Project LINK Storytime Kits

Originally started with grant funding from a New York State Parent and Child Library Services grant, Middle Country Public Library's Project LINK storytime kits are targeted to family childcare homes (including relatives who may care for children) as well as center-based childcare providers and early childhood teachers in the community (see Figure 12-3). They are intended to bring the resources of the public library right into the childcare setting to support early literacy development in a way that makes it as easy as possible for providers to utilize the materials.

Today, there are twenty conveniently prepackaged, themed Project LINK storytime kits, including:

ABC's and 1,2,3's
Animal Friends
Bears

12-3:   Project LINK Literacy Kit Flyer

PROJECT LINK LITERACY KITS

Experience the magic of library storytime at your family childcare or preschool.

Kit Themes:

Available Now:
Animal Friends
Bears
Circus
Colors
Family and Friends
Nursery Rhymes

Coming Soon:
Concepts
Creepy Crawlers
Dinosaurs
Celebrate Me
Food
Multicultural
Night Time
Pets
Rainforest
Seasons and Weather
Special Needs
Things That Go

Project link Literacy Kits were created for use with children ages three to five in an effort to promote early literacy development. Each thematic kit contains a selection of picture books, related literacy activities and educational props such as puppets, toys, and games. Kits are available to child-care providers in family childcare homes (including relatives who care for young children) childcare centers, nursery and preschools, and to primary grade teachers.

Middle Country Public Library
www.mcpl.lib.ny.us
(631) 585-9393 ext.108 Children's Services

Centereach:
101 Eastwood Blvd.
Centereach, NY 11720

Selden:
575 Middle Country Rd.
Selden, NY 11784

Celebrate Me
Circus
Colors
Concepts
Creepy Crawlers
Dinosaurs
Family and Friends
Farm Animals
Food
Multiculturalism
Night Time
Nursery Rhymes
Pets
Rainforest
Seasons and Weather
Special Needs
Things That Go

Kits are aimed at three- to five-year-olds and each kit contains some combination of:

Picture books and "big books"
Felt board and felt board story figures
Hand puppets, puzzles, or games
Music CDs or video story books
Songs and fingerplays
Activity sheets with suggestions for developmentally appropriate ways of extending the theme into science, food, art, music, and movement activities

Materials are labeled and circulated as a single unit in large, heavy-duty canvas tote bags. The inventory of each kit is checked upon the kit's return, and extras of easily lost items such as activity sheets and fingerplays are available for restocking. Whenever possible, items are laminated for durability and items are periodically cleaned or replaced as necessary.

A new variation, Library LINK Kits, has been developed for zero- to three-year-olds, substituting board books and developmentally appropriate younger-aged toys, puzzles, and activities in each of 11 themed kits:

Baby Signs
Colors
My World
Bilingual
Nursery Rhymes
Music
Babies
My Words
My Body

Mealtime
My Toys

Contact Information: Lisa G. Kropp, Middle Country Public Library, Centereach, NY. Phone: (631) 585-9393 ext. 230. Email: kropplisa@mcpl.lib.ny.us.

Deposit Collections

Many libraries place collections offsite in a variety of community settings to target special populations and support the literacy efforts of their fellow family support agencies. Deposit collections in health clinics and WIC sites, domestic violence shelters, pediatricians' offices, Head Start and Early Start programs, childcare centers, and family daycare homes ensure that high-quality early childhood books reach as many young children in the community as possible.

The Saratoga Springs Public Library, New York, has administered their "Picture Books Go to Town" outreach program for thirteen years. Twenty community sites receive rotating collections of ten to fifteen picture books, housed in plastic crates, to be put out in their lobbies and waiting rooms. Local sites include physicians', optometrists', dentists', and veterinarians' offices; mental health, physical therapy, and speech clinics; and two Head Start classrooms. Deposit collection books are checked out to "Children's Outreach" with extended loan periods. Sites are visited every three months, at which time damaged books are removed for repair or replacement. Each book is labeled: "This book is on loan from the Saratoga Springs Public Library. If you enjoyed it please visit us at 49 Henry St. where you will find many more." Sites are not held responsible for damaged or missing books but are periodically assessed for their suitability for the deposit collections. Sites at one time included the hospital emergency room and pediatric floor, local WIC site, and women's shelter, but the loss of books was so high that now these sites receive only discarded library books delivered by the Friends of the Library rather than the deposit collections which are intended to have a longer circulation life at the sites.

A similar effort, "Read Right Now," was developed in Washington County, Oregon (Lyons, 2001), to provide an opportunity for families to read to their children while waiting for their appointments at local social service agencies. Of obvious value to the children and families who read the books, these deposit collections can help build bridges between the library and area providers. Donna Dengel, reporting on a telephone survey her library conducted to determine what agencies referred their clients to library resources, found that most of the representatives answering positively were from the agencies that had "Books While You Wait" deposit collections in their lobbies (Dengel, 1998).

Adaptive Toy Collections

Libraries that have toy collections (see Chapter 10 for detailed information on establishing toy collections) may want to consider expanding the scope of their collection to include adaptive toys and special switches designed for children with disabilities. Very expensive and difficult to locate, these toys are often beyond the reach of parents of children with disabilities as well as the network of early intervention specialists and others working directly with young children and their parents. Middle Country Public Library's toy collection was initiated with a grant to establish an adaptive toy collection intended to encourage families of children with disabilities to utilize the library and its resources more fully. While the library expanded this idea and developed a circulating toy collection aimed at young children in general, an unintended consequence of the adaptive toy component was the popularity of these toys with the professionals (early intervention, healthcare workers, therapists) working with children and families with disabilities. They saw this collection as a resource for them as well, a heretofore unavailable way of introducing and demonstrating toys that stimulated specific developmental or therapeutic functions in children to the families they were working with. Illustrated catalogs of the adaptive toys and switches in the library's collection were made available to area schools with early intervention programs and access to this collection was extended to the professionals working with local families, regardless of their residency.

Access to Families

"As institutions, libraries are changing and responding to a full spectrum of community needs; at the same time, other community organizations are beginning to recognize the potential power for reaching families with young children that libraries provide" (Feldman and Jordan, 2001: 36). Libraries, with their open-door policies, extended hours, free access, and barrier-free appeal to all families with no needs-based limitations, can be very useful to family support providers who need access to families in their communities.

Libraries can help providers market their services by posting notices and distributing literature about their agency's services to families visiting the library. Local health departments and early intervention programs can have their staff participate in library programs to acquaint parents with developmental information. On Long Island, the Suffolk County Health Department used the network of libraries offering Parent/Child Workshops to promote their Scald Burn Prevention Campaign targeted at families with babies and toddlers. Cooperative Extension agents with their research-based information for parents and caregivers on nutrition and child development often partner with public libraries to reach families and get their message out. When the Pediatrics Department at Long Island's Winthrop University Hospital wanted their residents to get into the community and connect directly with young families, they turned to Family Place Libraries as a good place to start. Similarly, when Adelphi University, Garden City, New York, launched its Social Health Indicator's Community Voices Survey, they sought out a busy public library as one of their key points of contact to reach a representative cross-section of the community. Librarians who are "at the community table" have much to offer that is valuable to their partners, starting with access to families.

Information Fairs

With their neutral stance and available public space, libraries are in a great position to host various kinds of information expositions, giving providers access to families and a forum to promote their services. Nursery school or early childhood fairs which bring together representatives of all of an area's early childhood services can give providers exposure and parents an opportunity to speak firsthand to a variety of local caregivers. Family resource fairs and child health fairs broaden the scope of access to include providers of all kinds of services important to families, promoting networking among the organizations and awareness of local services among parents and caregivers (Feldman and Jordan, 2001).

Meeting Space

Another valuable commodity that libraries have to offer is space. Whether you can provide meeting room space to host coalition-building efforts or space to offer partners to extend their services into the community, never underestimate how useful an offer of space can be to family support providers. Libraries can be used as sites for developmental screening programs and health department immunization clinics. On Long Island, the response to facilitated enrollment sessions of the state-sponsored child and family health insurance programs was so successful that more library sites are being sought.

Libraries that open their doors and their meeting rooms to local organizations can expect requests from everyone from La Leche and Al-Anon groups to support groups of every stripe—a wonderful opportunity to really emphasize the library's role as a community center. Meeting room space was a main "draw" of the library–Mothers' Center partnerships described in Chapter 4. Offering space to family support agencies for parent education programs and ongoing child and family support activities is a good way of establishing closer connections between staffs and assures that their families are introduced to both the library and the local agency.

Space can also be offered to support an agency's training activities. Housing the public health nurses' in-service workshops, the Department of Social Service's efforts to recruit foster parents, or the mandatory childcare provider trainings provided by the local Child Care Council reinforces the library's importance as part of the family support landscape and puts it at the center of the action, ready to capitalize on the next collaborative opportunity that comes up.

Training, Education, and Networking Opportunities

Family support providers across all disciplines have an ongoing need to stay abreast of emerging issues affecting families, new research findings that have implications for their work with children and families, and opportunities for networking with each other that allow them to exchange information on best practices and new program models they may consider replicating or referring families to. Libraries, skilled at organizing informational programs for all types of audiences and with the requisite space available, may want to consider addressing this need to draw them closer to the family providers in their area.

Suffolk Coalition for Parents and Children: Interdisciplinary Forum for Continuing Education

The Suffolk Coalition for Parents and Children described in Chapter 4 fulfills the need for ongoing education and networking for the hundreds of interdisciplinary family support providers that participate in its five educational programs each year. Spearheaded by the efforts of a children's librarian more than twenty years ago, this coalition remains an important continuing education opportunity, as its programs are free and organized by the providers themselves. Every two years, interested coalition members meet to plan a two-year cycle of workshops, five bimonthly, two-hour programs each year, skipping the summer months. This totally voluntary effort, which could be taken on by a public library in partnership with a coalition of family support providers, can go a long way toward filling the need for education, training, and networking around child and family issues.

Particularly valuable for new practitioners eager to learn about new and existing resources and meet other providers in the area, Suffolk Coalition programs attract audiences (including librarians) from 25 to 100, depending on the topic. Each program is typically a panel presentation, with some speakers providing the content or subject overview and others focusing on specific programs and services available to the community that respond to the issue under discussion. This balance builds both the knowledge base and awareness of existing referral resources for the participants. A program cycle is provided in Figure 12-4.

Contact Information: Marci Byrne at Middle Country Public Library, Centereach, NY. Phone: (631) 585-9393 ext. 230. Email: byrnemarcellina@mcpl.lib.ny.us.

Distinguished Speakers Series (DSS)

Advertised as a way to support families by providing a "forum for Long Island practitioners to learn about current issues affecting children and teens today from specialists in the field," the Distinguished Speakers Series: Exploring Innovative Ideas in Family Support and Early Childhood Services was created by the Middle Country Library (MCL) Foundation as a way of melding the mission with the foundation's need to raise funds to support the Family Place Libraries initiative. Recognizing providers' need for ongoing training and education, the series offers three 1½-hour seminars each year, featuring local or regional authors and experts in the field. Workshops include a continental breakfast and fees are $25 per seminar. The MCL Foundation secures corporate and private sponsorships to further enhance the fundraising potential of the series, and these sponsorships cover the cost of speakers and scholarships to underwrite the seminar attendance of Family Place staff and those whose agencies cannot afford the fees.

12-4:   Suffolk Coalition for Parents and Children Workshop Schedule

Suffolk Coalition for Parents & Children

"...Because children are our most precious resource"

Mailing Address: Middle Country Public Library
101 Eastwood Blvd., Centereach, NY 11720
Phone: 631-585-9393 Fax 631-585-5035

MEETING DATES AND TOPICS
Winter 2005-Spring 2007

January 18, 2005	**Childhood Obesity**
March 15, 2005	**Child Development Birth-Five: Brain Development, Mother/Child Interaction, and Importance of First Year**
May 17, 2005	**Single Parents**
September 20, 2005	**Red Flags of Child Development: When & Where To Get Help**
November 15, 2005	**Services for Typically Developing Siblings and Families of Children with Mental, Physical, and Chronic Illnesses**
January 17, 2006	**Cultural Issues & Biases: Influence on Body Image & Eating Disorders**
March 21, 2006	**Child Witnesses: The Impact of Domestic Violence on Children**
May 16, 2006	**LGBT (Lesbian, Gay, Bisexual and Transgender) Teen Issues**
September 19, 2006	**Immigrant Issues: School Implications, Policies & Legal Issues, Facts & Myths, Bias & Attitudes**
November 21, 2006	**Health Literacy**
January 16, 2007	**Importance of Play, Imagination and Creativity in Child Development**
March 20, 2007	**Working with Challenging Family and Child Behavioral Issues**
May 15, 2007	**Racial Achievement Gap in Education**

A DSS advisory group, representing a cross-section of health and human service professionals, helps to identify and select the speakers and promote the programs to a wide audience. Seminars now regularly attract 80 to 100 participants, filling an important educational need and helping the MCL Foundation raise funds to support its Family Place Libraries regional initiative in the process. Offered since 1999, several recent series have included speakers such as:

Dr. Esther Fusco of Hofstra University on the "Important Role of Play in Early Literacy"

Author Meredith Wiley, New York State Director of Fight Crime: Invest In Kids, on "Ghosts from the Nursery: The Impact of Early Childhood Abuse and Neglect"

Maria Elisa Cuadra of COPAY, Inc., on "Working with Latino Families: Building Cultural Competence"

Dr. John Feierabend, Director of Music Education at the Hartt School of the University of Hartford, on "Endangered Musical Minds: Helping Children Develop Their Potential to Succeed with Music"

Sean Douglas, Adjunct Professor at the NYU School of Social Work, on "Understanding Culturally Diverse Parenting Styles"

Dr. Janet Fischel, Director of Stony Brook University's Reading and Language Laboratory, on "Promoting Optimal Developmental Literacy and School Success"

Author and psychotherapist Steven Levenkron on "Understanding and Treating Self-Mutilation"

Art educator and author Susan Striker on "Art: The Foundation for Reading, Writing and Self-Expression"

Asian educator and lecturer Lana Mar on "Living in a Multicultural World: Working with Asian-Americans"

Contact Information: Kathleen Deerr, National Coordinator, Family Place Libraries, Middle Country Public Library, Centereach, NY. Phone: (631) 585-9393 ext. 204. Email: deerrkathleen@mcpl.lib.ny.us.

Librarian-Led Training and Education for Family Practitioners

Brokering training and education opportunities provided by others is not the only service that children's librarians can provide for practitioners. Never underestimate the value of one's own skills and expertise that can be shared to improve the skills of others. A presentation for the staff of a partnering community agency on "Tips and Techniques for Reading Aloud," "Selecting Age-Appropriate Books and Toys for Children," "The Value of Nursery Rhymes and Fingerplays in Promoting Early Literacy," or "Navigating the Internet: Useful Sites for Parents and Professionals" are just a few of the ways librarians can teach and mentor practitioners in other fields who work with parents and young children. Offer to "trade-off" and do some cross-training, drawing from each other's skill sets to provide training for each other's staff. This kind of bartering is an economical way to fill continuing education needs, build respect, and cement relationships in the process.

Offsite Program Delivery

"Children's services librarians' roles have expanded significantly so that they are now teachers of adults, child advocates, collaborators, partners, and, sometimes, interventionists. . . . The sites for delivering children's services, traditionally the library and the classroom, now include a variety of community sites" (Wronka and Mahmoodi, 1992–93: 90). Extending library programs beyond the walls of the library to provide them onsite at various community locations is perhaps the ultimate support libraries can provide for other agencies and organizations. Many libraries send staff to provide storytimes for children in area hospitals, daycare and Head Start centers, shelters, or health clinics. Though labor intensive, offsite programs can help the library reach audiences that would not otherwise be able or would be less likely to utilize library resources, such as children of working parents, children of families with limited resources, or children of families who lack transportation or perhaps are unaccustomed to using libraries themselves or are unaware of their services.

Health Department–Public Library Collaboration

The Mastics-Moriches-Shirley Community Library, Shirley, New York, started working with their local County Health Center through a grant-funded Reach Out and Read project. The project also engaged the coordinator of the school district's Parent Child Home Program (PCHP), a home-based family literacy project. Both the library and the school district saw the contacts made at the health clinic as a way to reach families they would probably not otherwise see. While the initial funding was discontinued, the library's family literacy project coordinator continues to visit the health clinic every other week, reading aloud to families with young children in the waiting room and distributing information about the library's services and family literacy programs as well. The library continues to secure funding to provide a supply of books to the health center so that physicians can give them out to children as part of their well baby visits. The age range of these materials has been extended from birth through the third grade at the request of the health providers. They love the opportunity to introduce kids to books, so the supply now includes board books as well as easy readers and chapter books. In addition to the benefit of reaching new families, the library reports that this activity has really cemented the library's relationship to the staff at the health center and made the staff at the health center much more aware of the library as a community resource and partner. "To be effective we had to learn to become partners with the agencies we had sought to serve. In many cases the shift is more attitudinal than functional. The end result still may be that we provide a service or resource; the difference is that partners work together on its creation" (Dengel, 1998: 155).

Treasure Truck

Audience: Young children ages two through five in area daycare centers, public and private preschools, recreation centers, and shelters. During the school year visits are made to preschools and daycare centers and in the summer months to recreation centers and other community agencies. Although during the summer this may include school-age children, the primary target remains children of ages two through five.

12-5:   Norfolk Public Library Treasure Truck Logo

Purpose/Goals: To provide a positive literacy message and experience to all young children of Norfolk "as we create a city of readers."

Description/Program Overview: Norfolk's Treasure Truck visits more than 3,000 children each year through its outreach programs (see Figure 12-5). Children are presented a theme-related storytime, and each child receives a free packet that includes coloring sheets, stickers, a bookmark, pencils, and a free book to take home. Information about the Norfolk Public Library, getting a library card, and the importance of reading is provided for the child's guardian. Although generally the child is the one on the truck at the school or center visit, the program is focused on the whole family and the center staff as well. The literacy packet that is given out is intended to get parents excited about reading and using the library. Teachers and childcare staff also receive a bag containing helpful information on classroom literacy and reading development.

Partnering Organizations: In addition to Norfolk Library funding, the Treasure Truck has been supported by a variety of businesses, organizations, and individuals, including the Friends of Norfolk Public Library, the Ezra Jack Keats Foundation, Tidewater Children's Foundation, West Ghent Civic League, First Book, and Literacy Partnership.

Materials/Supplies: Each child's packet includes a new book for their "home library" and a coupon redeemable for another book at any Norfolk Public Library branch.

Marketing/Outreach: The Treasure Truck is a popular community service, loved by the childcare community. Many centers have limited public library visits due to transportation, staff, scheduling, and funding issues, so this program serves as a connection point between the centers and the library system. Parents and even the childcare staff can be unaware of all of the library's services, and this program serves as an introduction. An additional bookmobile service is utilized by some centers as a way for children to check out materials.

Staff: The Treasure Truck is managed by one outreach librarian, the only full-time staff assigned, assisted by one program assistant, a college student working fifteen hours per week. The outreach librarian usually takes the truck out on visits herself, only occasionally accompanied by her program assistant, who is primarily occupied preparing materials for the families.

Contact Information: Melanie Reeves, Norfolk Public Library, VA. Phone: (757) 441-1629. Email: Melanie.reeves@norfolk.gov.

Storymobile

Audience: Children in childcare centers, traditional and special preschools, and private kindergarten as well as the staff at visited schools and centers. During the summer, the Storymobile visits housing authorities, city parks, recreation centers, and other facilities reaching school-age and preschool children, as well as family childcare homes as time permits.

Purpose/Goals: To provide access to a variety of books and materials, establish the library habit, promote family literacy, encourage preschool teachers and childcare staff to read aloud daily, support preschool teachers' curriculum development, and deliver a summer reading incentive program.

Description/Program Overview: This eleven-year-old program of the James V. Brown Library, Williamsport, Pennsylvania, visits fifty different groups of children and their caregivers each week, circulating more than 50,000 items per year (see Figure 12-6). Storymobile visits are made every two weeks, during which a deposit collection for the school or center is left and a selection from the delivered materials is read aloud. Teachers may choose from books, magazines, CDs, curriculum guides, read-a-longs, learning kits, and puppets to support their classroom center activities. Children may borrow paperback picture books, board books, and nonfiction paperbacks. The coordinator reports that a tremendous degree of trust, interaction, and opportunities for referrals and recommendations has resulted from the familiarity established through this program between the library representative and the staff at various schools and centers. During the summer, the library's summer reading club is provided to these sites through the Storymobile.

Partnering Organizations: Visited sites include YMCAs and child development centers, preschools and nursery schools, and family childcare homes. The local

12-6:   James V. Brown Storymobile Photo

community college held an event that asked for new children's books as the price of admission, later donating some of the books to the Storymobile.

Program in Action: During visits, children use their own library cards to borrow up to two books for home use. Teachers may borrow unlimited materials. The Storymobile is equipped with a satellite dish to enable the "live" use of the library's online catalog.

Materials/Supplies: The library has developed twenty-five themed learning kits which include books, props, and lesson plan ideas which support the preschool curriculum and are available on loan to teachers both on the Storymobile and at the main library.

Marketing and Outreach: This is a very popular outreach service to childcare providers who advocated for the library with state legislators when the library faced budget cuts. The Storymobile provides a way to market all of the library's in-house programming as flyers are distributed advertising events at each visit.

Staff: Staffed by the children's outreach coordinator, a former preschool teacher.

Program Variations/Extensions: To extend the library's outreach to the early childhood community and address Pennsylvania's required continuing education credits for teachers, library staff offer the "Every Child Ready to Read" workshop for childcare providers and teachers along with a workshop on teaching art using books. Other teacher resources promoted via the Storymobile include the availability of an Ellison die-cut machine with dies to use on site at the library or to loan—a resource unaffordable by most childcare sites.

Contact Information: Pam Fink, James V. Brown Library, Williamsport, PA. Phone: (570) 323-7705. Email: pfink@jvbrown.edu.

The Portable Preschool Program

Audience: Family childcare providers who are registered in New York State, county certified, or listed with the local Child Care Council as well as the children in their care.

Purpose/Goals: To support the literacy efforts of family home childcare providers by providing access to literacy resources and modeling read-aloud techniques and to reach children who may not otherwise utilize the resources of the public library (and their families).

Description/Program Overview: The Portable Preschool Program (PPP) at the Patchogue-Medford Library, Patchogue, New York, has been providing monthly home visits to area family childcare homes for more than fifteen years (see Figure 12-7). A children's librarian conducts a half-hour story session at each visit and leaves a PPP kit with the provider to continue literacy activities throughout the month. Initiated with an in-house library innovation grant, the program is now institutionalized and is supported as part of the library's regular budget.

12-7: Patchogue-Medford Library Portable Preschool Program

Partnering Organizations: The PPP was one of the library's first outreach projects, connecting the staff to the local Child Care Council and to the Department of Social Services.

Practical Tips/Program in Action: Family home providers complete an application for the program, self-reporting where they are registered or listed and their identification number. There are usually three or more children of varying ages, infants and up, at each home visited, which requires flexibility in the selection of books, fingerplays, and activities to appeal to a multiage audience. The kits are checked out to the provider by the librarian prior to the visit for an extended six-week loan period. This kit is picked up and replaced by another at the next visit. This is the Patchogue-Medford Library's only home-visiting outreach activity, one that the staff has always expressed a great deal of comfort with due to the familiar, literacy-based nature of the interaction. The library does recommend calling ahead for directions and the number and ages of the children as well as to remind the provider of the visit. Sometimes they have forgotten or have a sick child that may require rescheduling the visit. The phone call also gives the provider an opportunity to share with the librarian something going on with one of the children in her care—a new sibling, death in the family, or any other issue that the librarian may choose to reflect in the books brought to the home.

Materials/Supplies: PPP kits are intended to support the literacy component of the provider's curriculum. There are eight themed kits to carry through the year (no summer or December visits). Each kit, housed in a sturdy canvas bag, includes six or more books, realia (puppets, a flannel board, sometimes a tape recorder and music), and a folder of suggested learning activities to continue through the month. Many of these activities are handmade to demonstrate for the provider that they can create learning activities using materials found in the home. Sometimes the pattern is included to encourage providers to create their own activities. Complimentary brochures and handouts are also included on child development, health, safety (often of seasonal interest), community resources, and library programs to be given to parents. Although no kits are delivered during the summer, a packet of summer fun activities is given to each provider.

Marketing/Outreach: When this program was first initiated, program flyers were sent to the local Department of Social Services and Child Care Council for distribution to family care homes known to these agencies in the library's district. Now the program is well established and homes are self-referred or identified by word of mouth or through notices in the library's newsletter.

Staff: Several children's librarians participate in the program, sharing the visit assignments.

Program Variations/Extensions: Some providers have gone on to participate in the Library's Systemic Training and Education of Parents (STEP) Parenting classes, or workshops on toilet learning and Discipline Is Not a Dirty Word, provided by Cornell Cooperative Extension. Many heavily use the library's professional collection which they are made aware of as part of the PPP visits. The librarian may occasionally bring along some material from this collection at the request of the provider. A special connection is formed between the visiting librarian and the children in the family homes. The importance of this bond is shown by the enthusiasm of the children who come in to the library with their parents and proudly point out the librarian who visited their home. While Patchogue-Medford Library has chosen to focus on the family home provider with the PPP, they also visit the Head Start and Early Head Start in their district as often as possible, leaving a deposit collection intended to be circulated from the center to the children's homes.

Contact Information: Toni Dean, Patchogue-Medford Library, Patchogue, NY. Phone: (631) 654-4700. Email: tdean@suffolk.lib.ny.us.

Conclusion

Clearly, there is a natural synergy between public libraries and librarians and the larger network of family support providers in communities and there are a variety of ways to provide support and nurture these connections for the ultimate benefit of the families we all strive to serve. While extolling the new "Age of Relationships" we find ourselves in, we are cautioned by the author that to make this a reality "We need to get out of our buildings and into our communities" (Link, 2001: 16). Similarly, one of the critical imperatives cited for successful community building reminds us that "to participate in community-building activities the librarian must leave the library" (McCook, 2000: 101). To position the library and its staff to address the needs of family support providers, in all the many ways this is possible, librarians need to be visible and accessible to their family support partners. If librarians and their family support partners work together, it is only a matter of time before new and effective and mutually beneficial initiatives will emerge.

References

Dengel, Donna. "Partnering: Building Community Relationships." *Journal of Youth Services in Libraries* 11, no. 2: 153–160, 1998.

Feldman, Sari, and Barbara Jordan. "Together Is Better: The Role of Libraries as Natural Community Partners." *Zero to Three* 21, no. 3 (December/January): 30–37, 2001.

Link, Terry. "Entering the Age of Relationships." *Public Libraries* (January/February): 15–16, 2001.

Lyons, Dianne Boulerice, ed. " 'Read Right Now' Turns Waiting Rooms Into Reading Rooms." *Public Libraries* 40, no. 1 (January/February): 20, 2001.

McCook, Kathleen de la Pena. *A Place at the Table: Participating in Community Building.* Chicago: American Library Association, 2000.

Wronka, Gretchen, and Suzanne H. Mahmoodi. "Children's Services Librarians: Collaborators and Teachers of Adults." *Minnesota Libraries* no. 30 (Autumn/Winter): 90–101, 1992–93.

Resource Listings

Recommended Sources for Developing Professional Collections

Child Care Providers/Early Childhood Educators:

Building Blocks
38 W. 567 Brindlewood
Elgin, IL 60123
(800) 233-2448

Gryphon House
P.O. Box 207
Beltsville, MD 20704
(800) 638-0928

High/Scope Press
600 North River St.
Ypsilanti, MI 48198-2898
(734) 485-2000

National Association for the Education of Young Children (NAEYC)
1313 L St. NW, Suite 500
Washington, DC 20005
(800) 424-2460

Redleaf Press
10 Yorkton Ct.
St. Paul, MN 55117-1065
(800) 423-8309

Family Support Providers:

Active Parenting
1955 Vaugh Rd., Suite 108
Kennesaw, GA 30144
(800) 825-0060

American Guidance Service
P.O. Box 99
Circle Pines, MN 55014-1796
(800) 328-2560

Brunner-Routledge
A Division of Taylor and Francis
47 Runway Rd.
Levittown, PA 19067
(800) 821-8312

Bureau for At-Risk Youth
135 Dupont St.
P.O. Box 9120

Plainview, NY 11803
(800) 999-6884

Center for the Improvement of Child Caring
11331 Ventura Blvd., Suite 103
Studio City, CA 91604-3147
(800) 325-CICC

Charles C. Thomas
2600 South First St.
Springfield, IL 62704
(800) 258-8980

Child Welfare League of America
440 First St. NW
Washington, DC 20001-2085
(202) 638-2952

Children's Defense Fund
25 E St. NW
Washington, DC 20001
(202) 628-8787

Family Development Resources
3070 Rasmussen Rd., Suite 190
Park City, UT 84098
(800) 688-5822

Family Support America
205 W. Randolph St., Suite 2222
Chicago, IL 60606
(312) 338-0900

Guilford Publications
72 Spring St.
New York, NY 10012
(212) 431-9800

Haworth Press
10 Alice St.
Binghamton, NY 13904-1580
(800) 429-6784

Hazelden
P.O. Box 176
Center City, MN 55012-0176
(800) 328-9000

Home Economics School Service
P.O. Box 802
Culver City, CA 90232
(310) 839-2436

Human Sciences Press
233 Spring St.
New York, NY 10013-1578
(212) 620-8000

JIST Life/Kidsrights
8902 Otis Ave.
Indianapolis, IN 46216
(800) 892-5437
www.kidsrights.com

Paul H. Brookes Publishing
P.O. Box 10624
Baltimore, MD 21285-0624
(800) 638-3775

Pro-Ed
8700 Shoal Creek Blvd.
Austin, TX 78757-6897
(512) 451-3246

Research Press
P.O. Box 9177
Champaign, IL 61826
(217) 352-3273

Sage Publications
P.O. Box 5084
Newbury Park, CA 91359-9924
(805) 499-0721

Search Institute
615 First Ave. NE, Suite 125
Minneapolis, MN 55413
(877) 240-7251
www.search-institute.org

Recommended Periodicals for Professional Collections

Child Care Providers/Early Childhood Teachers:

Childhood Education: Infancy Through Early Adolescence
Journal of the Association for Childhood Education International
17904 Georgia Ave., Suite 215
Olney, MD 20832
(800) 423-3563

Early Childhood Education Journal
Springer Science and Business Media
P.O. Box 2485
Secaucus, NJ 07096
(800) 777-4643

Early Childhood Research Quarterly
Publication of the National Association for the Education of
Young Children
1313 L St. NW, Suite 500
Washington, DC 20005
(800) 424-2460

Everyday TLC
TLC Press
P.O. Box 180
Wilmington, NC 28042
(800) 677-6644
www.everydaytlc.com

Exchange
P.O. Box 3249
Redmond, WA 98073-3249
(800) 221-2864
www.childcareexchange.com

High Scope ReSource: A Magazine for Educators
High Scope
600 N. River St.
Ypsilanti, MI 48198-2898
(734) 485-2000
www.highscope.org

Infants and Young Children: An Interdisciplinary Journal of Special
Care Practices
Lipincott Williams and Wilkins, Inc.
16522 Hunters Green Pkwy.
Hagerstown, MD 21740-2116
(800) 638-3030

The Mailbox: The Idea Magazine for Teachers
(available in Preschool, Kindergarten–Grade 1, Grades 2–3,
and Intermediate levels)
P.O. Box 9753
Greensboro, NC 27429-0753
(800) 334-0298

Scholastic Early Childhood Today
P.O. Box 54814
Boulder, CO 80322-4814
(800) 544-2917

School-Age Notes: Resources for After School Professionals
P.O. Box 476
New Albany, OH 43054-0476
(800) 410-8780
www.schoolagenotes.com

Teaching Pre K–8.
Early Years (subsidiary of Highlights for Children)
P.O. Box 54807
Boulder, CO 80322-4807
(800) 678-8793

Young Children
National Association for the Education of Young Children
NAEYC Subscriptions
P.O. Box 96270
Washington, DC 20090-6270
(800) 424-2460

Zero to Three
Journal of Zero to Three: National Center for Infants,
Toddlers and Families
P.O. Box 960
Herndon, VA 20172
(800) 899-4301
www.zerotothree.org

Family Support Providers:

Child and Adolescent Social Work Journal
Springer Science and Business Media, Inc.
101 Philip Dr.
Norwell, MA 02061
(866) 269-9527

Children and Youth Funding Report
8204 Fenton St.
Silver Spring, MD 20910
(301) 588-6380
www.cdpublications.com

Children's Health Care
Published by Lawrence Erlbaum Associates, Inc.
10 Industrial Ave.
Mahwah, NJ 07430-2262

Child Welfare
Publication of the Child Welfare League of America
P.O. Box 932831
Atlanta, GA 31193-2831
(800) 407-6273
www.cwla.org/pubs

The Evaluation Exchange
Harvard Family Research Project
(617) 496-4304
www.gse.harvard.edu

Families in Society: The Journal of Contemporary Social Services
P.O. Box 88814
Milwaukee, WI 53288-0814
(414) 359-1040
www.familiesinsociety.org

Journal of Child and Family Studies
Springer Science and Business Media, Inc.
P.O. Box 2485
Secaucus, NJ 07096
(800) 777-4643

Journal of Marital and Family Therapy
Publication of American Association for Marriage and Family Therapy
112 South Alfred St.
Alexandria, VA 22314-3061

Pediatrics
Official Journal of the American Academy of Pediatrics
P.O. Box 927
Elk Grove Village, IL 60007-0927
(866) 843-2271

Professional School Counseling
Publication of American School Counselors Association
P.O. Box 18136
Merrifield, VA 22118-0136
(800) 306-4722

Report
Quarterly Newsletter of the National Council on Family Relations
3989 Central Ave. NE, Suite 550
Minneapolis, MN 55421
(888) 781-9331
www.ncfr.org

School Social Work Journal
Sponsored by the Illinois Association of School Social Workers
341 N. Charlotte St.
Lombard, IL 60148

13

Limited-Literacy and Low-Income Families

"If you build it they will come" may not hold true even for libraries with the best of intentions. Developing family-centered collections, programs, and services is not enough if those families most in need and facing the greatest challenges are either unaware or underutilizing the resources available to them at their local library. This chapter will explore some of the issues facing libraries' often hardest to reach families as well as strategies, programs, collections, and services that address their unique needs.

The dual burden of poverty and limited education are often inextricably linked, and we know that children born to families facing these dual challenges are those most at risk for school failure and least likely to be fully utilizing the resources of the public library. However great the challenge, libraries that aim to reach those most in need will have to look at their library's services, collections, policies, and outreach strategies through a new lens. As always, strategic community partnerships and positive staff attitude will be critical.

Needs and Challenges

As Maslow's hierarchy of needs reminds us, families in poverty are facing life's requirements at its most basic level. Books and traditional library resources may not hold instant and readily apparent appeal, especially if school failure and limited literacy make reading and learning institutions unfriendly reminders of unhappy experiences. Lack of transportation, lack of time, fear of fines or fear of children damaging or losing library materials, a perception of an unwelcoming institutional environment like so many other unwelcoming institutions, a place with rules and restrictions suitable only for readers and the well educated—all of these may present barriers to reaching those families we most want to reach. Identifying families at risk may present the largest challenge because they are often "hidden," unknown to the library and its staff. As P. J. Capp of Leavenworth, Kansas, puts it, "The people we aren't seeing are the people we aren't serving. Sometimes you have to be a little creative" (Fine, 2001: 18).

Responding to the Challenges: Strategies That Work

1. Partner with agencies and organizations that can provide direct access to families most at risk, with whom connections and trust are already established. Secure their assistance in getting the word out about family resources at the library to the families you are trying to reach. Housing projects, Head Start programs, health clinics, the Salvation Army, WIC (Women, Infant and Child) sites, soup kitchens and food pantries, shelters, social service agencies, public health departments, and school personnel knowledgeable about students' home situations are all potential outreach partners. Leavenworth Public Library had the library designated an alternative WIC distribution site because its central location was convenient for families and the library sought the opportunity to serve an otherwise difficult-to-reach audience (Fine, 2001).

2. Provide training for staff to sensitize them to the fear, anxiety, added stress, and even shame that may accompany poverty and illiteracy. Families may require more time, assistance, and direction to acquaint them with the library facility and routines. Friendly, respectful, nonjudgmental, kind, and welcoming staff are the best ambassadors the library could have and are most likely to create the first impression of the library that will make or break future encounters with families. The way services are delivered can be as important as the services themselves. It must be acknowledged that working with families with lots of needs can require an extra dose of patience and dedication, and staff reinforcement needs to reflect the positive efforts to help in sometimes stressful situations.

3. Provide and promote library services that address issues that are high up on the family's list of priorities: GED (General Equivalency Diploma), employment assistance, job fairs, literacy instruction, access to computers and computer skills training, homework help and after-school activities for children, immunizations, health insurance and food stamp assistance, parenting classes, community service information and referrals to food, clothing, housing, health, and family support services. The more practical the service, the more receptive families are likely to be. In a 1999 study of the informa-

tion needs of low-income residents, the King County (Seattle) Library System found that career search, job advancement, culturally appropriate and translated materials, and Internet skills ranked the highest among participants' information needs (Armstrong, Lord, and Zeiter, 2000).

4. Capitalize on the library as a safe place for families and children and a refuge in an often dangerous world—"Stay cool with us this summer" or "Come in out of the cold." In communities rife with violence, there is much to be said for a comfortable, safe, and welcoming environment.

5. Emphasize what is free and fun at the library—free programs for family members of all ages, free access to learning materials that will help children to succeed—books, puzzles, and toys to use at the library and take home too. Homemade bookmaking workshops or programs such as "Create and Learn" described in Chapter 8 can be especially appealing to families with limited resources.

6. Recognize that fear of fines, rigorous library card application processes, and rigid program registration procedures may present a barrier for poor families or those with limited literacy. Reassurance may be needed that the library realizes that sometimes books are so well loved by children that they may become worn or damaged and that normal wear and tear is anticipated. Sensitivity to these underlying issues and allowing staff a degree of flexibility may minimize negative experiences. Staff may need to be empowered to seize the opportunity to engage a family in a program even if not preregistered, for instance. Families dealing at the subsistence level may not have the luxury of planning activities weeks in advance.

7. Assume parents' intrinsic desire for the best for their children. Providing parents opportunities to give their children all the experiences and activities the library has to offer is giving them the opportunity to be successful parents and nurturers of their child's early learning. They may not automatically understand their importance to their child's language development or recognize their role as their child's first teacher, especially if their own learning efforts met with failure. They may need to be convinced of the importance of coming to the library, continuing reading activities in the home, the long-term benefits of early language experiences, and their own ability to support these activities. And do not assume parents know how it is done—gently model literacy and language-learning activities; make recommendations for good read-alouds; reassure that "telling the story" to the pictures on the page is as valid a reading activity as any other and that talking to your child, sharing a conversation, and naming objects as one goes through the day are all ways to prepare a child for reading success.

8. Be realistic in measuring success. Traditional library output measures may not capture the strides made by families who begin visiting the library for the very first time, extending their stays and bringing along neighborhood children with each new visit.

9. Incentives do work. Everyone loves a free gift and special coupons to retrieve a free book at the library, get a free lunch at the local fast-food restaurant,

participate in a program that incorporates free books and toys. Similar giveaway incentives can be an important enticement, especially for families whose treats are few and far between. First Book (www.firstbook.org) and Reading Is Fundamental (www.rif.org) are good places to start.

10. The digital divide is real. Emphasize the library as a place where everyone in the family from tots to seniors can learn to use and have access to all the technology tools so necessary in today's world: computers, the Internet, software applications, information sources, and computer learning games that reinforce literacy for children and adults.

11. Reinforcement and extra efforts may be necessary to "prime the pump" for families that do not yet have the literacy and library-going habit. Reminder calls in advance of a program, follow-up calls, and personalized, mailed invitations all can help to foster the personal relationships that lead to trust and continued interest in the face of often serious obstacles. Other strategies, such as posting family photographs, stressing "membership" in the club or project, and the awarding of certificates of completion, are all morale boosters and create that sense of belonging and achievement that has often been lacking. Offer special tours of the library and encourage them to bring along neighbors and family members to get a thorough introduction to all of the library's resources. Opportunities to ask questions and get "special treatment" increase comfort level and goodwill.

12. Be flexible about allowing other family members and caregivers to accompany children in programs. Caregiving may be very much a shared responsibility among adults in the family, and the opportunity to involve as many caring adults in family literacy and library activities should be welcomed and encouraged. Make sure that families know that fathers and grandparents are welcome even if they can only occasionally participate. Word of mouth is often the best recommendation to others, and families in poverty living in close proximity to each other can be the best advertisements to encourage others' involvement.

13. Review library signage to see if more visual cues and symbols could be incorporated to aid access for those with limited reading skills. Sensitize staff to consider the possibility of limited literacy in giving directions, securing a library card, or registering for programs.

Collections for Parents and Caregivers with Limited Literacy

Making available information for parents with limited reading ability is particularly challenging. Look at your family support collection and area as a whole and see if you have included:

Books on parenting topics written at a low reading level as well as books that may not be specifically designated low literacy but which work well for this audience. These include those with limited text, larger type size, and more "white space" as well as those that rely heavily on illustrations, cartoons, or photographs for visual cues. A list of some low-literacy parenting titles is included at the end of this chapter.

Videotapes, DVDs, CDs, and books on tape on a wide range of parenting topics. Media levels the playing field for nonreaders, so they are recommended for a limited-literacy audience.

Free handouts with parenting information in simple, single-sheet flyer or brochure format, especially those featuring limited text and larger print that are aimed at a low-literacy audience. Prevent Child Abuse America (in partnership with Channing Bete Company) offers a variety of great brochures for parents suitable for limited-literacy populations. Phone: (800) 835-2671 or contact: http://pcaamerica.channing-bete.com.

Posters featuring simple parenting tips displayed around the children's room or family support area that provide simple parenting messages in a highly visual or limited text format. Parenting Resources, among the catalog sources listed at the end of this chapter, carries a line of parenting posters useful for this purpose.

Collections for Families with Limited Resources

Families in poverty can benefit tremendously from the wealth of free materials available for the entire family at the public library. Parents' attention should be especially directed to those items they might not expect to find at the library but which can be extremely helpful to parents who do not have the funds to purchase them for their home. These include:

Circulating toy, puzzle, game, and software collections.

Board books, card sets, alphabet and number sets, and so on.

Circulating literacy kits (often theme-related sets of books, puppets, music, flannel board stories, games, and suggested learning activities).

Bins of discarded magazines, catalogs, or craft materials for the taking (corrugated cardboard, paper, tubing, etc.), all of which make great additions to home literacy areas.

Parenting titles that focus on homemade toys, games, and learning activities that can be made using items commonly found around the house—conveying the important message that learning aids need not be store bought to be effective and may be more fun for the shared activity of creating them together. A list of these are included at the end of this chapter.

Programs for Families with Limited Income and Limited Literacy

Food/Transportation Programs

Special transportation assistance and food delivery programs that address fundamental issues for poor families may go a long way in helping the library reach targeted families. The Columbus, Ohio, Metropolitan Library offered a Reading Off Fines program where patrons could read to reduce money owed on their record.

They also arranged to have the city's Children's Hunger Alliance offer free lunches to children at the library—as many as sixty free lunches can be served on a busy day (Williams, 2005). The Harmon Branch of the Phoenix Public Library invites area residents, largely poor, for coffee at the "Harmon Cafe" every Friday and participates in a community garden project that helps residents raise fresh produce (Fransen and Adams, 2005). The Jacksonville Public Library System in Florida addressed the problem of transportation as a barrier to low-income families' use of the library by starting the Ride To Read program in partnership with the Jacksonville Transit Authority. "In Jacksonville, any child under seventeen years of age with a library card can receive coupons for free bus rides to and from any Jacksonville library" (Haller and Hayes, 2005: 327).

Early Literacy Book Incentive Programs

Programs that incorporate a book incentive or giveaway program have proven successful in reaching traditionally underserved families with very young children.

Reach Out and Read (ROR; www.reachoutandread.org) is a national program initiated by pediatricians to encourage doctors, hospitals, and child health facilities to incorporate reading aloud to very young children as a "healthy" practice, "prescribing" books to parents as part of their child's well baby visits. Program elements include free books to give parents at regular check-up visits and volunteers reading in waiting rooms. Many libraries have found ways to collaborate with ROR programs in their area, enhancing their ability to reach families served at local clinics and other facilities serving at-risk families that the library might not otherwise have an opportunity to reach.

Born to Read (www.ala.org/alsc/born.html) is a national project administered by the Association of Library Service to Children (ALSC), a division of the American Library Association. Libraries across the country have adopted the program's logo, materials, and activities to create unique local programs that promote reading aloud among young families, often in partnership with WIC sites, family centers, and clinics in an effort to reach those most in need in their communities.

Scores of similar programs function across the country to help libraries share the joy of books and reading with families hardest to reach in their communities. Begin with Books in Arapahoe Library District, Arapahoe County, Colorado, and Book Time with Your Baby in Duluth Public Library, Minnesota, are but two of many programs undertaken by libraries to reach families with young children. The Head Start/Library Partnership Project, Bell Atlantic/American Library Association Family Literacy Project, and hundreds of LSTA (Library Services and Technology Act)-funded projects across the country document libraries' efforts to serve families most in need of early literacy support.

Family Literacy Programs

Family literacy programs remain the most effective way for libraries to address the simultaneous needs of young children in need of a strong foundation for language learning and the need of their parents or caregivers for support in developing their own skills and to become an effective first teacher for their child. Family literacy programs incorporate all of the issues so critical to families where limited education, limited literacy, and poverty are a factor. Libraries are the perfect community setting to initiate family literacy efforts. Literacy is the library's mission, and libraries have resources for both adults and children with programs, collections, and services in place to address needs across the family spectrum—free and accessible to all with minimal barriers to those with limited resources. "Family literacy programs are now recognized as the most effective solution to the age-old problem of illiteracy. They work because they combine fundamental educational practices that foster the development of literacy and pre-literacy skills with sound parenting practices (such as modeling positive reading behavior in the home and stimulating language development from birth)" (Talan, 1999: vii).

By definition, family literacy initiatives incorporate:

An adult literacy component or opportunity for the adults to improve their own skills
Emergent literacy stimulation for children
Opportunities for intergenerational activities for parent and child to share
A parent education, modeling, family support component to bolster language-stimulating practices within the home and family context

Family literacy projects incorporate the best family-centered practices, building on family strengths, reflecting and respecting the culture, values, and heritage of the family, reinforcing the parents' role as first and most important teacher, and empowering parents by giving them a say in the pace and direction of learning activities so that more time can be spent on activities that seem to resonate with the parent and the child. Family literacy projects typically encourage and help families to develop literacy areas in the home, and library-sponsored family literacy projects may place a special premium on increasing families' utilization of the library, its resources, and its programs on a regular basis. This holds true for both adult and child, as family literacy programs encourage the continued growth and education for all generations participating.

Three family literacy program models follow: a home-visiting program that has been documented by longitudinal research studies to be extremely effective in producing long-term positive outcomes for both children and parents; a technology-based intergenerational family literacy program that increases computer literacy and basic literacy skills in adults and children simultaneously; and a nationally utilized family literacy curriculum that uses children's literature to reinforce literacy and parenting skills. All have been successfully implemented by public libraries and have been successful in helping libraries reach and serve families most in need in their communities—families with limited education, literacy, and often, limited income. Limited parental education is a key indicator for participation in all of these programs. "Recent research has indicated that the single most important factor in determining the life chances of children is the level of educational attainment of the parents, particularly the mother" (Talan, 1999: 5).

The Parent-Child Home Program

The Parent-Child Home Program (PCHP), a research-validated home-based literacy and parenting program strengthens families and prepares children to succeed academically and has been internationally replicated and successfully adapted by Middle Country Public Library, Centereach, New York, as well as three other public libraries on Long Island.

Audience: Children ages two and three years and parents or caregivers with limited education or literacy, low-income and often isolated teen parents, nonnative English speakers, and grandparents raising grandchildren.

Purpose/Goals: To improve school readiness, early literacy, and language skills among young children in order to effect their long-term ability to succeed in school by working intensively in the home and to support and strengthen parents' efforts to play, read, and share language with their children. The program assists the library to connect with families that may not be regular library users, to get them to increase the frequency of their visits to and their participation in library programs and services.

Program Overview: This family literacy program provides trained home visitors who make twice weekly visits to participating families throughout the school year over a two-year period. During the visit, the home visitor gently demonstrates how to read or use books and toys to have fun, create verbal interaction between the parent and child, and extend use of the books and toys with other fun learning activities. Home visitors alternate bringing either a new book or a new toy to the family each week, introducing the item during the first weekly visit and reinforcing and extending learning activities using the item during the second visit of the week. These books and toys are left with the family as a gift and are eventually augmented by materials borrowed from the library. Each visit is approximately one half hour. The ongoing relationship established between the family and the home visitor is intended to create the trust necessary to encourage parents to visit the library more frequently—often accompanied by the home visitor who can assist with obtaining a library card, touring the library, and providing an introduction to the library's programs and services for the entire family.

Partnering Organizations: To establish a PCHP it is necessary to have the coordinator be trained and certified by the staff of the National Center for the Parent-Child Home Program, a primary partner when establishing this program at your library. Each site will also want to collaborate with those organizations in their community who can help to identify families to participate in the program. Middle Country Public Library partners with the Pre-K program of the local school district and others to help identify families who can particularly benefit from this program (see survey in Tools, Section C). Head Start, clinics, and social services agencies or departments are other likely partners.

13-1: Parent-Child Home Program Logo

Soaring to Success
Through Books and Play...

The Parent-Child Home Program

The PCHP is replicated in cities and towns across the country. Libraries should check with the PCHP national office to see if there is an established PCHP in their vicinity, perhaps sponsored by a local school district, BOCES (Board of Cooperative Educational Services), or community agency, with whom they can create a connection. Although this segment has described libraries that have taken on the sponsorship of the program directly, there is equal value for libraries to make a strong connection with an existing program. The families participating in the PCHP are just those families at risk that libraries most want to reach, and forging a relationship with the staff working closely with these families, helping them to introduce families to the local library, and developing easy communication between librarians and the PCHP staff can accomplish results as desirable as implementing the program directly.

Practical Tips/Program in Action: Home visiting is a particularly intimate activity for library staff to engage in. It is necessary that home visitors be introduced to safe protocols for home visitors, be closely supervised, and have ample opportunity to debrief with the supervising librarian, discuss issues that may arise during the home visit, and review responses and perhaps referrals to other agencies to assist families with needs that arise. Referrals may include the need for services such as WIC programs, early intervention services, or access to an ESOL (English to Speakers of Other Languages) program. Flexibility in scheduling home visits is another important consideration, as it is necessary to accommodate the realities of families' lives, child illnesses, and other factors.

Identifying at-risk families poses a particular dilemma for libraries that do not inquire about patrons' income or education level. Middle Country Public Library staff developed a survey (see Tools, Section C) to help identify families for several family literacy programs which is distributed through the local school district to all families participating in the district's Pre-K program. Family referrals are also solicited from public health nurses, the social worker based at the library through a collaboration with a local family service agency, and adult literacy staff. Through these methods, the library identifies families for the PCHP and PACTT (Parents and Children Using Technology Together), which is described below.

Home visitors document each session spent with the family and report progress to the program site coordinator. For library-based PCHPs, this is usually the librarian in charge of the program. Participating sites can benefit from the evaluation and assessment tools that the program has developed over more than thirty years of practice. Good evaluation tools and well-established outcome measures can be especially important when seeking funding to support ongoing program implementation.

Materials/Supplies: In conjunction with the required training, the PCHP provides a list of suggested, developmentally appropriate toys and books that lend themselves well to the language stimulation activities that are central to the program and that will supply a family for a year's worth of home visits, based on one learning item per week per family across the school year with breaks for school vacations. Libraries have explored a variety of methods for purchasing books and toys for the program, including LSTA funding, soliciting support from the local Rotary and Kiwanis or Friend's group, or securing corporate underwriting from local banks or companies like Wal-Mart, Starbucks, and others that embrace literacy as part of their philanthropic mission. It is usually necessary for the library to underwrite the cost of the staff expenses, the home visitor(s) and the program coordinator, typically a children's librarian. The upside is that the purchase of the books and toys, which is clearly an integral program component and a critical incentive to family participation, is a very practical, necessary, and easily articulated expense to convey to potential funders.

Staff: Typically, home visitors are paraprofessionals, someone able to establish a good rapport with parent and child, perhaps warm, family-friendly library clerks or local community residents who may be parents themselves. As much as possible it is recommended that the home visitors reflect the communities in which they work and exhibit a kind, nonjudgmental, "gentle touch" as they model early literacy activities for parents and help parents to create a language-rich home environment.

Contact Information: Lisa Kropp, Middle Country Public Library, Centereach, New York. Phone: (631) 585-9393. Email: kropplisa@mcpl.lib.ny.us.

Additional Resources: Contact Sarah Walzer, Executive Director, Parent Child Home Program, 800 Port Washington Blvd., Port Washington, NY 11050. Phone: (516) 883-7480. Email: info@parent-child.org or check out www.parent-child.org.

Parents and Children Using Technology Together (PACTT)

Target Audience: Parents and caregivers with limited education, literacy, income, and limited technology and computer literacy skills and their children age three and four years.

Purpose/Goals: To improve the literacy and technology skills of both adults and children through the use of quality early childhood learning software and to reinforce the parents' role as their child's first teacher.

Description/Program Overview: PACTT is an intergenerational, technology-based family literacy program which introduces basic computer skills to adults through the use of early childhood software and then provides opportunities for the adults to support their child's learning by introducing and sharing early learning activities on the computer. The program accepts that computer literacy is as much a requirement for school and workplace readiness as print literacy, that adults lacking one or both of these skills are at a severe disadvantage, and that parents' ability to support their children's learning can be enhanced by improving both skills simultaneously.

Each program runs for six weeks and each session is 1½ hours long. Computer instructors introduce parents to basic computer skills as well as a particular early childhood software program for the first half of each session while children participate in early literacy activities in another room. For the second half of the program, children join their parents at the computer and the parent introduces the child to the software program of the day, which they then explore together. Reading and learning activities are taken home each week to reinforce basic literacy concepts, and additional "Skill Sharpener Sessions" provide opportunities for parents and children to practice on the computer outside scheduled program sessions. During the program parents are introduced to the concepts of Every Child Ready to Read, a joint project of the Public Library Association and the Association for Library Service to Children, and the importance of reading aloud to children at home. Families become familiar with the library's public access catalog, parenting resources on the Internet, additional computer skills classes for adults and children, and other programs for children and families available at the library. Taking photos of each family pair is also recommended. Posting participant pictures creates a sense of pride and belonging. At the end of the program, each family creates a book based on the literacy lessons and activities they participated in, and the photos can be used as part of the book's decoration. A celebration is held at the end of the program and certificates of completion are presented, another important morale booster.

Partnering Organization: PACTT is based on a model program developed by the Center for Applied Special Technology (CAST), in Peabody, Massachusetts, which found that through the use of computers and early childhood software, adults with little or no computer experience and often limited print literacy could improve their own technology and literacy skills and simultaneously introduce these skills to young children. The program provides training for the adults to use technologies in ways that support their children's and their own learning.

Practical Tips/Program in Action: The Pre-K survey (Appendix C) is utilized to identify families for PACTT, and referrals to these programs are also solicited from school and library staff. The number of parent-child participants in the program will be governed by the number of computer stations available for the group sessions. For groups of ten families or more it is advisable to have at least two staff members present during computer sessions to assist. Those very new to computers can get easily frustrated without someone nearby to help them on to the next step. The learning curve is usually quite fast and confidence grows rapidly, but during the first session or two having an extra pair of hands is helpful. As everyone knows, computers often have a mind of their own, and it is helpful to have someone to troubleshoot technical glitches while the group moves on. A computer instructor and children's librarian working in tandem are ideal.

Materials/Supplies: Sufficient copies of early childhood software to be loaded on all of the computer stations used by the parents (grandparents) and children are necessary. Middle Country Public Library's PACTT Program uses software programs such as Dr. Seuss ABC; Elmo's Preschool; Winnie the Pooh and the Honey Tree; Dora's Backpack Adventures; Caillou Alphabet Preschool; Arthur's Reading Race; Ready to Read with Pooh; Madeline's Preschool; Franklin's Activity Center; Berenstain Bears Living Books-In the Dark; Mickey Mouse Toddler; and Dr. Seuss Preschool. Other supplies include weekly handouts for families (e.g., take home literacy activities for parents and children to share). When grant funding is available, each family is given a paperback picture book to take home each week, but this is an optional addition and is not necessary to run the program.

Staff: The children's librarian coordinates and oversees the program, identifies and establishes relationships with families, selects and orders software and literacy materials, creates supplemental literacy activities for children's sessions and for home use, adapts and implements the program curriculum, and identifies and schedules staff. A computer instructor provides the course content during both the parent sessions and the parent-child sessions. This could also be a librarian sufficiently comfortable with technology to introduce computer concepts and the early childhood software programs. The staff must be sufficient for the number and age of the children participating in the emergent literacy-based childcare session in the first half of the program while the parent is receiving computer training. At Middle Country Public Library, a minimum of two staff members is utilized at each session, usually a library clerk assisted by a library page. A Spanish-speaking library staff member can also be called upon to participate in the program to translate and assist parents if Spanish-speaking families are registered.

Contact Information: Ann Swedish, Middle Country Public Library, Centereach, NY. Phone: (631) 585-9393 ext. 271. Email: swedishann@mcpl.lib.ny.us.

GrandPACTT

Target Audience: Grandparents who are providing primary childcare for or raising their grandchildren, age two through four years.

Practical Tips/Program in Action: All components of the program were consistent with PACTT (described above) except that it was found that some grandparents, though not all, were particularly anxious about using new technology, requiring in some cases significantly extra time and assistance to help them gain comfort with the mouse and keyboard functions. This also became one of the most rewarding aspects of GrandPACTT as the pride at mastering what had for some been a totally foreign skill opened up a whole new world for the participants who went on to take other computer classes, got email accounts, and thoroughly enjoyed being able to share the world of technology with their grandchildren. For the library, GrandPACTT represented a way to reach out to grandparents in the community in a positive, fun, proactive way that encouraged them to share the library and its resources with their grandchildren.

Partnering Organizations: Middle Country Public Library adapted the PACTT program with grant funding from Generations United, an organization interested in promoting intergenerational shared site programming. The library also spoke to and widely distributed a flyer to senior organizations, senior housing facilities, and senior centers throughout the community; developed a newspaper ad targeting grandparents; and enlisted the assistance of an organization working specifically with grandparents raising their grandchildren in the area.

Contact Information: Lori Abbatepaolo, Middle Country Public Library, Centereach, NY. Phone: (631) 585-9393 ext. 295. Email: Abbatepaololori@mcpl.lib.ny.us.

Motheread, Inc.

Motheread, Inc. is a national training and curriculum development organization with programs (based on their curricula) offered in a variety of settings across the country, including some that are library based.

Audience: Parents and caregivers of children ages two through eleven, particularly families with low literacy from low-income, high-stress families. Special curriculum units are available for incarcerated fathers, expectant and new parents, immigrants, and adults with developmental disabilities.

Purpose/Goals: Motheread, Inc. helps adults improve their own literacy skills and those of their children within a context that also helps develop life skills, using literature and stories as its basis for instruction.

Description/Program Overview: Motheread combines the teaching of literacy skills with child development and family empowerment issues, helping parents and children learn to use the power of language to discover more about themselves, their families, and their communities. Motheread curricula utilize commercially available multicultural children's literature, teaching adults to be story readers, writers, storytellers, and reading role models for their children and children to be storysharers in an environment that encourages reading, critical thinking, and problem solving. All Motheread curriculums use children's literature to learn literacy skills and examine themes and life lessons through these simply written stories. Programs are typically eight to twelve weeks (20 instruction hours on average) with eight to twelve adults in each class. Individuals interested in teaching Motheread or Fatheread classes for adults or storysharing classes for children must attend a four-day Motheread training institute and become certified instructors.

At the Peoria Public Library in Peoria, Arizona, two librarians attended the necessary training prior to implementation of the program. In this community, the Motheread program takes place at a district elementary school located in close proximity to the public library. After dropping their children off at school, parents are invited into the school for the program. The program consists of an eight-week session, each 1½ hours, and one additional session in which participants are invited to the library to tour and learn about materials and services. During each session of the program, parents are introduced to a new picture book, practice reading it as a group, and are given assistance on effective ways to read and discuss the story with their children. Parents are given a copy of the book to keep. As the Motheread philosophy stresses the importance of "story," librarians relate each picture book to the lives of the parents and encourage parents to share their stories. In Peoria, many families speak Spanish as their primary language, and therefore bilingual books are used. In addition, librarians provide a craft or activity related to the story to act as an ice-breaker and that can be shared with their children at home. The library considers the program a success, as many families who have participated in it continue to be active library users and have formed friendships and relationships with one another and the library staff. Funding for the Peoria Public Library Motheread program was provided through the Arizona Humanities Council for staff training and duplicate copies of books for parents.

Partnering Organizations: Humanities councils are Motheread's primary affiliates, but programs are held in many different community settings, including schools, childcare centers, community colleges, correctional facilities, family resource centers, churches, public housing, and libraries. Peoria Public Library also works with the local elementary school in order to identify and reach parents and families for the program.

Materials/Supplies: The basic Motheread curriculum includes the Literacy and Parent Education Teacher's Guide, the Storysharing Handbook, and a Storysharing Plan for use by parents with their children in the home. The program requires a large selection of children's literature from a wide variety of cultural backgrounds. The number of titles and number of copies per title are determined by the local program's budget and number of students involved. In general, programs are encouraged to purchase multiple copies of books for use in adult classes and those implementing the Storysharing curriculum. Additional curriculums are available for use with specific audiences: for example, B.A.B.Y. (Birth and Beginning Years), F.A.T.H.E.R. (Fathers Acting To Heal, Educate, and Reconnect), and My United States.

Staff: The program requires staff members who have attended a Motheread, Inc. training institute and understand the program philosophy and approach. The national program recommends that two program leaders conduct the program.

Contact Information: Dawn Marie Schmidt, Peoria Public Library, Peoria, AZ. Phone: (623) 773-7562. Email: DawnM@peoriaaz.com.

Additional Resources: Visit www.motheread.org or write to: Motheread, Inc., Suite 7, 3924 Browning Place, Raleigh, NC 27609. Phone: (919) 781-2088.

Conclusion

A great deal of information has been shared to acquaint the reader with suggested strategies for connecting with hard-to-reach families and programmatic and collection resources that can be developed to support them. What should be stressed is that it is not the job of just those few designated as "outreach" staff; all children's librarians should think of themselves as the frontline of library efforts to reach those constituencies who most need all of the wonderful resources the library has to offer.

References

Armstrong, Annie Laurie, Catherine Lord, and Judith Zeiter. "Information Needs of Low-Income Residents in South King County." *Public Libraries* (November/December): 330–335, 2000.

Feinberg, Sandra, and Sari Feldman. *Serving Families and Children Through Partnerships.* New York: Neal-Schuman, 1996.

Fine, Jane. "From the Field: Reaping the Benefits of Partnership." JOYS (Fall 2001): 16–22, 2001.

Fransen, Pattie, and Sabrena Adams. "Phoenix's Harmon Branch Extends a Helping Hand." *Public Libraries* (November/December): 323–324, 2005.

Haller, Anita, and Keith Hayes. "Jacksonville Public Library Service to Low-Income Urban Areas." *Public Libraries* (November/December): 327–328, 2005.

Motheread, Inc. www.motheread.org.

Parent-Child Home Program. www.parent-child.org.

Talan, Carole. *Founding and Funding Family Literacy Programs: A How-To-Do-It Manual for Librarians.* New York: Neal-Schuman, 1999.

Walzer, Sarah. "The Parent-Child Home Program and Libraries." 2000/2001. *Zero to Three* (December/January): 8–9, 2001/2002.

Williams, Cathy. "Serving Urban Populations." *Public Libraries* (November/December): 320–321, 2005.

Wronka, Gretchen, and Suzanne H. Mahmoodi. "Children's Service Librarians: Collaborators and Teachers of Adults." *Minnesota Libraries* no. 30 (Autumn/Winter): 90–101, 1992/1993.

Resource Listings

Low Literacy Parenting Books/Series

Baby Tips Series. Tucson, AZ: Fisher Books.

Barns, Rebecca Beall. *20 Ways To Calm a Crying Baby.* Charlottesville, VA: Thomasson Grant, 1994.

Johnson's Child Development Series. New York: DK Publishing.

Meyer, Gloria. *What To Do When Your Child Gets Sick.* Whittier, CA: Institute for Healthcare Advancement, 2001.

Peinkofer, J. *101 Ways To Soothe a Crying Baby.* Lincolnwood, IL: Contemporary Books, 2000.

Play and Learn Series. Torrance, CA: Totline Publications.

Play with Purpose Series. Ontario, Canada: Brighter Vision Publishers.

Steelsmith, Shari. *Peekaboo! and Other Games to Play with Your Baby.* Seattle: Parenting Press, 1994.

Stewart, Deborah, and Christine Evans. *Baby and Me: The Essential Guide To Pregnancy.* Palo Alto, CA: Bull Publishing, 1997.

Tools for Everyday Parenting Series. Seattle, WA: Parenting Press.

Williams, Frances. *Babycare for Beginners.* New York: Harper Perennial, 1996.

Low Literacy Catalog Sources

Capstone Press
P.O. Box 669
Mankato, MN 56002-0669
(800) 747-4992
www.capstone-press.com.
Offers a series for teens on parenting skills that are written in a high interest/low reading level style and also has some Spanish-language materials.

Meld: Parenting That Works
219 North Second St., Suite 200
Minneapolis, MN 55401
(612) 232-7563
Fax: (612) 344-1959
info@meld.org.
Each offering in the catalog is accompanied by a "literacy scale," which assesses the readability of the title from very basic to mid-level. Great resources for low-literacy parents and teen parents.

Morning Glory Press
6595 San Haroldo Way
Buena Park, CA 90620-3748
(888) 612-8254
Fax: (888) 327-4362
infor@morninggplorypress.com or www.morninggplorypress.com
Comprehensive catalog focusing on materials for pregnant and parenting teens, much of it written at a low-literacy level.

New Readers Press
U.S. Publishing Division of Laubach Literacy
Department FS02, P.O. Box 35888
Syracuse, NY 13235-5888
(800) 448-8878
www.newreaderspress.com
Offers low-level literacy materials in areas such as parenting, family literacy, pregnancy, and health issues.

Parenting Press
P.O. Box 75267
Seattle, WA 98175-0267
(800) 992-6657
Fax: (206) 364-0702
www.parentingpress.com
Resources include the "Tools for Everyday Parenting" series of books for parents, small format and highly illustrated, suitable for low-literacy audiences.

Parenting Resources
P.O. Box 138299
Chicago, IL 60613
(773) 525-5977
Fax: (773) 525-6532
www.parenting-resources.com
This catalog, which is targeted to Even Start, Head Start, and family literacy programs, provides a great assemblage of some of the best resources for parents, including those with limited literacy, including a number of posters as well as parenting materials in Spanish.

SBS Prevention Plus
649 Main St., Suite B
Groveport, OH 43125
(800) 858-5222

Fax: (614) 836-8359

www.sbsplus.com or sbspp@aol.com

This catalog of Shaken Baby Syndrome materials also includes information on other general parenting topics. The "Child Behavior Management Cards" (30 topics) make great handouts for low-literacy readers, each offering important information on a different parenting topic in a simple format, from toilet training to biting. Cards lend themselves to a countertop displayer.

Totline Publications

Division of Frank Schaffer Publications

P.O. Box 37267

Boone, IA 50037-2267

(800) 264-9873

www.mhteachers.com/cgi-bin/gradeprod.cgi?imp=tot

Totline is a good source of low-literacy early childhood resources.

Zero to Three

Suite 200, 2000 M St., NW

Washington, DC 20036-3307

(800) 899-4301

www.zerotothree.org

This national organization is the nation's leading resource on the first three years of life. The organization's aim is to strengthen and support families, practitioners, and communities to promote the healthy development of babies and toddlers. Several titles, including "Learning and Growing Together" and "You Make a Difference," are good resources for the early years, written in accessible language.

Suggested Titles for Homemade Play and Learning Materials

Anderson, Rita, and Linda Neumann. *Partners in Play: Homemade Toys for Toddlers: An Owl Book.* Glen Ellyn, IL: Partners Press, 1991.

Baratta-Lorton, Mary. *Workjobs for Parents: Activity-Centered Learning in the Home.* Menlo Park, CA: Addison-Wesley, 1975.

Baratta-Lorton, Mary. *Workjobs II: Number Activities for Early Childhood.* Menlo Park, CA: Addison-Wesley, 1979.

Blose, Dee. *Thrifty Nifty Stuff for Little Kids: Developmental Play Using Home Resources.* Tucson, AZ: Communication Skill Builders, 1995.

Miller, Linda, and Mary Jo Gibbs. *Making Toys for Infants and Toddlers: Using Ordinary Stuff for Extraordinary Play.* Beltsville, MD: Gryphon House, 2002.

Miller, Linda, and Mary Jo Gibbs. *Making Toys for Preschoolers.* Beltsville, MD: Gryphon House, 2002.

Miller, Linda, and Mary Jo Gibbs. *Making Toys for School-Age Children.* Beltsville, MD: Gryphon House, 2002.

Redleaf, Rhoda. *Learn and Play the Recycle Way: Homemade Toys That Teach.* St. Paul, MN: Redleaf Press, 1999.

14

Culturally Diverse Families

Libraries across the country recognize that demographics are changing. We live in a global world with new populations emerging in our communities seemingly overnight. Minnesota reports on efforts to reach out to Hmong and Somali families, even as the rates of Spanish-speaking and Asian immigrants soar from California to New York. In some communities there is still a great divide that leaves African American families and families of color isolated in their own hometowns. Clearly libraries have a role to play in helping families acclimate and gain access to the resources and skills they and their children need to succeed. For family-centered libraries, reaching out to culturally diverse populations is a high priority.

Needs and Challenges

Culturally diverse families, particularly those new to this country, often struggle to be understood in a language that is not their own, in a country with unfamiliar cultural traditions and mores, expectations that may not be readily understood, and sometimes amid a cloud of legal uncertainty that creates a fear of institutions and government agencies. All of these can lead to insecurity, stress, and anxiety.

Though libraries may eagerly await greater use of their resources by these new populations, families may come from countries where there is not a tradition of

239

free, public libraries and may be totally unaware of the resources available to them at the local library. Teachers and the education system in general may be held in such high esteem that speaking directly to a teacher or getting involved in one's child's school would seem almost disrespectful. Libraries may have been reserved for the elite and the educated and may be viewed in much the same respectful but distant view. Cultural mores may limit women's independent access to programs and services, or families may be impeded by all of the struggles referenced in the previous section due to limited income, transportation, and time. There may be anticipated or real limitations in the library's ability to address their needs, particularly in the areas of foreign language resources or the presence of staff with whom they can speak and convey their needs. Taking into consideration the economic realities within which libraries must operate, libraries must at least consider how they might improve access to services for culturally diverse populations, particularly families with young children who may benefit the most from early intervention and assistance.

Responding to the Challenges: Strategies That Work

1. Actively look for staff who can speak other languages and who reflect some of the diverse cultures of the community. "One of the most important factors that librarians mention over and over for attracting Spanish-speaking patrons is having staff who speak the language" (Moller, 2001: 18). Trust is built over time, and word of mouth from one community or family member to another may be the most successful form of advertising. Having members of various ethnic groups employed at the library can jumpstart this process. The Arlington County, Virginia, Public Library instituted a Cultural Ambassadors Program. Library staff who are members of specific immigrant communities and fluent in other languages, volunteer to be liaisons to their communities, bringing back feedback, publicizing library programs, placing notices in non-English media, helping to plan cultural events, and agree to have their phone numbers listed as library contacts (Osborne, 2004: 100–101). Library staff who speak other languages can help explain "how the library works" and help families negotiate getting a library card and registering for programs appropriate to their needs.

2. Encourage staff to participate in language training and consider offering language instruction for staff at the library along with cultural awareness and sensitivity training. A sixteen-hour basic conversation and functional Spanish instruction course has been developed especially for library staff. For information about "Spanish That Works . . . In a Library," contact www.thelearninglight.com or call (866) 391-8901.

3. Offer programs that reflect the family orientation of many new immigrant groups and emphasize the intergenerational nature of programming in advertising, demonstrating a respect for the importance of extended family relationships. Encourage all to attend—grandparents, cousins, siblings, and parents or caregivers with babies and toddlers—keeping in mind that best

practice in family support takes a "strengths-based" approach and respects the multigenerational context of child rearing in many cultures as a strength to be respected and encouraged.

4. Connect with local school English as a Second Language (ESOL) teachers; reach out to churches and other houses of worship, trusted leaders, community agencies, food establishments, markets, and cultural associations that can help the library gain access to ethnic communities; and take advantage of community festivals and foreign language media (print, TV, and radio) to reach new populations. "The library's fliers and posters need to be in the neighborhood grocery store, video store, and local bakery. The library's programs should be announced at Sunday Mass or service" (Cuesta, 2003: 5).

5. Let parents know that children need exposure to language in all its forms and parents should be encouraged to sing, talk, and read to their children in their first language even as they seek mastery of English. Encourage parents' use of children's materials to reinforce their own skills and their child's at the same time.

6. Locate foreign language and bilingual materials in highly visible, easy-to-access areas and be sure to include periodicals and newspapers in the languages most predominant in the community.

7. Make efforts to really learn about the new populations in the community (what countries, how many, experiences with and perceptions of the library, obstacles, collection and program interests, important holidays and cultural events, points of contact, community leaders, media, and other information sources utilized). Middle Country Library in Centereach, New York, undertook an informal Community Diversity Survey of library users from a variety of countries over a period of time (see Appendix C) and used the information to develop and expand collections and eventually plan a large Asian Heritage Festival. Feedback also led the library to add a Spanish Speaking Literacy Assistant position, available to help individuals and families learn about all of the resources at the library and help them utilize collections, programs, and services more fully.

8. Provide programming that will have practical appeal: ESOL and citizenship classes, financial literacy, computer skills training, how the education system works, and library programs for children and parents that will help prepare children to succeed in school, and, of course, family literacy programs that address the multigenerational need for language and literacy support.

9. Offer events and exhibits reflecting the art, history, music, and culture of various ethnic groups to demonstrate the library's interest in helping the community members get to know each other and position the library as a community institution interested in promoting education and multicultural awareness.

10. Offer bilingual story hours and incorporate songs, repetitive verses, and folktales reflecting a variety of cultures.

11. Consider Sunday programs to attract families that may work six days of the week.
12. Review library signage and forms and consider having some translated into languages other than English, especially a Welcome sign that signals an enthusiastic greeting to newcomers.

Collections for Culturally Diverse Parents and Caregivers

Libraries need to look critically at their family support collections and areas to see if they have created an environment and collections that reflect the cultural diversity of their communities, one that sends a welcoming message to all families. Look at such things as the area's artwork and posters, the collection as a whole, the items selected for display, free handout material, and the dolls, puppets, flannel boards, and other materials that are used in the children's room and in library programs to be sure that all children see themselves reflected in the library's surroundings. Does the parents' collection reflect a broad cultural perspective? If there is a significant non-English-speaking population, are there materials in other languages available? Has attention been drawn to their existence? Admittedly, parenting material in other languages and written from a variety of cultural perspectives may not be easy to locate, but the effort will result in a balanced, diverse collection that offers something for all families in the community (Feinberg and Feldman, 1996). A list of culturally diverse parenting books and catalog sources for culturally diverse family materials is included at the end of this chapter.

Culture/Language Kits

The Davenport, Iowa, Public Library promotes greater multicultural awareness and understanding by circulating "Culture Kits" to families, schools, and organizations that include clothing, games, musical instruments, and family items representing the cultures of countries such as Nigeria, Colombia, Russia, China, Saudi Arabia, and Kenya (Lyons, 2001). In Ontario, the Hamilton Public Library developed Family Language Kits to promote reading, language development, and library use among new immigrants. The library has created more than 100 dual language kits in fifteen languages, each kit containing print and nonprint materials (bilingual picture books and folktales, puppets, picture dictionaries) to promote fun, interactive language learning. Families are encouraged to use the kits together, to help improve their English as a group effort. Kit themes include nutrition, safety, health, and the neighborhood. Mothers with young children were a special target for the kits when they were conceived, and parents are asked to provide input in the kit development. Translations of materials are double-checked for accuracy and great care is taken to assure that materials are culturally sensitive and accurate (Osborne, 2004: 35–37). A programmatic variation on these kits has been developed by Shippensburg Public Library in Pennsylvania. Their Passport Program introduces families to countries around the world through games, crafts, and hands-on exploration of materials associated with the featured country. Held several Saturdays each year, the program utilizes high school exchange students, foreign students from nearby Shippensburg University, and community volunteers from a variety of countries to assist as volunteers and provide a real face and human context to the cultural activities being shared.

Programs for Culturally Diverse Families

It should be noted that all programs for parents and children described in this book and especially those family literacy programs described in the previous chapter that are targeted for low-literacy audiences (PCHP [Parent-Child Home Program], PACTT [Parents and Children Using Technology Together], and Motheread) are all suitable for culturally diverse families. The following are included here because they are specifically targeted to families whose primary language is other than English.

Bilingual Storytime

Audience: Families with preschool-aged children and their siblings.

Purpose/Goals: To welcome Spanish-speaking families to the library at a time that is convenient for working parents; to reinforce the language skills of both parents and children.

Description/Program Overview: At Central Islip Public Library, New York, the Bilingual Storytime is held once a month from October through May and lasts forty-five minutes to one hour, offering stories and songs, read and sung in both English and Spanish. The extended family is invited, so siblings, grandparents, and all other family members are welcome to participate, and a simple craft activity which the entire family can do together rounds out the program. The Bilingual Storytime was initiated as a partnership between the library and the local PCHP and later, the local Even Start Program. The library hosts the program and the children's librarian is at the door of the community room to welcome families as they enter. Bilingual staff members from the PCHP and Even Start have conducted the storytime from its inception. Now that these programs have been defunded, the library is picking up the cost of the Spanish-speaking storyteller.

The library reports major positive change following implementation of this programmatic outreach to the Spanish-speaking families in the community. The Library's Spanish-language and bilingual materials for both parents and children have increased as a result of increased demand and frequent use, and the staff reports that Spanish-speaking families who rarely ventured into the library now think of it as their "second home." In the evenings and on Saturdays in particular, the Family Place space is filled with parents and children, talking with each other and using the library's board books and picture books.

Partnering Organizations: Initially, the PCHP and Even Start program helped to identify and recruit families for the program. Their early involvement was critical as they served as ambassadors to the library for families that were not already using its resources.

Practical Tips/Program in Action: This program is offered on a drop-in basis, eliminating any barriers that might be caused by requiring registration. Because the exact numbers attending are unknown, the library must have sufficient craft materials on hand for a large crowd. This is a family program, and parents or caregivers are required to accompany and participate with children. The library has the room ready and provides nametags, sign-up sheets, and a book display in the room. The room is set up with tables and chairs in the back of the community room. This arrangement leaves plenty of room for the families to sit on the floor in front of the presenters.

Materials/Supplies: The library provides crayons, glue sticks, scissors, and whatever other materials for the craft of the day are necessary, making available books requested by the presenters and a book display to encourage parents to take books home. Something is given to families at the end of each program—a bookmark, a flyer on other programs coming up, or some other handout.

Staff: A librarian is available to meet and greet the families, and a bilingual staff member acts as a translator and assists with nametags and sign-in sheets. Two presenters participate, alternating the stories, songs, and fingerplays—first in one language and then the other.

Contact Information: Lili-Ane Bukowy at Central Islip Library, Central Islip, NY. Phone: (631) 234-9333. Email: LBukowy@suffolk.lib.ny.us.

Learning English: A Family Affair (LEFA)

Audience: Parents participating in the library's ESOL classes and their children age two through second grade (siblings welcome).

Purpose/Goals: To give parents the skills needed to be their child's first and most important teacher by providing an enjoyable library experience in conjunction with parents' ESOL instruction and to reach children in homes where English is not the first language before they enter school and provide additional English enrichment to those already in school.

Description/Program Overview: This family literacy program simultaneously addresses the instructional needs of adult learners of English and their young children. While parents attend ESOL classes at the library, children are playing and participating in early literacy activities with library staff. The program is two hours long and runs weekly throughout the school year. Parents and children are separated for the first hour and forty-five minutes. Midway through the session the librarian engages the children in a circle time including songs, fingerplays, and a brief story. Parents and children are reunited during the last fifteen minutes of the session for snacks, socializing, and a parent-child circle time in which a gift book is read that parents have been introduced to during their ESOL session. Families go home with this gift book, which is purchased by the library's Family Literacy Project, Inc., a 501(c)(3) set up to raise money for special purchases such as these. Parents are encouraged to explore the library and are made aware of other library activities and services, including books, toys, and other resources that may be checked out. LEFA runs continually, one morning each week throughout the school year, in order to meet the growing demand.

Partnering Organizations: The Mastics-Moriches-Shirley Library received a New York State Parent and Child Services Grant to initiate this program but now maintains it (staffing, refreshments, supplies, etc.) out of the regular library budget. Literacy Suffolk, Inc. partners with the library's adult literacy staff as trained and experienced Literacy Suffolk volunteers conduct the ESOL group sessions with parents for the LEFA program.

Practical Tips/Program in Action: LEFA requires two separate, adjoining rooms or spaces for separate adult and child activities. The staff is especially supportive and sensitive to both parents and children as the parents and children attempt to separate for, perhaps, the first time. As families arrive, children and parents go into their respective rooms when they are comfortable doing so. Families are recruited through all of the existing ESOL classes, billing this as a family opportunity as well as an early childhood and parenting program. The program is advertised through flyers, brochures, the library newsletter, and the library catalog in both English and Spanish.

Materials/Supplies: The adult literacy class requires tables and chairs; a TV and VCR; blackboard; and adult learning materials focused on life skills activities (making appointments, reading a bus schedule, going to the bank, etc.). These adult literacy materials are from the library's collection of literacy resources. The children's activity and interaction portion of LEFA requires age-appropriate toys which may include puppets, Legos, blocks, a pretend play or dress-up area, musical instruments, paper and crayons or markers, picture books and board books, an area rug for circle time, and a table for snacks and refreshments on a weekly basis.

Staff: The program requires an ESOL instructor and library staff to facilitate the child activity and interaction session and to run the circle time. Two staff members are present with the children at all times, one clerk and one page. The children's librarian participates in the program for approximately thirty to forty minutes of each session.

Contact Information: Eileen Curtin at the Mastics-Moriches-Shirley Community Library, Shirley, NY. Phone: (631) 399-1511. Email: ECurtin@suffolk.lib.ny.us.

Conclusion

Finding innovative ways of reaching out to new families, bridging cultures, overcoming language barriers, and introducing entire generations to the wealth of resources that the library can provide are some of the most stimulating, albeit challenging, experiences a librarian can face. Success can sometimes be measured only in small, slow steps, but the rewards are great, and not just for the recipients of these services. The entire community benefits when the library reflects the full cultural spectrum of its service area. It is the essence of the democratic ideal on which our public libraries are founded. For libraries challenged to make their services meaningful in a dramatically changing world, the welcoming spaces, dynamic programs, and rich array of resources that family-centered libraries offer are just what is needed to help young families from diverse cultural backgrounds find a sense of community and help their families thrive.

References

Cuesta, Yolanda J. "Marketing to Latinos: It's About Building Trust." *Marketing Library Services* (May/June): 4–5, 2003.

Feinberg, Sandra, and Sari Feldman. *Serving Families and Children Through Partnerships.* New York: Neal-Schuman, 1996.

Lyons, Dianne Boulerice, ed. "Tales from the Front: Culture Kits Available at Davenport PL." *Public Libraries* (January/February): 20, 2001.

Moller, Sharon Chickering. *Library Service to Spanish Speaking Patrons.* Englewood, CO: Libraries Unlimited, 2001.

Osborne, Robin, ed. *From Outreach to Equity: Innovative Models of Library Policy and Practice.* Chicago: American Library Association, 2004.

Resources for Culturally Diverse Families

Parenting Books

Abner, Allison. *The Black Parenting Book: Caring for Our Children in the First Five Years.* New York: Broadway Books, 1999.

Alcaniz, Lourdes. *Waiting for Bebe: A Pregnancy Guide for Latinas.* New York: Ballantine Books, 2003.

Alperson, Myra. *Dim Sum, Bagels and Grits: A Sourcebook for Multicultural Families.* New York: Farrar, Straus and Giroux, 2001.

Beshir, Ekram. *Meeting the Challenge of Parenting in the West: An Islamic Perspective.* Beltsville, MD: Amana Publications, 2000.

Beshir, Mohamed Rida. *Muslim Teens: Today's Worry, Tomorrow's Home: A Practical Islamic Parenting Guide.* Beltsville, MD: Amana Publications, 2001.

Brown, Dennis, and Pamela A. Toussaint. *Mama's Little Baby: The Black Woman's Guide to Pregnancy, Childbirth, and Baby's First Year.* New York: Dutton, 1997.

Comer, James P. *Raising Black Children: Questions and Answers for Parents and Teachers.* New York: Plume, 1992.

Hale, Janice E. *Learning While Black: Creating Educational Excellence for African American Children.* Baltimore, MD: Johns Hopkins University Press, 2001.

Harris, Phyllis Y. *From the Soul: Stories of Great Black Parents and the Lives They Gave Us.* New York: G. P. Putnam's Sons, 2001.

Hopson, Darlene Powell, and Derek S. Hopson. *Different and Wonderful: Raising Black Children in Race-Conscious Society.* New York: Fireside Books, 1992.

Kunjufu, Jawanza. *Restoring the Village, Values and Commitment: Solutions for the Black Family.* Chicago, IL: African American Images, 1996.

Paratore, Jeanne R. *What Should We Expect of Family Literacy?: Experiences of Latino Children Whose Parents Participate in an Intergenerational Literacy Project.* Newark, DE: International Reading Association, 1999.

Rand, Donna, and Toni Trent Parker. *Black Books Galore: Guide to More Great African American Children's Books.* San Francisco, CA: Jossey-Bass, 2001.

Rodriguez, Gloria G. *Raising Nuestros Ninos: Bringing Up Latino Children in a Bicultural World.* New York: Fireside, 1999.

Stevenson, Howard, Gwendolyn Davis, and Saburah Abdul-Kabir. *Stickin' To, Watchin' Over, and Gettin' With: An African American Parent's Guide to Discipline.* San Franciso, CA: Jossey-Bass, 2001.

Tan, Amy Lin. *Chinese American Children and Families.* Olney, MD: Association for Childhood Education International, 2004.

Tarazi, Norma. *The Child in Islam: A Muslim Parent's Handbook.* Plainfield, IN: American Trust Publications, 1995.

Toussaint, Pamela. *Great Books for African-American Children.* New York: Plume, 1999.

Vazquez, Carmen Inoa. *Parenting with Pride, Latino Style: How to Help Your Child Cherish Cultural Values and Succeed in Today's World.* New York: Rayo, 2004.

Ward, Janie Victoria. *The Skin We're In: Teaching Our Children to Be Emotionally Strong, Socially Smart, Spiritually Connected.* New York: Free Press, 2000.

Williams, Kelly. *Single Mamahood: Advice and Wisdom for the African-American Single Mother.* Secaucus, NJ: Carol Publishing Group, 1998.

Winbush, Raymond A. *The Warrior Method: A Program for Rearing Healthy Black Boys.* New York: Amistad Press, 2001.

Wright, Marguerite A. *I'm Chocolate, You're Vanilla: Raising Healthy Black and Biracial Children in a Race-Conscious World.* San Francisco, CA: Jossey-Bass Publishers, 1998.

Catalog Sources for Culturally Diverse Materials

Asia For Kids
Master Communications, Inc.
4480 Lake Forest Dr., Suite 302
Cincinnati, OH 45242-3726
(513) 563-3100
Fax: (513) 563-3105
www.afk.com
Offers a wide selection of bilingual books for children in a variety of Asian languages as well as resources for children (and adults working with children) on

Asian folklore, culture, and traditions, including multicultural CDs, videos, dolls, puppets, wall hangings, cards, and accessories.

Avicenna Books
#116 Bldg. 80 JFK
Jamaica, NY 11430
Email: usoffice@iran-books.com or www.avicennabooks.com
This online Iranian bookstore provides publications in Farsi (Persian). Click on "books" for a listing of materials for children and teens. The site comes up in Farsi—click on "English version" in the upper left-hand corner.

Bilingual Publications Company
270 Lafayette St.
New York, NY 10012
(212) 431-3500
Fax: (212) 431-3567
Email: lindagoodman@juno.com
Spanish language books for adults and children, including parenting titles.

Center for the Improvement of Child Caring
11331 Ventura Blvd.
Studio City, CA 91604
www.ciccparenting.org
Publisher of several culturally specific parent education curricula, Effective Black Parenting, and Los Ninos Bien Educados.

Child Development Media
5632 Van Nuys Blvd., Suite 286
Van Nuys, CA 91401
(818) 994-0933
Fax: (818) 994-0153
Extensive collection of previewed and selected videos on parenting and child development topics. A separate listing of both Spanish-language videos and closed-captioned titles adds to the catalog's usefulness.

Culture for Kids
4480 Lake Forest Dr., #302
Cincinnati, OH 45242
(800) 888-9589
Fax: (513) 563-3105
Email: Info@cultureforkids.com
Multicultural and multilingual books and videos for children, as well as dolls, posters, games, and other items celebrating multicultural themes.

Family Development Resources
3160 Pinebrook Rd.
Park City, UT 84060
(800) 688-5822
Publisher of *Multicultural Parenting Educational Guide: Understanding Cultural Parenting Values, Traditions, and Practices* by Stephen J. Bavolek, which includes Parenting Values and Practices of Korean Families, Japanese Families, El Salvadoran Families, Mexican Families, Hawaiian Families, Puerto Rican Families, Chinese

Families, Vietnamese Families, Hmong Families, Chilean Families, Laotian Families, Cambodian Families, and Filipino Families.

Far Eastern Books
P.O. Box 846
Adelaide Street Station
Toronto, Ontario, Canada M5C 2K1
(905) 477-2900 or (800) 291-8886
Fax: (905) 479-2988
www.febonline.com
Board books and other titles for children in Arabic, Somali, Serbo-Croatian, Bengali, Turkish, Chinese, Hindi, Gujarati, Urdu, Vietnamese, Farsi, and other languages.

Flame Company
31 Marble Ave.
Pleasantville, NY 10570
(800) 535-2632
www.flamecompany.com
Check out the Parents' Library, offered in dual language and in Spanish, with titles for adults on parenting information for children of all ages.

Greek Baby
(877) 600-8400
www.greekbaby.com
This Web site offers children's educational products in Greek. Books are listed for ages one through three and four through twelve years. Also includes books for parents and teachers.

Just Us Books
356 Glenwood Ave.
East Orange, NJ 07017
(973) 672-7701
www.justusbooks.com
Children's books featuring African American families and themes.

Lectorum Publications, Inc.
111 Eighth Ave., Suite 804
New York, NY 10011
(800) 345-5946
www.lectorum.com
Lectorum has an extensive collection of fiction and nonfiction for children and adults in Spanish.

Libros Sin Fronteras
P.O. Box 2085
Olympia, WA 98507-2085
(800) 4-Libros (800) 234-2767
Fax: (360) 357-4964
www.librossinfronteras.com
A wide selection of parenting books and several videos in Spanish.

Madera Cinevideo
311 South Pine St., Suite 102
Madera, CA 93637
(800) 828-8118
Email: video@psnw.com or www.cinevideo.com
Catalog of Spanish-language videos, including parenting topics.

Mazda Publishers, Inc.
P.O. Box 2603
Costa Mesa, CA 92626
(714) 751-5252
www.mazdapub.com
Publisher to try if looking for Persian materials.

Meld
219 N Second St., Suite 200
Minneapolis, MN 55401
(612) 232-7563
Fax: (612) 344-1959
info@meld.org or www.meld.org
Both Spanish and Hmong parenting resources. Each offering in the catalog is accompanied by a "literacy scale," which assesses the readability of the title from very basic to mid-level.

Milet Books
Milet Publishing Ltd.
6 North End Parade
London W14 OSJ, England
Phone: 442076035477
Email: infor@milet.com or www.milet.com
Publishes a wide range of bilingual children's books in more than a dozen languages.

Multi-Cultural Books and Videos, Inc.
28880 Southfield Rd., Suite 183
Lathrup Village, MI 48076
(800) 567-2220
www.multiculbv.com
This distributor offers materials (books, videos, newspapers, and magazines) in over twenty languages (including Hindi, Punjabi, Urdu, Bengali, Gujurati, Tamil, and others) for both adults and children. Also carries materials for ESL (English as a Second Language) learners.

National Black Child Development Institute
1023 15th St. NW
Washington, DC 20005
(202) 387-1281
www.nbcdi.org
Several publications, posters, a calendar, and curriculums related to the development of African American children.

Ninos
P.O. Box 1603

Secaucus, NJ 07096-1603
(800) 634-3304
Fax: (201) 583-3644.
Bilingual and Spanish-language books and audiovisual items for children, as well
as art and music activities and teacher tools.

NoorArt
(888) 442-5687
www.noorart.com
Billed as "The Best Products for Little Muslims," this catalog includes books,
games, dolls, videos, and audios for children celebrating the Islamic religion and
culture, including several board books in English-Arabic translation.

Pan Asian Publications
29564 Union City Blvd.
Union City, CA 94587
(800) 909-8088 or (510) 475-1185
Fax: (510) 475-1489
www.panap.com
Khmer, Lao, Hmong, Chinese, Korean, Japanese, Vietnamese, and Tagalog adult
and children's books, as well as bilingual books. Some parenting titles available.

Parenting Resources
P.O. Box 138299
Chicago, IL 60613
(773) 525-5977
Fax: (773) 525-6532
www.parenting-resources.com
A good source of low-literacy parenting resources, including Spanish-language
parenting materials.

Positive Images Children's Books
593A Macon St.
Brooklyn, NY 11233
(718) 453-1111
Black culture and multicultural titles.

Programas En Espanol
AGC Educational Media
1560 Sherman Ave., Suite 100
Evanston, IL 60201
(800) 421-2363
Fax: (847) 328-6706
www.agcmedia.com
Good source of videos in Spanish on parenting, childhood development, childcare, health, nutrition, and safety issues.

Salina Bookshelf, Inc.
Flagstaff, AZ 86001
www.salinabookshelf.com
Salina Bookshelf, founded in 1994, is an independent publisher of textbooks,
children's picture books, reference books, and electronic media in Navajo and
English (dual language).

SBD Spanish Book Distributor, Inc.
8200 Southwestern Blvd., #1316
Dallas, TX 75206-2180
(800) 609-2113
En Espanol: (214) 369-1655
www.sbdbooks.com
Focusing on books for adults, this catalog contains a large collection of books on child care and parenting in Spanish.

Tsai Fong Books
3711 Briarpark, Suite 200
Houston, TX 77072
(713) 974-6226
Fax: (713) 974-1164
Email: infor@bookswindow.com or www.bookswindow.com
Korean, Vietnamese, and other Asian-language books and bilingual books for children and adults, including some parenting titles.

15

Teen Parent Families

"Though pregnancy, birth and abortion rates among teenagers in the United States have declined over the past decade, they still remain an endemic public health issue" (Sexual Information and Education Council of the United States, 2002). "The United States has the highest rate of teen pregnancy and births in the western industrialized world. Each year 750,000 teenage women aged 15–19 become pregnant" (Guttmacher Institute, 2006). Eight in ten of these pregnancies are unintended and 81 percent are to unmarried teens (National Campaign to Prevent Teen Pregnancy, 2006).

While experts agree that poverty is a cause as well as a consequence of early childbearing, statistics clearly show having a baby during adolescence intensifies and often perpetuates poverty. Fifty-two percent of all mothers receiving welfare had their first child as a teenager and two thirds of all families begun by young unmarried women are poor. Teen mothers are less likely to complete the education necessary to qualify for well-paying jobs. Only 41 percent of teen mothers complete high school.

The children of teen mothers bear the greatest burden and are at significantly increased risk for a number of economic, social, and health problems including low birth weight, chronic illness, developmental delays, and learning disabilities. They have more difficulty in school, are less likely to complete high school, and are at greater risk for abuse and neglect. Sons of teen mothers are 13 percent more likely to end up in prison, and daughters are 22 percent more likely to become teen mothers themselves (National Campaign to Prevent Teen Pregnancy, 2002).

Teen parents and their children are among the neediest populations in our society. They are also among the most challenging to reach. Libraries and librarians have much to offer to help meet these needs but must be willing to go beyond the library walls to connect these fragile young families with resources that may dramatically impact their future.

Needs and Challenges

Teen parents face the dual challenge of mastering the developmental tasks of adolescence and becoming parents at the same time. They need opportunities, resources, and support to continue and complete their own education to gain the workforce skills necessary to secure good jobs. Simultaneously, they need opportunities, resources, and support to develop their parenting capacity, including serving as their child's first teacher. Teens need programs and services that provide pregnancy prevention information, counseling, life skills training (financial and household management), educational and vocational preparation, prenatal care, and parenting education, as well as appropriate childcare and social support systems. They also need assistance in identifying and accessing healthcare services, social services assistance, and social support (e.g., extended family, neighbors, and friends). Finally, teen parents need opportunities to continue their adolescent development so they can successfully transition from childhood to adulthood.

Isolation and Dependence

At a time when teens need to separate from parents, exert more control and power over their lives, develop some degree of confidence as independent persons in the world, learn to form new attachments with peers, and formulate their own ideas and ideals, teen parents find themselves isolated from their peers and more dependent on parents or other authorities for their own and their baby's basic needs.

Teen parents are caught between two worlds, yet do not really fit into either one. The responsibilities of parenthood prevent them from participating in activities with their nonparenting peers, and their young age makes it difficult for them to relate to other parents who are adults. Without the support of a peer group, teen parents are unlikely to seek out and participate in programs and services on their own. Lack of childcare and transportation pose additional barriers to such participation.

Prior Library Experiences

Pregnant and parenting teens with limited or no library experience are often unaware that public libraries have information and services for them and their children. They are unlikely to even think of the library as a resource. Teens with a childhood history of lost or long overdue items may assume they would have to pay large fines before they could get a library card. For others, past negative experiences with library rules and regulations and perhaps even staff in public or school libraries are enough to negatively impact their view of libraries and deter them from venturing in.

Developmental Stage of Teens

One of the greatest challenges for those working with teen parents is to assume that because they are parents they have the same capacity as most adult parents. Though teen parents are parents with adult responsibilities, one must keep in mind that teen parents are still teenagers going through major physical, cognitive, social, and emotional changes. They are concrete thinkers who live in the here and now and view the world as black and white; are typically self-centered and impulsive; and developmentally need to begin taking more control over their lives. While those are certainly not ideal traits for parents, this developmental stage is necessary for teens to transition from children into autonomous adults. Research on adolescent brain development provides further insight into teenage behavior. Recent studies reveal that the development of the most advanced parts of the brain—those dealing with emotional control, impulse restraint, and rational decision making—occurs during adolescence. Furthermore, we now know that substantial growth in the brain structure that connects all parts of the brain, building the capacity to make good decisions, does not happen until late teens (Bradley, 2002). These findings provide answers to the age-old question adults pose to teens, "What were you thinking?" We now know it is not that they are purposefully not thinking, but that their thinking capacity is still in development.

Staff Attitude

Attitudes projected by staff can either encourage or discourage library participation (see Chapter 3). Like those of many other adults, staff attitudes toward and assumptions about teen parents may be counterproductive to creating a welcoming library environment. Because adolescent sexuality is such an emotionally charged issue for most adults, developing and maintaining a nonjudgmental attitude is particularly challenging. Library staff must not allow their personal moral, religious, or ethical beliefs to color their interactions with pregnant and parenting teens. Staff need to remain open, neutral, and supportive, both in their verbal interactions and body language. How often have teens commented, "I don't like the way that lady looked at me?" A disapproving expression can belie even the best customer service language.

Responding to the Challenges: Strategies That Work

1. One of the most effective strategies for reaching teen parents is to work collaboratively with agencies and organizations that are already serving them.

Through such partnerships libraries can integrate library programs and collections into settings where teen parents are living or already receiving services or agencies can transport teen parents and their children from their sites to the library. Potential partnering agencies include:

- Local school districts—especially those with alternative programs for pregnant and parenting teens
- Head Start, Early Head Start, and Even Start programs
- Women Infant and Child (WIC) programs
- Teen shelters and group homes for pregnant and parenting teens
- Lamaze birthing classes for teens
- Hospital programs for teen parents
- Local youth and family service organizations who serve pregnant and parenting teens
- Social Service (government-sponsored) programs for teen parents

Many of these agencies provide ready audiences of teen parents who are participating in ongoing classes or groups, or the agencies may be able to provide incentives for participation in library programs in the form of educational credits or some other desirable product or service. Other collaborations provide opportunities to engage teen parents and their children in waiting rooms through personal one-on-one conversations or through brief programs such as storytimes and Mother Goose. Such programs allow library staff to model appropriate, engaging early literacy activities and provide an opportunity to share information about library programs and services. Perhaps most important, they allow for personal connections between the teen parent and library staff that are often crucial to getting them to visit the library.

2. Examine library policies, rules, and procedures that may pose barriers to service. "Public libraries should be places where pregnant teens feel comfortable to visit without the lack of confidentiality being a factor" (Anderson, 2005: 44). Questions to help begin the process include: Does your library have a policy regarding confidentiality and under-age teens? Can teens obtain library cards for themselves and their children if they have outstanding fines from their younger years or are not yet eighteen years old? Are there provisions for lengthening loan periods to coincide with scheduled outreach or group library visits? Does the library provide deposit collections at offsite community settings frequented by teen parents? Look beyond policies, practices, and rules to identify the purposes behind them and be willing to explore options and make adaptations to better meet the needs of teen parents and their children.

3. Educate staff about the underlying causes of teen pregnancy and the role library resources (including staff) and services play in helping teen parents meet challenges. Increase staff awareness and knowledge of the physical, emotional, and financial challenges facing teen parents. Books such as *You Look Too Young to Be a Mom: Teen Mothers Speak Out on Love, Learning and*

Success (2004), edited by Deborah Davis, can be helpful in providing insight into how life changes when girls become mothers.

4. View teen parents as teens first and parents second. Though parents, teens are developmentally still teens and need opportunities to continue their adolescent development so they can successfully transition from childhood to adulthood. Viewing teen parents within the context of adolescent development informs program and service development and lessens unrealistic expectations by library staff and administration.

5. Treat teens with acceptance and respect. Teen parents are entitled to the same good customer service provided to all library visitors. Greeting them with smiles, a warm welcome and genuine desire to serve them and their children is a must for all library staff. As adults and professionals we need to keep in mind teen parents are often scared, unsure, and embarrassed in new situations. Providing clear information in a caring, respectful manner will lessen their anxiety and let them know the library is a trusted, safe, and supportive place.

6. Assume teens want the best for their children even though they may not be fully aware of how to provide it. Offer opportunities and materials that not only inform and educate but also engage and empower teen parents to be their child's first teacher. Serve as a model and guide rather than an instructor, and remember positive reinforcement is as important for the teen as it is for the child.

7. Adapt programs and services to meet the developmental needs of the teen parent as well as their child. For instance, take advantage of their creative side and need to be physically engaged. Rather than providing a formal presentation on a topic, start a conversation while the girls are engaged in a craft activity. This creates a comfortable, informal atmosphere where the teens can voice their opinions and reflect on what is being said. It also allows the librarian to guide the discussion, gently engage reluctant teens, and contribute information and materials on the topic.

8. Involve teen parents in the planning, delivery, and evaluation of programs and services for themselves and their children. This not only gives teens a sense of ownership but also builds their self-esteem and connection to the program and the library.

9. Treat each teen as a unique person. Remember teen parents are individuals, not just someone's mother or father or a member of the teen parent group. Treating teens as individuals helps to build relationships between the teen and library staff and increases a teen's sense of self-worth.

10. Feed them and their children and, if possible, allow them some decision making in the choice of refreshments. Allowing them to vote or take turns in deciding what will be served at a following program is often an incentive to future attendance.

11. Provide incentives geared to both the teens and their children. Whether it is a stuffed animal or a gift certificate for a manicure, free gifts are effective incentives. Once teens become parents, most gifts they receive are for their ba-

bies. Gifts for teens indicate the librarian recognizes and values them as individuals, not just someone's mother or father.

12. Rethink how you measure impact. Attendance does not tell the whole story. Use of observation and information gathered through informal discussions and anecdotal information provide a truer picture of impact.

13. Rethink traditional marketing tools. In her book *Extreme Teens*, Sheila Anderson exhorts us to "invade the traditional world of marketing by packaging the library and its services, collections, and staff as a product that all teens, regardless of extremes, want to open and experience! . . . You need to be on the cutting edge in your approach to promoting library services to a population that is typically difficult to reach" (Anderson, 2005: 137). Traditional publicity may reach professionals and older adults, but it is not effective with teens. A flyer advertising an early literacy program explaining phonemic awareness and phonological sensitivity is not likely to attract a teen parent. A flashing icon on the library's Web page stating something to the effect of, "You have the power to make your child succeed!" is more likely to get their attention. Because teens are egocentric it is often more effective to appeal to their interests and concerns rather than only highlighting the benefits a program or service will have for their babies.

14. Take advantage of popular media outlets. Local radio stations may provide free public service announcements. A program announcement by a popular DJ may catch their ears. Local cable stations often feature community members on their shows. This is a wonderful opportunity to promote library services and resources. Teaming up with a teen parent and baby promotes both the library and a more positive view of teen parents.

15. Prepare yourself and your staff for the challenge of working with teens (see Figure 15-1). Preparing oneself for such work is important to successfully serving teens and their children. The following are some insights to working with teen parents adapted from a briefing paper, "Working with Teen Parents and Their Children: The Importance of School-Based Programs and Guidance for Child Care Professionals in the Field," from the Center for Assessment and Policy Development, 1996.

Collections for Teen Parents

Just like materials for any teen, those for teen parents need to reflect the audience and be available in a variety of formats to address their abilities and preferences. Growing up in the high-tech, fast-paced world of computers, Ipods, DVDs, and sound bites, media and electronic formats are often the preferred format for parenting resources. The demands of schoolwork, jobs, parenting responsibilities, limited literacy, and lack of English-language proficiency will most likely preclude reading lengthy books on child development and parenting. Print formats such as magazines, cartoon or graphic materials, and eye-catching posters are better suited to the needs of teen parents. Colorful, easy-to-read materials, such as the "Born

15-1:   Preparing to Work with Teen Parents: Insights from the Field

Discussions with child care providers serving children or teens have identified some insights for others preparing to work with this population.

Many of the issues related to serving children of teens are common to all first time mothers.

Styles of communication are important.
Teens are concrete thinkers and, as a result, tend to take things very seriously. Simple, direct and frequent communication may work best. Communication styles that respect and give equal weight to a teen's opinion are often more effective that paternalistic styles.

Celebrate successes and provide support
Adolescent parents are often the subject of criticism by adults and need a great deal of critical praise and support to build confidence and motivation.

Be patient and accessible
Trusting relationships with adults are important. However, it takes time to build trust and librarians must find the time to develop relationships with teen parents. This requires a certain level of flexibility to accommodate the teen's schedule.

Respect for parental role
Teen parents struggle with being both an adolescent and a parent. Programs must find ways to balance respecting the rights and wishes of young parents with doing what is best for the child.

Counsel them on quality
Many teens do not know what to look for in early childhood programs and materials. These skills are important so they can make good choices for their children.

Prepare for emotional, behavioral, developmental issues
Children of teen parents may be sick more frequently than other children. They may also develop slower. Librarians need to be aware of possible delays, look for signs of illness and develop strategies to connect teen parents to community service providers to address these issues.

Prepare for dealings with other family members
Tensions between the teen mother and grandmother (the teen's mother) around child rearing practices are not uncommon. Issues of "who is the real mother?" may come up. Strategies to work with grandmothers and teen parents must be developed which respect the roles of each and their love for the child.

Expect conflicts of authority
In some respects, conflicts with service providers are ways in which teen parents exercise the power that they are encouraged to exert regarding their children. Adolescent parents are repeatedly told to take responsibility for their children and librarians may be one of the few groups of people with whom they can exercise this power.

Focus on peer involvement
Acceptance and approval by their peer group is critically important to adolescents. Many have lost their old friends and are isolated and depressed. Focusing on activities that involve their peers helps address this isolation and allows them to learn from each other.

Realize here and now is important
Expect some frustration when asking teens, particularly younger adolescents, to plan ahead. Over time, adolescents move from concrete to operational thinking where they begin to focus on their future and consider the long-term implications of their current actions.

Don't expect praise
While providers working with this population go out of their way to be understanding and flexible, these behaviors are expected by teens and they may not show gratitude. Over time, adolescents begin to understand the impact that adults have had on their lives; however, as teens they (and their friends) are the center of attention.

Have fun
Teen parents are children themselves and need and want to have fun. Providers should have a sense of humor and enjoy the time spent with this special group of young people.

Adapted with permission from "Working with Teen Parents and Their Children: The Importance of School-based programs and Guidance for Child Care Professionals in the Field: A briefing Paper." Center for Assessment and Policy Development, 1996.

Learning Tools" (distributed nationally through United Way—Success By Six), quick fact sheets, postcards, posters, and pamphlets produced by a variety of local and national organizations that assist pregnant and parenting teens are examples of more accessible formats. And do not forget to let them know about circulating toy collections (see Chapter 10). Not only are they a great resource for teen parents with limited budgets, but teen parents still have a lot of "kid" in them, and encouraging them to play with their children is helping them be better parents in a way that is an especially good fit for them.

Collections also need to include up-to-date information and referral resources of local agencies that provide information and assistance on topics such as prenatal care, adoption, housing, legal assistance, financial assistance, rape, family planning, abortion and abortion alternatives, parenting, childcare, family support, healthcare, education options, and job training.

Sources for information and materials specifically geared to teen parents are located at the end of this chapter. Additional information can also be found in Chapter 13, "Limited-Literacy and Low-Income Families."

Programs for Teen Parents

The design of all programs and services must take into consideration the characteristics and challenges faced by teen parents. Programs and services need to be accessible, engaging, and developmentally appropriate for all children in a teen parent family—the teen parents as well as the baby. It is also important to reach out to those who provide care for the children as well as the teen parents. This may include grandparents and formal and informal childcare providers.

The following are some examples of library programs for teen parents.

Teen Parent/Child Workshop

Audience: Pregnant and parenting teens and their children.

Purpose/Goals: To increase awareness of library and other community agency resources and services for teen parents and their children; to increase knowledge of child development, early literacy, and parenting; to model early literacy behaviors and provide early learning experiences for parents, children, and program childcare providers; to foster early literacy activities among teens and their children; to increase library usage by teen parents.

Description/Program Overview: Ongoing for twenty years, this program is an adaptation of the Parent/Child Workshop (see Chapter 8) that is designed especially for teen parents. The workshop is held one evening per month (October–June) on the same day and time as the weekly Teen Parent Program of the local youth agency. The actual program begins after an informal dinner and includes a librarian-facilitated parent and child play and circle time and interaction with resource professionals. In addition to participating in the Teen Parent/Child Workshop, teens are also introduced to a full range of library materials and services for themselves and their children, including a tour of the library's teen area and the specially designed and welcoming Family Place space. Teen families are eligible to continue participating until they age out of the Teen Parent Program at twenty-one years of age. This enables library staff to build close relationships with the teens.

Practical Tips/Program in Action: Over the years, input from the teens, program staff, and resource professionals has resulted in a number of adaptations to better meet the needs of the group. It was determined that teen parents were better able to focus on what the resource professionals had to say if they met with them and the librarian in an adjoining room while childcare workers remained with the babies and toddlers in the workshop area. Resource professionals take care to use hands-on activities with the teens to share information. For instance, rather than talking about or watching a DVD on nutrition, the girls might input information on the food they and their child had eaten that day into a computer program that analyzes nutritional content and discover for themselves the pros and cons of what they and their babies have eaten. That might be followed by a tasting party for the parents and children featuring healthy alternative foods. It has been found that the more hands-on involvement, the better. In addition to the core topics of the Parent/Child Workshop (see Chapter 8), teen input has led to the addition of new topics, such as child custody and support, mommy and me exercise, how to obtain a GED (General Equivalency Diploma), dealing with pediatricians, and career planning.

Additional time and childcare were built in before the program to allow teens the opportunity to hang out with each other, purchase items at the supermarket and drug store located next to the library, and meet privately with the social workers if needed. A rap group facilitated by the social workers was added on at the end of the workshop. While the actual Parent/Child Workshop portion of the program remains about 75 minutes, the additional components increase the overall time the families are at the library to about 2 ½ hours.

Partnering Organization: Colonial Youth and Family Services is the primary partnering agency, providing transportation, social workers, and childcare workers as well as dinner for participants donated by the local Subway restaurant.

Materials/Supplies: At each session, library resources on the specific workshop topic as well as materials for babies and toddlers are displayed. Pamphlets, flyers, and fact sheets on child development, early literacy, nutrition, baby safety, healthcare, childcare, discipline, immunization, exercise, stress reduction, alternative education, and vocational and college preparation are also displayed for easy access. Items specific to a particular workshop topic are compiled and distributed directly to the parents during the session. Other supplies vary. The workshop featuring nutrition offers samples of healthy foods. Cakes are often provided for celebrations of births, graduations, and other milestones. Additional supplies include typical arts-and-crafts materials. Girls new to the group receive an Infant Kit (see Chapter 11) welcoming the girls and their babies to the library.

Marketing and Outreach: Word-of-mouth advertising by participating teens, referrals from both the library and Teen Parent Program staff, and listings of the program in the literature and newsletters of both organizations publicize the program.

Staff: The program is staffed by one or two social workers and two childcare providers from the Teen Parent Program, a children's librarian, and a resource professional secured by the library (varies depending on the theme of the week). Resource professionals include staff from the local health center, Cornell Cooperative Extension, and the staff of legal and educational agencies. A library page sets up and takes down the interactive play area.

Additional Information: Contact Eileen Curtin at the Mastics-Moriches-Shirley Community Library, (631) 399-1511.

Teen Parent Outreach

Audience: Pregnant and parenting teens attending the Norfolk (VA) School System's alternative school for pregnant and parenting teens.

Purpose/Goals: To reach an underserved population and provide parent education to increase awareness of and participation in early literacy activities and library programs and services.

Description/Program Overview: Teens are transported to the library as part of their school day to participate in one of three parent-focused library programs, Alpha Seeds (based on ALSC/PLA's Every Child Ready to Read); Motheread (www.motheread.org), a program that combines the teaching of literacy skills with child development and family empowerment issues (described in Chapter 13); and Reading Rockets (www.readingrockets.org), a six-week, thirty-minute literacy program to assist parents in helping their children, from preschoolers through early elementary students, with reading. Teens are also introduced to a full range of library materials and services for themselves and their children, including the library's Family Place space known as the Kids' Zone. A fourth offering, Babygarten (www.babygarten.com), for teens and their babies together (see Chapter 8), is provided on-site at the school due to the complication and expense of transporting babies and toddlers to the library.

Partnering Organizations: The Norfolk Public School System provides transportation and collaborates with the library in the scheduling of programs to allow for the integration of the offsite programs into the typical school day. The district also provides scheduled time and space on school grounds for the delivery of the Babygarten program.

Materials/Supplies: Curriculum materials guiding the four individual programs as well as fifteen copies of individual books recommended by the programs are utilized. Additional supplies include basic arts-and-crafts materials, and Babygarten also requires boxes of toys and manipulatives appropriate for babies.

Marketing and Outreach: Because the program is limited to students at the Coronado School, publicity is limited to a flyer providing program information for teachers. The library contacts the school administration at the beginning of each school year to schedule the programs. Post-program articles emphasizing Norfolk

Public Library's commitment to creating readers are published in the library newsletter and local press.

Staff: Alpha Seeds utilizes one library staff member or one trained volunteer. Motheread requires one library staff member certified in the Motheread program, and Reading Rockets and Babygarten each utilize one librarian trained in the particular program.

Practical Tips/Program in Action: Curriculums are often embellished to make them more hands-on. For instance, a craft component has been added to each session of Alpha Seeds so teen parents can create simple early literacy items (e.g., flannel boards) to bring home and use with their children. During all programs, but especially Motheread and Reading Rockets, the staff is conscious of guiding questions and discussions toward the teen's life experiences and providing a high level of positive reinforcement. Librarians also take advantage of opportunities to deliver quick, informal sound bites on information regarding child development, parenting, and early literacy as well as promoting the resources of the parents' collection.

Additional Information: Visit Norfolk Public Library's Web site, www.npl.lib.va .us, or contact Terry Wanser at (757) 664-7328 or teresa.wanser@norfolk.gov.

Teen Parent Program: Building New Generations

Audience: Teen parents and their children.

Purpose/Goals: To reach an underserved population on the Navajo Indian Reservation and increase their awareness of and participation in early literacy activities and library programs and services.

Description/Program Overview: Using the Arizona State Library early literacy program, Building New Generations, the library staff shares information with parents on the importance of early literacy and models how to share books with babies, toddlers, and preschoolers. Volunteer students provide childcare for accompanying children in the Family Place space. The program is offered quarterly, lasting about an hour and a half, and attracts six to ten teen parent families.

Materials/Supplies: Early childhood books; Building New Generations program pamphlets; information sheets on early literacy and brain development; DVD on infant brain development (Infant Brain Development, the Critical Intervention Point featuring Dr. Jill Stamm of the New Direction Center for Infant Brain Development); refreshments; and donated books and toys in good condition.

Marketing and Outreach: A flyer advertising the program is distributed at the reservation post office, hospital, schools, and library. Word of mouth and personal invitations are often more effective than the flyer in this small, close-knit community.

Staff: One library staff member conducts the program and volunteer students provide childcare.

Program Tips/Program in Action: Refreshments and giveaway toys and books are major motivators for teen parent participation.

Addtional Information: Contact Eileen Curtin at the Mastics-Munches-Shirley Community Library, (631) 399-1511.

Conclusion

Pregnant and parenting teens and their children are part of our communities and impact all of our lives. The early support, encouragement, and empowerment they receive may well determine the outcomes for these families. Working in collaboration with other health and human services agencies, libraries can help diminish the future social, educational, and financial risks of teen families and help to build stronger, healthier families and communities.

References

Anderson, Sheila B. *Extreme Teens: Library Services to Nontraditional Young Adults.* Westport, CT: Libraries Unlimited, 2005.

Bradley, Michael J. Yes, *Your Teen Is Crazy!* Gig Harbor, WA: Harbor Press, 2002.

Center for Assessment and Policy Development. "Working with Teen Parents and Their Children: The Importance of School-Based Programs and Guidance for Child Care Professionals in the Field: A Briefing Paper." Center for Assessment and Policy Development. Available: www.capd.org/pubfiles/pub-1996-04-01.pdf, 1996.

The Guttmacher Institute. "U.S. Teenage Pregnancy Statistics National and State Trends and Trends by Race and Ethnicity." New York: The Guttmacher Institute. Available: http://www.guttmacher.org/pubs/2006/09/12/USTPstats.pdf, 2006.

National Campaign to Prevent Teen Pregnancy. www.teenpregnancy.org/resources/data/genlfact.asp, 2006.

National Campaign to Prevent Teen Pregnancy. "Not Just Another Single Issue: Teen Pregnancy Prevention's Links to Other Critical Social Issues." Available: www.teenpregnancy.org/resource/data/pdf/notjust.pdf, 2002.

Sexual Information and Education Council of the United States. SIECUS Report. www.siecus.org/pubs/fact/fact0010.html, 2002.

Resources

Ordering Sources

Adolescent Wellness and Reproductive (AWARE) Foundation
1015 Chestnut St., Suite 1225

Philadelphia, PA 19017-4302
(215) 955-9847
http://www.awarefoundation.org
The mission of the foundation is to educate and empower adolescents to make responsible decisions regarding their wellness, sexuality, and reproductive health.

AIMS Multimedia
Discovery Education
20765 Superior St.
Chatsworth, CA 91311-4409
(800) 367-2467
http://www.aimsmultimedia.com/
Offers DVDs on teen pregnancy and parenting.

Born Learning
www.bornlearning.org/files/bornlearningtools.pdf
Provides easy-to-use research-based materials that help parents make learning fun and take advantage of everyday moments. Available in English and Spanish.

Film Media Group, Films for the Humanities
P.O. Box 2053
Princeton, NJ 08543
(800) 257-5126
www.films.com
Offers DVDs on teen pregnancy and parenting.

Healthy Teen Network
509 Second St. NE, Suite 200
Washington, DC 20002
(202) 547-8814
healthyteens@healthyteennetwork.org
Healthy Teen Network's mission is to provide leadership, education, training, information, advocacy, resources, and support to professionals and organizations in the field of adolescent health, with an emphasis on teen pregnancy, pregnancy prevention, and teen parenting.

Injoy Videos
7107 La Vista Place
Longmont, CO 80503
(303) 447-2082
(800) 326-2082 ext. 2
www.injoyvideos.com
Offers DVDs addressing childbirth, breastfeeding, child abuse prevention, parenting, postpartum, prenatal care, teen pregnancy, and teen pregnancy prevention. Available in English and Spanish.

Kidsrights
Jist Publishing
8902 Otis Ave.
Indianapolis, IN 46216
(800) 648-5478
http://www.jist.com/kidsrights/

Publishes and distributes books, booklets, pamphlets, videos, and games on a variety of topics for professionals and the families they serve, including teen parents.

Medline Plus
www.medlineplus.gov
8600 Rockville Pike
Bethesda, MD 20894
A service of the U.S. National Library of Medicine, this site includes information on a wide variety of health topics including materials for and about pregnant and parenting teens.

MELD
219 North Second St., Suite 200
Minneapolis, MN 55401
(612) 332-7563
Fax: (612) 334-1959
Provides publications, programs, and training workshops for professionals working with parents including materials for parents under twenty-one years of age.

Morning Glory Press
Buena Park, CA
www.morninggglorypress.com
Offers books and board games specifically designed for pregnant and parenting teens on a range of topics from prevention to child development and discipline.

Web Sites Created by and for Teen Parents

Girl-Mom
www.girl-mom.com
A site designed and moderated by and for young mothers, Girl-Mom supports and empowers young mothers of all backgrounds, and is dedicated to fighting stereotypes about teenage mothers.

Teen Pregnancy Place
http://members.aol.com/mnn1121/index.html
Offers peer support, pregnancy information, a discussion board, and links to a wide variety of Web sites for pregnant and parenting teens.

Young Mommies Help Site
http://www.youngmommies.com/
Offers support, information, and a link to other young mothers to increase their ability to develop healthy parenting techniques and a positive sense of self.

Young Positive Parenting Organization
www.yppo.com
Offers information and fact sheets on pregnancy, childbirth, and toddler safety and peer support through penpals and message boards for both moms and dads.

16

Families and Children with Special Needs

The birth of a child with a disability or the discovery that a child has a disability can have profound effects—emotionally, physically, socially, and financially—on a family. An estimated 652,000 children under the age of five have developmental delays or physical disabilities (U.S. Census Bureau, 2002). Though great strides have been made in the provision of early intervention and special education services during the last two decades, many families of children with special needs are still isolated and not generally included in typical community life, including the programs and services offered by libraries and other community agencies. Reaching out to families of children with special needs and providing a truly inclusive environment that integrates all families is an important and natural role for family-centered libraries. This chapter will look at some of the unique challenges facing these families, outline the laws that govern early intervention services, and provide ideas and strategies that family-centered libraries can employ to reach and serve special families.

As with all services for families, staff attitude is critical. The following definition of inclusion provides a look at the philosophy that underscores service to families of children with special needs.

Definition of Inclusion

Inclusion advocates that all children, regardless of their abilities, have the right to participate and will benefit from participation in natural community settings with typically developing children. Aiming to reverse the isolation children with disabilities often experience, inclusion encourages their participation in playground activities, childcare settings, nursery school programs, and activities in local settings, such as the public library. Inclusionary practices focus on celebrating diverse abilities and having respect for the contributions *all* children can make. Maximizing on the openness and nonjudgmental attitudes of young children, inclusion in the earliest years allows all children to learn from one another and provides the foundation for a future where people of all abilities value and respect each other.

Special Needs and the Law

Two federal laws, the Individuals with Disabilities Education Act (IDEA) and the Americans with Disabilities Act (ADA), address the needs of people who have disabilities. These laws are designed to increase our awareness of diverse cultures and populations, increase the productivity of all members of society, eliminate discrimination based on differences, and ensure that all children enter school ready to learn.

IDEA ensures that all children (up to the age of twenty-one) receive a free and appropriate education regardless of their disability. The most recent version of IDEA was passed by Congress in 2004 and the final regulations went into effect in October 2006.

For children under the age of three receiving services, these services must be contained within an Individualized Family Service Plan (IFSP). An IFSP documents and guides the early intervention process for children with disabilities and their families. The IFSP is the vehicle through which effective early intervention is implemented in accordance with Part C of the Individuals with Disabilities Education Act (IDEA). It contains information about the services necessary to facilitate a child's development and enhance the family's capacity to facilitate the child's development. Through the IFSP process, family members and service providers work as a team to plan, implement, and evaluate services tailored to the family's unique concerns, priorities, and resources (Bruder, 2000).

At age three the focus of service changes from family centered to child centered. Beginning at age three, each public school child who receives special education and related services must have an Individualized Education Program (IEP). Each IEP must be designed for one student and must be a truly individualized document. The IEP creates an opportunity for teachers, parents, school administrators, related services personnel, and students (when appropriate) to work together to improve educational results for children with disabilities (U.S. Department of Education).

The library can play several roles in the design of a child's IFSP or IEP: as a resource and information center for parents, as a place for service providers to offer therapy to the child, and as an inclusive environment in which a young child with a disability can participate with typically developing children.

The Americans with Disabilities Act (ADA) is a federal law that encourages a proactive approach to serving people with disabilities. Its main mission is to protect those with disabilities from discrimination in public access and accommodations, employment, housing, and transportation. All public agencies and private businesses are under obligation to make accommodations for the needs of the disabled, unless they can prove that making those accommodations creates a financial hardship or seriously alters the nature of their business.

The key areas of ADA compliance, relative to libraries, involve:

Assuring nondiscrimination in employment of persons with disabilities
Assuring equity of access to services and information
Removing physical and environmental barriers that restrict patrons with disabilities from using the library
Training staff and the general public in disability awareness issues and the regulations of the law (Feinberg et al., 1999: 16).

Needs and Challenges

All families come to the library with their own needs, issues, and concerns. Some are typical and shared by most families. Others are unique to individual families. Families of children with disabilities are no different. Librarians need to remember that, just like any other parent, the parents of a special needs child are looking for information, peer support in their parenting role, a safe and nonjudgmental place to bring their child, and opportunities to get involved in community life with their child. Parents of children with special needs, however, often face major obstacles in fulfilling these needs. An ordinary event, like finding the right haircutter for a child's first haircut, can be a major issue for parents of a child who experiences seizures, needs a breathing tube, or simply cannot sit still.

Raising a child with special needs often places many additional and unexpected challenges and demands on parents and other family members. It is critical for parents to have access to complete, current, and unbiased information about their child's disability, currently available services as well as services their child may need in the future, financial assistance, trained childcare providers, assistance with family functioning, and how to connect with other families who have children with similar conditions.

Families also need the interaction, support, and acceptance of a wider social network than that provided by the early intervention and medical communities. Yet lack of time, due to medical and early intervention appointments, fear of being stared at, the parents' perception that they and their child may not be welcome, and concern that their child may not be able to use regular materials and equipment or be able to keep up with their typically developing peers often deter families from participating in library and other community programs and services. Engaging these parents and providing an environment in which they and their children feel welcome and successful may be the greatest challenges libraries face in serving special needs families.

Responding to the Challenges: Strategies That Work

1. Partner with agencies and organizations providing services to families of children with special needs. Though confidentiality issues preclude them from providing individual family information, these agencies can distribute library information and inform parents about library programs, resources, and services. Potential partnering agencies include school district preschool education departments, health departments, health clinics, hospitals, Special Education Parent Teacher Associations (SEPTA), and early intervention agencies. In addition to promoting services and programs, these agencies can provide demographic information about the early childhood special needs population in a community. Knowing the number of children with disabilities, the types of disabilities present, and when and where most children are receiving services can help librarians develop collections, programs, and services designed for this audience.

2. Utilize these agencies to promote services for families with special needs to community, civic, and religious groups. These groups are often willing to publicize information on their Web site and in their newsletters or bulletins, and their members may know of families within the library's service area who can benefit from such services, programs, and resources. This also helps build community awareness and sensitivity.

3. Offer the library as a natural community setting for the delivery of some individualized early intervention services. This can be especially appealing to providers and parents who are looking for alternatives to home-based service delivery. Parents may be more willing to venture into the library accompanied by a trusted early intervention provider. In some instances, families have included library programs and visits as part of their IFSP.

4. Provide training for staff to sensitize them to the fear, anxiety, sadness, and financial, emotional, physical, and social stresses that often impact a family with a special needs child. Information on the spectrum of disabilities present in the community and effective communications training (see Chapter 6) will increase staff knowledge and skills, helping them feel more capable and confident when serving the special needs population (adults and children).

5. View the child as a child first. A disability needs to be addressed only when it poses a barrier to access and participation. If adaptations are necessary, consult the child's parents and early intervention providers for suggestions. See the "Programming for Special Needs Children" section of this chapter for adaptation guidelines.

6. Be flexible and creative. Look at policies, rules, and procedures that pose barriers to inclusion. Adding staff or allowing a parent or early intervention provider to participate in a "child only" program may be all that is needed to create a positive library experience for everyone.

7. Seek out advice and support from early intervention and special education providers. These professionals know the children they are serving and, along with parents, can provide valuable insights and assistance.

8. Exhibit a nonjudgmental attitude of acceptance and respect for both the parent and the child. Remember that while some disabilities are visually obvious, others such as learning disabilities and behavioral conditions may not be apparent. Library staff who view the parent of a hyperactive child as ineffectual and have a critical attitude—"If I were that child's parent, she would behave"—will undermine a successful inclusionary experience. The staff needs to remain neutral and supportive at all times.

9. Provide a climate that supports staff members as they go through the inclusion process. Set the tone by listening to staff members' concerns, validating their feelings and working together to find effective strategies to address challenging situations. Consider including an early intervention provider at a staff meeting where these issues are discussed to suggest possible strategies.

10. Begin where the staff is most comfortable. Collection and space development and the creation of brochures and bibliographies can often be the first step for staff members who may feel inadequate and uncomfortable. Knowledge of appropriate materials not only provides information that helps educate staff members, but also boosts their confidence levels.

11. Create a space that is welcoming and accessible to children with special needs and their families (see Chapter 7).

Collections

Collections that nurture various styles and modes of learning, respond to individual needs and preferences, and are appropriate for children with a range of developmental abilities are a must for family-centered libraries. Children with special needs can often utilize the same materials as their nondisabled peers. For instance, cloth books, while often used with infants and toddlers, are easier for an older preschool child with a physical disability to hold and turn pages in than a traditional book, which does not display the same type of flexibility. Chapter 9 provides a listing and sources for books, audiovisual materials, and electronic resources in a variety of formats, many appropriate for young children with special needs. Chapter 10 covers the development of a toy collection including both commercial toys and adaptive toys, as well as capability switches and alternative input devices for electronic equipment. Sources for ordering are also provided.

While information on establishing a parents' collection is found in Chapter 11, parents of children with special needs require additional and more specialized materials often not found in a general parenting collection. A listing of resources in-

16-1:   Special Needs Collection Bookmark

The Special Needs Collection at the Farmingdale Public Library

Please come and visit our extensive collection of materials. This collection is designed to assist all members of the community, including parents and family members, educators, all therapists, social workers, paraprofessionals, and psychologists in understanding and addressing the issues of the developmentally disabled from infancy through adulthood. There are DVDs, videos, curriculum guides, periodicals, books, flash cards

Also included are:

Inclusion
Individual Differences
Multiculturalism
Advocacy & Legal Issues
Learning Disabilities
Dyslexia
Attention Deficit
Hyperactivity Disorder
Autism, Asperger Syndrome
Down Syndrome
Epilepsy
Cystic Fibrosis
Muscular Dystrophy
Anger Management
Feeding & Nutrition
Toilet Training
Speech & Language
Activities, Games,
Stories & Songs
Infant & Child Development
Social Skills
Individual Education Plans
Transitions & Vocational
Training
Behavior Management
Sibling & Family Relationships

**The Farmingdale Public Library
116 Merritts Road
Farmingdale NY 11735
516.249.9090
www.farmingdalelibrary.org**

cluding books, periodicals, Web sites, and pamphlets, as well as ordering sources, can be found at the conclusion of this chapter.

Specialized collections for families of children with special needs will be utilized only if families and professionals who work with them are aware of these resources. The bookmark in Figure 16-1 and the following Early Intervention Parent Resource Kit are two examples of products that help inform your community.

Early Intervention Parent Resource Kit

Intended as a resource for parents who are concerned about their young child's development or who know that their young child has a disability or developmental delay, Early Intervention Parent Resource kits are designed as a giveaway items. The kits are packaged in 9×12 office envelopes, are labeled appropriately, and include the following types of brochures and information:

Early intervention brochures
Child development guidelines
Advocacy center information
Information on local early intervention agencies
Information on local early childhood education sources
Contact information for national organizations focusing on children with special needs
Resource directories for children with special needs
Parenting and early childhood library services brochure
Parent's guide to the New York State early intervention program

Programming for the Special Needs Child

Including families and children with disabilities into library programming may require some adaptations. These adaptations will often be successful if the children's librarian takes the time to meet with the children's parents and other family support agencies in order to collaborate and plan together the best environment for the participating child. Flexibility is the underlying principle in making library programs accessible to the special needs child. Often, the materials and supplies that are already on hand in the library can be utilized in new ways to accommodate a child with special needs. For instance, supplying sponges for a child with tactile sensitivity allows the child to still experience "finger painting" during an art activity and requires little cost. The following adaptation guidelines are useful to consider when creating more inclusive programs:

Be willing to adjust age and other requirements to make an appropriate program placement. Keep in mind that it is usually advisable to have children of the same chronological age remain together whenever possible.
Eliminate any program eligibility requirements that would screen out children with disabilities.

Suggest to parents that they may want to adjust their arrival or departure time. Arriving early can help a child acclimate to a new experience and surroundings, while leaving early allows a child with a shorter attention span to still enjoy a program.

Permit parents to accompany their child into programs, even those designated "for children only."

Be open to the possibility that a parent may want the child's service provider to also participate in the program. This can be a wonderful opportunity for the library staff to learn from the expertise of a specialist in another discipline.

Reduce group size or add an additional staff person to increase your staff-to-child ratio.

While inclusion is every family's right, it is also every family's choice. Some families are more comfortable attending programs geared specifically for special needs children. These programs are often the first steps in future parent-child participation in typical library programs. The following provides examples of programs that allow such a choice.

My Fun Place

Audience: Children of all ages with special needs and their families.

Purpose/Goals: To entice families and children with special needs to use the library as a fun place to bring their children and ultimately to integrate these children beyond My Fun Place into the regular program offerings.

Description/Program Overview: My Fun Place is a grouping of different programs for special needs children and their families. One program brings outside programmers, such as puppeteers, physical movement specialists, and musicians to the library on a weekly basis on either Monday evenings or Sunday afternoons. Another program, Playtime at My Fun Place, an adaptation of the Parent/Child Workshop (see Chapter 8), meets twice annually for five consecutive weeks. A parent support group meets weekly at the library in the evening.

Partnering Organizations: The local chapter of Special Education Parent Teacher Association (SEPTA) works with the children's staff to publicize programs and services available at the library. Staff members from the library attend SEPTA board meetings to talk about the variety of programs and collections that the library offers.

Practical Tips/Program in Action: Every other month, a brochure listing approximately five to seven programs being offered for this targeted audience is distributed.

Staff: A children's librarian facilitates all My Fun Space programs (see Figure 16-2). In addition, outside program presenters conduct individual, one-time pro-

My Fun Place
Programs for Children with Special Needs

September/ October 2006

Farmingdale Public Library
116 Merritts Road
Farmingdale, NY 11735
516-249-9090
www.farmingdalelibrary.org

My Fun Place

The Fun Bus
Ages:4 years-2nd grade
The Fun Bus returns for another fun-filled day of bouncing, jumping, spinning, and more.
Pre-registration required. Proof of age required to pre-schoolers.

Musical Moppets
Ages 3 1/2 -up and a parent
By singing, dancing, playing instruments marching, and puppet play, children will
delight in this fun-filled musical adventure. Pre-registration required.

The Danna Banana Show
All Ages
Join us for an afternoon of original tunes and well known favorites that will have you tapping, clapping, and singing along. Seating is first come, first served.

Lil Playmates
Ages: 3 1/2-12 years and a parent
A physical, fun program for you and your child. Pre-registration required.

Fun and More with Will Shaw
All Ages
Will Shaw is back by popular demand. Come join us for an afternoon of fun and entertainment. Seating is first come, first served.

Playtime at My Fun Place
All ages and their families
A fun-filled program of play and art. Pre-registration required.

Just for Parents
Parents Only
Join us as we share tips, discuss strategies for everyday issues and share information about resources available in our community. All are welcome.

grams such as yoga, staff from local family serving agencies serve as resource professionals during Parent/Child Workshops, and a SEPTA member facilitates the parent support group.

Contact Information: Christa Lucarelli, Farmingdale Public Library, Farmingdale, NY. Phone: (516) 249-9090. Email: youthservicesfal@yahoo.com.

Something Special

Audience: Children with special needs and their families.

Purpose/Goals: To provide a time for the family and child with special needs to interact in an unstructured, relaxed environment meant solely for recreation and to help families network with one another and gain some valuable interactive experience with other parents.

Description/Program Overview: The program is an adaptation of the Parent/Child Workshop (see Chapter 8) and held seasonally three times a year for four consecutive Saturday mornings. Each session meets for 1½ hours and ends with a brief circle time incorporating songs, nursery rhymes, and fingerplays. A family outreach worker from the library's Family Center (see Chapter 4) attends one session to introduce families to support services offered at the library and through other community agencies.

Materials/Supplies: Suitable play materials from the library's adaptive toy collection are displayed, along with Legos, blocks, puzzles, musical instruments, and creative play items.

Practical Tips: Display different books each week from the Parents Collection so that families can browse materials during the program. Consider passing around an informal phone list, so that interested families can exchange contact information with one another. The program is advertised through early intervention agencies.

Staff: The program is staffed by two professionals.

Contact Information: Lisa Kropp, Middle Country Public Library, Centereach, NY. Phone: (631) 585-9393 ext. 230. Email: kropplisa@mcpl.lib.ny.us.

Toddler Learning Centre

Audience: Parents and children age eighteen months through three years, including children with special needs and typically developing children.

Purpose/Goals: To have typically developing and special needs children interact in a small group community setting in which therapists are able to provide therapy and to provide parents an opportunity to develop support networks with one another and observe behavior models that they can incorporate into their daily routines.

Description/Program Overview: This cooperative program, an adaptation of the Parent/Child Workshop (see Chapter 8), is conducted by the library and an early intervention program. It runs for four weeks and provides opportunities for children with developmental delays to play with age-appropriate toys, interact with typically developing children, and receive therapy in a group setting. A child development specialist and a speech/hearing specialist partner with the children's librarian to facilitate group interactions in a welcoming and informal atmosphere. Parents develop support networks and receive information each week about library resources and programs and learn developmentally appropriate ways to play with their children. The librarian concludes each session with a read-aloud book to model reading techniques and a song or rhyme. The Toddler Learning Centre provides one of the only group gatherings in the area for very young children with developmental delays.

Partnering Organizations: The County Early Intervention Program: Strawberry Field, State College, PA.

Materials/Supplies: Age-appropriate toys shared with the Parent/Child Workshop and parenting information handouts.

Staff: A children's librarian and an early intervention therapy staff member.

Contact Information: Anita Ditz, Schlow Memorial Library, State College, PA. Phone: (814) 235-7817. Email: aditz@schlowlibrary.org.

Conclusion

The public library is a place for lifelong learning for everyone regardless of age, income, race, or ability. Including children and families with special needs promotes this basic mission and benefits everyone involved—families and children with disabilities and those families, children, and library staff without disabilities who participate together in an inclusive setting. By serving all families and bringing all segments of the community together, libraries are helping to create more tolerant, accepting, and healthy communities.

References

Bruder, Mary Beth. "The Individualized Family Service Plan (IFSP)." Available: www.ericec.org/digests/e605.html, 2000.
Feinberg, Sandra, et al. *Including Families of Children with Special Needs.* New York: Neal-Schuman, 1999.

U.S. Census Bureau. "Survey of Income and Property Participation, June–September." Available: www.census.gov/hhes/www/disability/sipp/disable02.html, 2002.

U.S. Department of Education. "A Guide to the Individualized Education Program." Available: www.ed.gov/parents/needs/speced/iepguide/index.html.

Resources for Parents of Children with Special Needs

Books

Baker, Jed E. *Social Skills Training for Children and Adolescents with Asperger Syndrome and Social Communications Problems.* Shawnee Mission, KS: Autism Asperger, 2003.

Brinkerhoff, Shirley. *Why Can't I Learn Like Everyone Else? Youth with Learning Disabilities.* Broomall, PA: Mason Crest Publishers, 2004.

Citro, Theresa A., ed. *The Experts Speak: Parenting the Child with Learning Disabilities.* Waltham, MA: Learning Disabilities Association of Massachusetts, 2001.

Dykens, Elisabeth M., et al. *Genetics and Mental Retardation Syndromes: A New Look at Behavior and Interventions.* Baltimore, MD: Brookes Publishing, 2000.

Gargiulo, Richard M. *Young Children with Special Needs: An Introduction to Early Childhood Special Education.* Albany, NY: Delmar Learning, 2005.

Geralis, Elaine, ed. *Children with Cerebral Palsy: A Parent's Guide.* Bethesda, MD: Woodbine House, 1998.

Harris, Sandra L., and Beth Glasberg. *Siblings of Children with Autism: A Guide for Families.* Bethesda, MD: Woodbine House, 2003.

Kathiresan, M. *The ABC's of Autism.* Lansing: Autism Society of Michigan, 2000.

Kumin, Libby. *Classroom Skills for Children with Down Syndrome: A Guide for Parents and Teachers.* Bethesda, MD: Woodbine House, 2001.

Maanum, Jody L. *The General Educator's Guide to Special Education: A Resource Handbook for All Who Teach Students with Special Needs.* Minnetonka, MN: Peytral Publications, 2004.

Mordaini, Don. *Wild Child: How You Can Help Your Child with Attention Deficit Disorder (ADD) and Other Behavior Disorders.* New York: Haworth Press, 2000.

Naseef, Robert A. *Special Children, Challenged Parents: The Struggles and Rewards of Raising a Child with a Disability.* Baltimore, MD: Brookes Publishing, 2001.

Nekola, Julie. *Helping Children with Special Needs: Resources for Parenting and Teaching Children with Emotional and Neurological Disorders.* Wayzata, MN: Nekola Books, 2001.

Niemann, Sandy, and Namita Jacob. *Helping Children Who Are Blind: Family and Community Support for Children with Vision Problems.* Berkeley, CA: Hesperian Foundation, 2000.

Ozonoff, Sally, et al. *A Parent's Guide to Asperger Syndrome and High Functioning Autism: How to Meet the Challenges and Help Your Child Thrive.* New York: Guilford Press, 2002.

Pueschel, Siegfried M. *A Parent's Guide to Down Syndrome: Toward a Brighter Future.* Baltimore, MD: Brookes Publishing, 2001.

Quill, Kathleen A., et al. *Do-Watch-Listen-Say! Social and Communication Intervention for Children with Autism.* New York: Delmar Publishers, 1995.

Rief, Sandra F. *How to Reach and Teach Children with ADD/ADHD: Practical Techniques, Strategies, and Intervention.* San Francisco, CA: Jossey Bass, 2005.

Robledo, S., et al. *The Autism Book: Answers to Your Most Pressing Questions*. New York: Avery, 2005.

Sandall, Susan R., et al. *Building Blocks for Teaching Preschoolers with Special Needs*. Baltimore, MD: Brookes Publishing, 2002.

Shaywitz, Sally E. *Overcoming Dyslexia: A New and Complete Science Based Program for Reading Problems at Any Level*. New York: Alfred A. Knopf, 2003.

Siegel, Bryna. *Helping Children with Autism Learn: Treatment Approaches for Parents and Professionals*. New York: Oxford University Press, 2003.

Smith, Sally L. *The Power of the Arts: Creative Strategies for Teaching Exceptional Learners*. Baltimore, MD: Brookes Publishing, 2001.

Spungin, Susan J., et al., eds. *When You Have a Visually Impaired Student in Your Classroom: A Guide for Teachers*. New York: AFB Press, 2002.

Stillman, William. *The Everything Parent's Guide to Children with Asperger Syndrome*. Avon, MA: Adams Media, 2005.

Strichart, Stephen S., and Charles T. Mangrum. *Teaching Learning Strategies and Study Skills to Students with Learning Disabilities, Attention Deficit Disorder, or Special Needs*. Boston, MA: Allyn and Bacon, 2002.

Swartz, Sue. *The New Language of Toys: Teaching Communication Skills to Children with Special Needs*. Bethesda, MD: Woodbine House, 1996.

Webster, Alex, and Joao Roe. *Children with Visual Impairments: Social Interaction, Language and Learning*. London: Routlege, 1998.

Widerstrom, Anne H. *Achieving Learning Goals through Play: Teaching Young Children with Special Needs*. Baltimore, MD: Brookes Publishing, 2005.

Wilkins, Julia. *Group Activities to Include Students with Special Needs: Developing Social Interactive Skills*. Thousand Oaks, CA: Corwin Press, 2001.

Woodrich, David L. *Attention-deficit/hyperactivity Disorder: What Every Parent Wants to Know*. Baltimore, MD: Brookes Publishing, 1994.

Periodicals

ADRH Report
Guilford Press
72 Spring St.
New York, NY 10012
(800) 365-7006

Attention! C.H.A.D.D. (Children and Adults with Attention Deficit Disorder)
8181 Professional Place, Suite 150
Landover, MD 20785
(800) 233-4050

Brown University Child and Adolescent Behavior Letter
Wiley Subscription Services Inc.
111 River St.
Hoboken, NJ 07030
(888) 378-2537

Candlelighters Quarterly Newsletter
Childhood Cancer Foundation

c/o American Cancer Society
7910 Woodmont Ave., Suite 460
Bethesda, MD 20814-3015
(301) 657-8401 or (800) 366-2223

Children's Health Care
Journal of the Association for the Care of Children's Health
Lawrence Erlbaum Associates Inc.
10 Industrial Ave.
Mahwah, NJ 07430-2262
(800) 926-6579

Countdown
Juvenile Diabetes Foundation International
120 Wall St.
New York, NY 10005-4001
(800) 533-2873 or (212) 785-9500

Down Syndrome News
National Down Syndrome Congress
1370 Center Dr., Suite 102
Atlanta, GA 30338
(800) 232-NDSC

Early Childhood Report: Children with Special Needs and Their Families
LRP Publications
747 Dresher Rd.
P.O. Box 980
Horsham, PA 19044-0980
(215) 784-0860

Early Intervention
Illinois Early Childhood Intervention Clearinghouse
830 South Spring St.
Springfield, IL 62704
(217) 522-4655

Endeavor
American Society for Deaf Children
3820 Hartzdale Dr.
Camp Hill, PA 17011
(800) 942-2732

Exceptional Children
The Council for Exceptional Children
1110 North Globe Rd., Suite 300
Arlington, VA 22201
(866) 915-5000

Exceptional Parent
P.O. Box 3000
551 Main St.

Johnstown, PA 15907
(877) 372-7368

Families and Disability Newsletter
University of Kansas
Beach Center on Families and Disability
3111 Haworth Hall
Lawrence, KS 66045-7516
(785) 864-7600

Future Reflections
National Federation of the Blind Magazine for Parents of Blind Children
1800 Johnson St.
Baltimore, MD 21230
(410) 659-9314

Inclusive Education Programs: Advice on Educating Students with Disabilities in
Regular Settings
LRP Publications
747 Dresher Rd., Suite 500
Horsham, PA 19044-0980
(215) 784-0860

LDA Newbriefs
Learning Disabilities Association
4156 Library Rd.
Pittsburgh, PA 15234
(412) 341-1515

LD Essentials
National Center for Learning Disabilities
381 Park Ave. South, Suite 1401
New York, NY 10016
(212) 545-7510 or (888) 575-7373

M A Report, Allergy and Asthmatics Network
Mothers of Asthmatics, Inc.
2751 Prosperity Ave., Suite 150
Fairfax, VA 22031
(800) 878-4403

Mainstream: Magazine of the Able-Disabled
P.O. Box 370598
San Diego, CA 92137-0598

NICHCY News Digest
National Information Center for Children and Youth with Disabilities
P.O. Box 1492
Washington, DC 20013-1492
(800) 695-0285

Pacesetter
PACER Center

8161 Normandale Blvd.
Minneapolis, MN 55437-1044
(952) 838-9000

Pediatric Mental Health
Pediatric Projects
P.O. Box 571555
Tarzana, CA 91357
(800) 947-0947

Pediatrics for Parents
P.O. Box 63716
Philadelphia, PA 19147
(215) 625-9609

Pediatricsofficial
American Academy of Pediatrics
P.O. Box 927
Elk Grove Village, IL 60009-0927
(866) 843-2271

Sibling Information Network Newsletter
University of Connecticut
263 Farmington Ave.
Farmington, CT 06030
(860) 679-1315

Washington Watch
United Cerebral Palsy Associations
1660 L St. NW, Suite 700
Washington, DC 20036
(800) 872-5827 or (202) 776-0406

Web Sites

American Foundation for the Blind
http://www.afb.org

The ARC
http://thearc.org

Children and Adults with Attention Deficit Disorders
http://www.chadd.org

Council for Exceptional Children
http://www.cec.sped.org

DisabilityInfo.gov
http://www.disability.gov

Disability Solutions
www.disabilitysolutions.org

Down Syndrome WWW Page
http://www.nas.com/downsyn

Epilepsy Foundation of America
http://www.efa.org

Family Center on Technology and Disability
http://www.fctd.info

Family Village
www.familyvillage.wisc.edu

Internet Resources for Special Children
http://www.irsc.org

Learning Disabilities Association
http://www.ldanatl.org

March of Dimes Birth Defects Foundation
http://www.modimes.org

MUMS: National Parent-to-Parent Network
http://www.netnet.net/mums

National Early Childhood Technical Assistance Center
http://nectac.org

National Family Association for Deaf-Blind
http://www.nfadb.org

NICHY (National Dissemination Center for Children with Disabilities)
http://www.nichcy.org/

Parent Advocacy Coalition for Educational Rights (PACER) Center, Inc.
http://www.pacer.org

Tourette's Syndrome "Plus"
http://tourettesyndrome.net

United Cerebral Palsy
http://www.ucpa.org

Wrightslaw
http://www.wrightslaw.com

Ordering Sources for Early Intervention Parent Resource Kit Materials

A.D.D. Warehouse
300 NW 70th Ave., Suite 102
Plantation, FL 33317
(800) 233-9273
www.addwarehouse.com

Alexander Graham Bell Association for the Deaf
3417 Volta Place NW
Washington, DC 20007-2778
(202) 337-5220
www.agbell.org

American Academy of Child and Adolescent Psychiatry
2615 Wisconsin Ave. NW
Washington, DC 20016
(202) 966-7300
www.aacap.org

American Academy of Pediatrics
141 Northwest Point Blvd.
Elk Grove Village, IL 60007-1098
(847) 434-4000
www.aap.org

American Diabetes Association
ATTN: National Call Center
1701 N Beauregard St.
Alexandria, VA 22311
(800) 342-2383
www.diabetes.org

American Foundation for the Blind
11 Penn Plaza, Suite 300
New York, NY 10001
(212) 502-7600
www.afb.org

American Printing House for the Blind
P.O. Box 6085
1839 Frankfurt Ave.
Louisville, KY 40206-0085
(800) 223-1839
www.aph.org

American Speech-Language-Hearing Association
10801 Rockville Pike
Rockville, MD 20852
(800) 638-8255
www.asha.org

Autism Society of America
7910 Woodmont Ave., Suite 300
Bethesda, MD 20814-3067
(800) 328-8476
www.autism-society.org

Autism Society of North Carolina
505 Oberlin Rd., Suite 230

Raleigh, NC 27605-1345
(919) 743-0204
www.autismsociety-nc.org

Beach Center on Families and Disability
University of Kansas, Haworth Hall
1200 Sunnyside Ave., Room 3136
Lawrence, KS 66045-7534
(785) 864-7600
www.beachcenter.org

Blind Children's Center
4120 Marathon St.
Los Angeles, CA 90029
(323) 664-2153
www.blindcntr.org

Books on Special Children (BOSC)
P.O. Box 3378
Amherst, MA 01004-3378
(413) 256-8164
www.boscbooks.com

Brookes Publishing Company (formerly Paul H. Brookes)
P.O. Box 10624
Baltimore, MD 21285-0624
(800) 638-3775
www.brookespublishing.com

Brookline Books
34 University Rd.
Brookline, MA 02445
(617) 734-6772
www.brooklinebooks.com

Brunner-Mazel
19 Union Square West
New York, NY 10003
(800) 825-3089
www.routledgementalhealth.com

Candlelighters Childhood Cancer Foundation
P.O. Box 498
Kensington, MD 20895-0498
(800) 366-2223
www.candlelighters.org

Center for Speech and Language Disorders
552 South Washington St., Suite 109
Naperville, IL 60540
(630) 530-8551
www.csld.com

Centering Corporation
7239 Maple St.
Omaha, NE 68134
(866) 218-0101
www.centeringcorp.com

Charles C. Thomas Publisher
P.O. Box 19265
2600 South First St.
Springfield, IL 62704
(800) 258-8980
www.ccthomas.com

Child Development Media
5632 Van Nuys Blvd., Suite 286
Van Nuys, CA 91401
(800) 405-8942
www.childdevelopmentmedia.com.

Children and Adults with Attention Deficit Disorders (CHADD)
8181 Professional Place, Suite 150
Landover, MD 20785
(301) 306-7070
www.chadd.org

Comforty Media Concepts
2145 Pioneer Rd.
Evanston, IL 60201
(847) 475-0791
www.comforty.com

Communication Skill Builders
c/o Psychological Corporation
555 Academic St.
San Antonio, TX 78204
(800) 211-8378

Compassionate Friends
P.O. Box 3696
Oak Brook, IL 60522
(877) 969-0010
www.compassionatefriends.org

Council for Exceptional Children
1110 North Glebe Rd., Suite 300
Arlington, VA 22201
(888) 232-7733
www.cec.sped.org

Educational Productions
9000 SW Gemini Dr.
Beaverton, OR 97008-7151

(800) 950-4949
www.edpro.com

Epilepsy Foundation of America
8301 Professional Place
Landover, MD 20785-7223
(800) 332-1000
www.epilepsyfoundation.org

Exceptional Parent Library
551 Main St.
Johnstown, PA 15901
(800) 372-7368 x 110
www.eplibrary.com

Fanlight Productions
47 Halifax St.
Boston, MA 12130
(800) 937-4113
www.fanlight.com

Federation for Children with Special Needs
1135 Tremont St.
Boston, MA 02120
(800) 331-0688 (MA) or (617) 236-7210
www.fcsn.org

Films for the Humanities and Sciences
P.O. Box 2053
Princeton, NJ 08543-2053
(800) 257-5126
www.films.com

Guilford Publications
72 Spring St.
New York, NY 10012
(800) 365-7006
www.guilford.com

HEATH National Clearinghouse on Postsecondary Education for Individuals
With Disabilities
George Washington University
2121 K St. NW, Suite 220
Washington, DC 20037
(800) 544-3284
www.heath.gwu.edu

Health Resources and Services Administration
National Maternal and Child Health Bureau
Parklawn Building, Room 18-05
5600 Fishers Lane
Rockville, MD 20857

(301) 443-2170
www.mchb.hrsa.gov

James Stanfield Publishing Company
Drawer 124
P.O. Box 41058
Santa Barbara, CA 93140
(800) 421-6534
www.stanfield.com

Learner Managed Designs
P.O. Box 747
Lawrence, KS 66044
(800) 467-1644
www.lmdusa.com

Learning Disabilities Association of America
4156 Library Rd.
Pittsburgh, PA 15234
(412) 341-1515
www.ldanatl.org

Let's Face It Resource List
P.O. Box 29972
Bellingham, WA 98228-1972
(360) 676-7325
www.faceit.org

March of Dimes Birth Defects Foundation
1275 Mamaroneck Ave.
White Plains, NY 10605
(914) 997-4488
www.marchofdimes.com

National Association for Parents of the Visually Impaired
P.O. Box 317
Watertown, MA 02471
(800) 562-6265
www.spedex.com/napvi

National Association of the Deaf
8630 Fenton St., Suite 820
Silver Spring, MD 20910-3819
(301) 587-1789
www.nad.org

National Center for Learning Disabilities
381 Park Ave. South, Suite 1401
New York, NY 10016
(888) 575-7373
www.ncld.org

National Down Syndrome Society
666 Broadway
New York, NY 10012
(800) 221-4602
www.ndss.org

National Easter Seals Society
230 West Monroe, Suite 1800
Chicago, IL 60606
(312) 726-6200
www.easterseals.com

National Hemophilia Foundation
116 West 32nd St., 11th Floor
New York, NY 10001
(212) 328-3700 or (800) 424-2634
www.hemophilia.org

National Information Center for Children and Youth with Disabilities (NICHCY)
P.O. Box 1492
Washington, DC 20013-1492
(800) 695-0285
www.nichcy.org

National Lekotek Center
3204 West Armitage Ave.
Chicago, IL 60647
(773) 276-5164 or (800) 366-7529
www.lekotek.org

National Organization for Rare Disorders (NORD)
55 Kenosia Ave.
P.O. Box 1968
Danbury, CT 06813-1968
(203) 744-0100 or (800) 999-6673
www.rarediseases.org

Pacer Center, Inc.
8161 Normandale Blvd.
Minneapolis, MN 55413
(952) 838-9000
www.pacer.org

Parents Helping Parents
3041 Olcott St.
Santa Clara, CA 95054
(408) 727-5775
www.php.com

Pro-Ed International Publishers
8700 Shoal Creek Blvd.

Austin, TX 78757-6897
(800) 897-3202
www.proedinc.com

TASH: The Association for Persons with Severe Handicaps
29 West Susquehanna Ave., Suite 210
Baltimore, MD 21204
(410) 828-8274
www.tash.org

Tourette Syndrome Association, Inc.
42-40 Bell Blvd., Suite 205
Bayside, NY 11361-2820
(718) 224-2999
www.tsa-usa.org

United Cerebral Palsy Association
1660 L Street NW, Suite 700
Washington, DC 20036-5602
(202) 776-0406 or (800) 872-5827
www.ucp.org

Universal Health Communications, Inc.
The Colonial Center, Suite 202
1200 S. Federal Hwy.
Boynton Beach, FL 33435
(561) 731-5881
www.universalhealthonline.com

Vida Health Communications, Inc.
6 Bigelow St.
Cambridge, MA 02139
(800) 550-7047
www.vida-health.com

Visually Impaired Preschool Services
1906 Goldsmith Lane
Louisville, KY 40218
(502) 636-3207 or (888) 636-8477
www.vips.org

VORT Corporation
P.O. Box 60132-W
Palo Alto, CA 94306
(650) 322-8282
www.vort.com

Woodbine House
6510 Bells Mill Rd.
Bethesda, MD 20817
(800) 843-7323
www.woodbinehouse.com

Young Adult Institute (YAI)
460 West 34th St.
New York, NY 10001
(212) 273-6100
www.yai.org

PART IV

Tools for Family-Centered Libraries

A

Professional Development Tools

A-1: Self-Study for Children's Librarians

It is important for children's librarians or professionals assigned to work with children in the library, particularly with regard to those who work with young children and families, to identify their own strengths and weaknesses. To assist in this self-study process, the following tool is provided. It is intended that the librarian/professional will complete the checklist and, if desired, share the information with people who can assist in obtaining technical assistance and training to enhance those skills that need improvement, and to offer assistance to others in areas where the librarian feels competent.

THE SELF STUDY IS DIVIDED INTO EIGHT SKILL AREAS:
Program and Service Strategies
Program Development and Implementation
Materials and Collections Development
Family Involvement
Support Staff
Administrative Aspects
Interagency Cooperation
Self-Development

THE TOOL LISTS FOUR POSSIBLE REACTIONS:
⇒ HELP! Help is needed as soon as possible. This is something I can learn but I need education and training.
⇒ NEED MORE: No emergency, but perhaps a workshop or conference could help fill this gap in knowledge and skill. Seek help from an experienced colleague.
⇒ OK: No technical assistance is needed. I can and do an adequate job.
⇒ COMPETENT: I feel competent in this area and could serve as a mentor and potential resource to other librarians.

After reading the skill, check the box which best reflects your "level" of need. After you have marked all the items, review the needs assessment and circle the item you would like to work on first. Outline a plan of self-training, research the topic and read relevant materials, talk to colleagues that you feel could provide advice and guidance, and look for training opportunities.

Adapted from: Gaetz, Joan and others. *To Be the Best That We Can Be: A Self-Study Guide for Early Childhood Special Education Programs and Staff.* Poulsbo, WA: Educational Services District 114, Marine Science Center and Oak Harbor School District, 1987.

(continued)

A-1:　Self-Study for Children's Librarians (*continued*)

PROGRAM AND SERVICE STRATEGIES

	Help!	Need More
	Okay	Competent

	H	N	O	C	COMMENTS
State the philosophy and long range goals of the early childhood and family support programs in the library					
Justify the program strategy that you utilize within each early childhood/parent program.					
Effectively use resources to help plan your program content.					
Structure the physical setting to meet the needs of young children and their parents/caregivers.					
Design and implement appropriate schedules and program content.					
Cooperatively plan and carry out programs with staff members, parents, and other related professionals.					
Apply program/service strategies to meet the needs of young children and their families individually.					
Apply program/service strategies to meet the needs of young children and their families in groups.					
Modify program/service strategies to serve children with special needs and their families.					
Describe strategies to educate children in the least restrictive environment.					
Develop and use a system for evaluating the effectiveness of your program/service.					
Effectively use the expertise of other library professionals in program planning for young children and their families.					
Implement an effective communication system to share information and concerns with staff.					

Other needs and concerns related to program/service strategies:

PROGRAM DEVELOPMENT AND IMPLEMENTATION

	Help!	Need More
	Okay	Competent

	H	N	O	C	COMMENTS
Perform a task analysis of a long term goal.					
Describe the steps leading to the development of a program or service.					
Understand child development at all stages so that library programs and policies can reinforce the child's growth.					
Produce a written outline and summary of the program or service.					
Select activities and resources from professional materials and children's collection that best meet the needs of the intended audience.					
Describe the various elements that affect an individual's learning style.					
Modify program/service content to accommodate children with special needs.					
Effectively organize group activities for children, birth through age 8, and their parents.					
Provide opportunities and follow-up activities to reinforce specific program/service.					
Use ongoing evaluation to improve program/service.					
Provide appropriate supervision and management of other staff.					

Other needs and concerns related to program development and implementation:

MATERIALS AND COLLECTIONS DEVELOPMENT

Help! Need More
Okay Competent

H N O C   COMMENTS

Select appropriate commercially produced materials for an early childhood program/service.

Produce "staff-made" materials to facilitate the achievement of program objectives.

Effectively develop materials which foster independence in learning (learning packets, kits, stations, handouts for home use, etc.)

Effectively use technology with young children and parents.

Select, order and catalogue materials for young children and their families.

Train support staff and parents to use materials effectively.

Modify materials to make them accessible to children with special needs.

Evaluate the appropriateness of materials used in programs.

Other needs and concerns related to materials and collections development:

Help! Need More
Okay Competent

FAMILY INVOLVEMENT

H N O C   COMMENTS

Communicate with parents regarding their child's reading interests

Understand the "parent as teacher" role and its relationship to library service

Understand the "family centered" approach to library service

Have knowledge of cultural issues relevant to the population served.

Develop your own rationale for involving families in the program.

Define the staff's responsibilities and the program's resources in implementing a parent involvement component.

Initiate and maintain effective communication with the child and his/her family.

Identify factors in the home that have a positive effect on the child's academic performance.

Train parents in the process of parenting as it applies to their child's education, particularly with regard to literacy, language development, computer literacy, creativity and independent learning.

Promote positive parent/child interactions.

Model appropriate discipline techniques to use with young children.

Develop creative strategies to encourage participation from all family members.

Evaluate the effectiveness of involving families in programs.

Other needs and concerns related to family involvement:

(continued)

A-1:   Self Study for Children's Librarians (*continued*)

	Help!	Need More
	Okay	Competent

SUPPORT STAFF

	H	N	O	C	COMMENTS
Justify the need for a family service program.					
Help recruit, interview and place volunteers/support staff appropriately according to needs and abilities.					
Orient new assistants to the program.					
Delegate effectively and in an orderly and gradual manner.					
Provide training opportunities for support staff.					
Facilitate positive interpersonal communication among staff.					
Manage staff time efficiently throughout daily program.					
Implement an effective communication system to relay instruction to and receive information from staff.					
Assess the performance of assistants.					

Other needs and concerns related to support staff:

ADMINISTRATIVE ASPECTS

	H	N	O	C	COMMENTS
Demonstrate knowledge of standards, guidelines and roles regarding public library service to young children and families.					
Demonstrate knowledge of budget and funding sources for early childhood and parent education services.					
Maintain appropriate internal records relating to the administration of early childhood and parent programs/services.					
Use effective communication strategies with the library administration.					

Other needs and concerns related to adminstrative aspects:

	Help!	Need More
	Okay	Competent

INTERAGENCY COOPERATION

H N O C   COMMENTS

	H	N	O	C	COMMENTS
Exchange program and referral information with other community agencies.					
Understand the referral process as it relates to the role of information and referral in a public library setting, particularly regarding families and young children.					
Identify all agencies in the community who work with young children and families.					
Develop an awareness of public and private agencies providing educational, recreational, and informational services to young children and their families.					
Develop an awareness of local family support programs.					
Develop a channel to disseminate information on library programs to the general public.					
Provide relevant information to the child and his/her family.					
Assist staff in other departments within the library in understanding the goals and functions of the library's early childhood and parent programs.					
Understand the laws concerning child abuse and the services that are provided to help young children and their families with abuse problems.					
Understand the meaning of advocacy as it relates to young children and their families.					
Help coordinate and cooperate with agencies to improve services to the child and his/her family.					
Cooperatively develop programs with other agencies.					
Participate on interagency task forces, coalitions, agency boards, etc. that advocate and work for children and families.					
Integrate library service with other services to families within the community.					

Other needs and concerns related to inter-agency cooperation:

(*continued*)

A-1:   Self-Study for Children's Librarians (*continued*)

	Help!	Need More
	Okay	Competent

SELF-DEVELOPMENT

	H	N	O	C	COMMENTS
Understand the basic needs of human beings.					
Act relaxed and comfortable with parents and children.					
Maintain good eye contact, often getting down to child's eye level.					
Speak with a voice that is gentle, quiet, calm, and firm sending messages that are direct and clear.					
Use a special voice for talking with young children.					
Exhibit a clean, healthy professional appearance and wear clothes appropriate to the day's work.					
Listen carefully and respectfully to children and parents.					
Exhibit a high tolerance for variety of noise and movement and don't expect order every moment.					
Touch children often with movements that soothe, guide, redirect, reassure, reinforce.					
Identify factors which you need to consider for personal self-growth.					
Examine your personal attitudes towards being a librarian.					
Describe qualities of an effective early childhood and family support professional.					
Analyze professional behavior to understand its impact on child and parent behaviors.					
Create a positive atmosphere that promotes learning.					
Describe stages of librarian development.					
Evaluate your performance in program and service delivery.					
Secure resources to aid you in staff development.					

A-2: Professional Development Resources				
Agency	Description	Conferences	Resources	Professional Development
American Library Association (ALA) 50 E. Huron St. Chicago, IL 60611 (800) 545-2433 www.ala.org	Provides leadership for the improvement of library services around the country, resulting in improved learning opportunities, as well as equal access to information for all.	X	X	X
Association for Library Services to Children (ALSC) 50 E. Huron St. Chicago, IL 60611 (800) 545-2433 Ext.2163 www.ala.org/alsc	The division of ALA devoted to helping libraries provide the highest caliber of library services to children of all ages.	X	X	X
Child Care Exchange P.O. Box 3249 Redmond, WA 98073 (800) 221-2864 www.childcareexchange.com	Promotes the exchange of ideas among leaders in early childhood programs worldwide.	X	X	X
Cooperative Extension Services 1400 Independence Ave. SW, Stop 2201 Washington, DC 20250-2201 (202) 720-7441 www.csrees.usda.gov/index.html	Offers integrated research, education, and extension perspectives and provides national leadership for programs addressing critical issues relating to families, youth, and communities. Many states have state and local offices.	X	X	X
Families and Work Institute (FWI) 267 Fifth Ave., Floor 2 New York, NY 10016 (212) 465-2044 www.familiesandwork.org	A center for research that provides data to inform decision-making on the changing workforce, changing family, and changing community. Initiated Mind in the Making: The Science of Early Learning, an initiative focused on early learning.		X	
Family Institute of Cambridge (FIC) 51 Kondazian St. Watertown, MA 02472 (617) 924-2617 www.familyinstitutecamb.org	An educational resource for psychologists, social workers, family therapists, mental health counselors, and others working to help families in need.	X	X	X
Get Ready To Read! (GRTR!) National Center for Learning Disabilities 381 Park Ave. S., Suite 1401 New York, NY 10016 (212) 545-7510 www.getreadytoread.org	Brings research-based strategies to parents, early education professionals, and childcare providers to help prepare children to learn to read and write.		X	

(continued)

A-2: Professional Development Resources (*continued*)		Conferences	Resources	Professional Development
Agency	*Description*			
Harvard Family Research Project (HFRP) 3 Garden St. Cambridge, MA 02138 (617) 495-9108 www.gse.harvard.edu/hfrp	Assists philanthropies, policymakers, and practitioners in developing strategies to promote the educational and social success and well-being of children, families, and their communities.	X	X	X
Latino Family Literacy Project 1107 Fair Oaks Ave., Suite 225 South Pasadena, CA 91030 (626) 799-7341 www.latinoliteracy.com	Offers training workshops for professionals who work with Latino parents and their children in building a regular family reading routine and developing strong English-language skills.	X	X	X
Lee Y Seras-Ready for School, Ahead for Life 557 Broadway New York, NY 10016 (212) 545-7510 www.leeyseras.net	Supports Latino families as the first teacher in their child's life and provides professionals who work with these families the tools and resources needed to create an environment conducive to learning.		X	X
National Association for the Education of Young Children (NAEYC) 1509 16th St. N.W. Washington, DC 20036 (800) 424-2460 www.naeyc.org	Dedicated to improving the well-being of all young children, with particular focus on the quality of educational and developmental services for all children from birth through age 8.	X	X	X
National Center for Family Literacy (NCFL) 325 West Main St., Suite 300 Louisville, KY 40202-4237 (502) 584-1133 www.famlit.org	Works in cooperation with communities and educators to achieve the optimal literacy potential for all families.	X	X	X
National MultiCultural Institute 3000 Connecticut Ave. NW, Suite 438 Washington, DC 20008-2556 (202) 483-0700 www.nmci.org	Works with individuals, organizations, and communities in creating a society that is strengthened and empowered by its diversity.	X	X	X
National Scientific Council of the Developing Child Brandeis University Mail Stop 077 Waltham, MA 02454-9110 (781) 736-3822 www.developingchild.net	Enhances the early development of children through the design and implementation of effective public and private policies and programs.		X	

Agency	Description	Conferences	Resources	Professional Development
New Directions Institute for Infant Brain Development (NDI) 4500 N. 32nd St., Suite 206 Phoenix, AZ 85018 (602) 371-1366 www.newdirectionsinstitute.org	Provides parents and caregivers with trainings and tools to help infants, toddlers, and preschoolers develop a healthy brain and enter school ready to learn.		X	X
Ounce of Prevention 122 S. Michigan Ave., Suite 2050 Chicago, IL 60603-6198 (312) 922-3863 www.ounceofprevention.org	Works to ensure healthy lives for young children at-risk by providing early childhood programs and extensive training to early childhood professionals and educating state and federal policymakers.	X	X	X
Parents as Teachers 2228 Ball Dr. St. Louis, MO 63146 (314) 432-4330 www.parentsasteachers.org	Enhances child development and school achievement through parent education.		X	X
Public Library Association 50 E. Huron St. Chicago, IL 60611 (800) 545-2433 Ext. 5752 www.pla.org	Supports public library services including services for very young children and parents.	X	X	X
Zero To Three 2000 M St. NW, Suite 200 Washington, DC 20036 (202) 638-1144 www.zerotothree.org	Promotes the healthy development of our nation's infants and toddlers by supporting and strengthening families, communities, and those who work on their behalf.	X	X	X

B

Program Curricula

B-1: Off to a Good Start

Opening:	Book—*It Looked Like Spilt Milk* by Charles G. Shaw
	Encourages perceptual and verbal skills by identifying shapes
Art Activity	Have children drop or splatter white paint onto blue construction paper and fold in half to create their own "cloud" picture.
Learning Stations:	Duplo blocks
	Sequence cards
	Rhyming cards
	Sort a Number
	Bristle blocks
	Learning games, such as Chutes and Ladders
	Nesting shapes
	Opposite concepts flannel board
	It Looked Like Spilt Milk flannel board
	Cloud match (homemade game to model ideas to parents)
	Face Game
	Memory Match cards
Music:	Hap Palmer—"Put Your Hands Up in the Air"
Handouts:	Cloud poems
	Cloud activities packet to do at home

B-2:   Circle Time

Meet and greet parents and children. Have everyone sit in a circle with the parachute in the middle.

Activities to help familiarize children with the parachute:

Lift parachute up and down.

Walk around in a circle holding the parachute.

Activities/Songs:

"Old MacDonald" with the parachute—throw animal puppets in the middle of the parachute while singing the song.

"Wheels on the Bus"—Pretend that the parachute is the different object mentioned in the song and make the appropriate motions with the parachute.

Popcorn—Many toy catalogs have parachute sets that come with vinyl popcorn kernels. Throw them it in the middle and shake the popcorn so that it looks as if the popcorn is being popped.

Beach Ball Game—Bounce the balls on the parachute. Create different games using the same beach balls.

Five Little Monkeys—Use the popular song "Five Little Monkeys Jumping on the Bed" but have them jump on the parachute instead.

End the program with giving the children a ride on the parachute. Have the children sit in the middle (in small groups) while parents and facilitator(s) create a ride by pulling the parachute around in a circle.

B-3:   Mother Goose Stories

Opening Rhyme:	Hello Song
	Apple Peaches Pumpkin Pie
Finger Rhymes:	I have 10 Fingers
	Shake Your Hands
	Head, Shoulders, Knees, and Toes
	Open, Shut Them
	Wiggle My Fingers
Peek-a-Boo:	Big A
	Peek-a-Boo!
	Book: *Peek-a-Moo* by Marie Torres Cimarusti
Rhymes/Songs:	"Humpty Dumpty"
	"Jack and Jill"
	"Two Little Blackbirds"
	"Five Little Monkeys"
	"Pat-a-Cake"
	"I'm a Little Teapot"
	"Old MacDonald"
	"Hickory, Dickory Dock"
	"Hey Diddle Diddle"

B-4:   Toddler Tales

Opening Song:	"The More We Get Together"
Additional Songs:	"Itsy Bitsy Spider"
	"I'm a Little Teapot"
	"The Wheels on the Bus"
	"Clap, Clap, Clap Your Hands"
Opening Finger Play:	Open Shut Them
Book to Share:	*Silly Little Goose* by Nancy Tafuri
Music CD and Activity:	Have children and adults dance with shaker eggs.
Book Sharing:	Take five minutes for parents and children to sit on the floor with baskets of board books. Play soft music in the background.
Open Playtime:	Change the music to a more upbeat tempo, open the toy chests, get out the riding toys, and let the children loose with their parents for approximately fifteen minutes. Sing clean-up song after a five-minute warning, and close the toy chest at the end.
Teaching Point:	Print Awareness—Encourage your child to explore books. Give your child sturdy books to look at, touch, and hold. Allow her to turn the pages, look through the holes, and so forth, and keep them on a low shelf so she can choose her favorites.
Closing Song:	"Story Time Was Fun"
Props Needed:	Book selection for the week, guitar, and baskets of board books, shaker eggs, toy chest, CD player, and CDs.

B-5:   Four and More

Week Theme: Letter Knowledge	
Group Time Opening:	Name song with name cards—Talk to parents about using the first letter of the child's name and the names of people important to him such as mom, dad, and siblings to teach the letters of the alphabet.
Story:	*Chicka, Chicka, Boom, Boom*—Have children use rhythm sticks whenever they hear "chicka, chicka, boom, boom" in the story.
Music:	"Greg and Steve's ABC Song"
Learning Stations:	Reading area: ABC books
	Letter stamps
	Magnetic letters
	Shaving cream (to trace letters in) and Play Doh to make letters with *Chicka, Chicka, Boom, Boom* flannel board story for retelling
	ABC Seas game
	ABC floor puzzles
	ABC Picture Bingo
	Spilt Milk Caps (matching lowercase letters)
	Sorting straights and curves—Use macaroni
	Sorting letters—Alphabet cereal
	Make It Take It—Visors—Children decorate and write name on a visor
Closing:	*Alligator ABC* story and closing song

C

Surveys

EXPLORING OUR DIVERSITY
Getting to Know the People In Our Community

---

1. How often do you use the library?

    _ daily   _ 3–4 times a week   _ weekly   _ 3–4 times a month   _ occasionally

2. How long have you been using the library?

    _ 1–5 months   _ 6–11 months   _ 1–2 years   _ 3–5 years   _ for a long time

3. I usually visit the library on (please check all that apply):

    Monday   _ morning   _ afternoon   _ evening
    Tuesday   _ morning   _ afternoon   _ evening
    Wednesday   _ morning   _ afternoon   _ evening
    Thursday   _ morning   _ afternoon   _ evening
    Friday   _ morning   _ afternoon   _ evening
    Saturday   _ morning   _ afternoon   _ evening
    Sunday   _ morning   _ afternoon   _ evening

4. Check the main reasons you use the library

    _ For information or materials related to school, job, or career
    _ For information related to personal interests or needs
    _ To use/borrow Children's Department materials
    _ To use/borrow Adult Department materials
    _ To participate in Adult Department Programs
    _ To participate in Children's Department Programs
    _ To use computers
    _ To use the photocopier
    _ For fun or recreation
    _ Other _____

5. What is your primary interest?

    _ Videos   _ Library services
    _ Books/Newspapers/Magazines   _ Library programs
    _ CDs   _ Other _____

6. Who normally accompanies you to the library?

    _ Your children   _ Your friends
    _ Your parents   _ Other family members
    _ Your husband/wife   _ Other

7. What types of interactions do you have with library staff?

_ Request assistance for a search _ For general advice _ None	_ For more information about the community _ Other: _____

8. Have you ever attended library programs or used any of the specialized services?
    (please check all that apply)

    _   Parent-child programs   _   Computer classes

_ Children's programs   _ Citizenship
_ Adult programs   _ ESOL classes
_ CRD   _ Other _____
_ GED classes

9. How did you first hear about these programs (please check all that apply)?

    _ Word of mouth   _ In-library advertisements
    _ Public Service Announcement   _ Other _____

10. If you have never attended a library program before, please tell us why?

    _ No transportation   _ No program that matches your interests/needs
    _ Language barrier   _ Other _____

11. Do other members of your family attend library programs or use the specialized services?

    _ Yes   _ No

    Describe: _____

12. What other programs do you wish the library would offer or other services that would be useful to you?

    _____

13. Would the addition of any foreign language materials be useful to you?

    If so, what language: _____

    What format(s): Newspaper, books, videos, etc. _____

    Would special programs/translators be helpful? _____

14. Do you feel the library offers an open and friendly environment?
    _ Yes   _ No

    Comment: _____

15. What is the best way for us to communicate to you and your family about new programs and services?

    _____

    _____

16. Please tell us about cultural community centers and other places we should know about to help us
reach families of other cultures who may not be using the library (e.g., houses of worship, clubs, businesses,
food establishments: _____
_____

(continued)

17. Are there any barriers to your using the library more fully (e.g., transportation, language, child care, time of programs, etc.)? _____

_____

_____

Demographic Information (optional)

I. Would you be interested in participating in future initiatives and/or discussion on diversity issues?
   _ Yes   _ No   Comments: _____

   If so, please provide us with the following information:

   Name: _____

   Address: _____

                  _____

   Phone Number: _____

II. Age Group

   _ 3–12   _ 13–19   _ 20–29   _ 30–39   _ 40–49
   _ 50–59   _ 60–69   _ 70–79   _ 80–89   _ 90+

III. How do you get to the library?

   _ Walk   _ Own Vehicle   _ Public Transportation   _ Other _____

IV. Education

   _ Less than high school   _ 2-year college degree   _ Technical degree
   _ High school   _ 4-yr college degree   _ Professional license/certificate
   _ Some college   _ Advanced degree   _ Other _____

V. Employment

_ Government	_ Education	_ Business/Industry
_ Industry	_ Self-employed	_ Domestic Help
_ Health field	_ Office/Clerical	_ Other

V. Ages of children: _____

VI. Country of origin: _____

VII. Languages spoken: _____
   Languages read: _____

VIII. Town of residence: _____

Middle Country Public Library
Parent Child Home Program/PACTT/Library Links Survey

The Middle Country Public Library is surveying parents in the school district to identify families who may be eligible to participate in the following library outreach programs:

The Parent Child Home Program (PCHP), a 25 week in-home program in which trained library staff home visitors bring a new toy or book to your home and spend thirty minutes twice a week sharing and reading with you and your child.

Parents and Children Using Technology Together (PACTT), a six-week program designed for families and their preschool aged children. While childcare is provided, parents learn computer basics with the use of literacy-based early childhood software. The parents are then given the opportunity to teach these new skills to their children.

Library Links: Connecting Family Child Care Providers and the Library, increases early literacy experiences of young children in family child care homes by building one on one partnerships between family child care providers and librarians, and by introducing the wealth of resources, programs, and services the public library offers. Funded by a NYS Parent Child Services Grant.

IF YOU HAVE A CHILD, OR WATCH A CHILD BETWEEN THE AGES OF 1–5, PLEASE COMPLETE THIS SURVEY AND RETURN IT TO YOUR CHILD'S TEACHER BY SEPTEMBER 30, 2005. Thank you for your cooperation.

1. How long has your family lived in the Middle Country School District? _____Less than 1 year _____1–3 years _____4–9 years _____10 years or more

2. Please list the age of each child in your home: _____

3. What is the yearly family income? (**N/A for child care providers**) _____Below $20,000 _____$20,000–$35,000 _____$36,000–$50,000 _____$51,000–$70,000 _____Over $70,000

4. Circle the highest grade or education level you have completed: 6th 7th 8th 9th 10th 11th 12th Some College   Associates Degree   Bachelors Degree   Post Graduate Courses   Masters Degree   PhD   Vocational School/Other

5. Do you have a Middle Country Public Library (MCPL) card? _____YES _____NO
   Do any of your children have library cards? _____YES _____NO

6. Please list the language(s) regularly spoken in your home: _____

7. How often do members of your family use MCPL? ____Never __Rarely ___Several times a year _____1–2 times per month _____Once a week _____Several times per week

8. Who is completing this form? ____Mother ___Father ____Grandparent ___Child Care Provider ____Other

9. If chosen to participate in the **PCHP**, would you and your child be available for two 30-minute visits per week in your home with a trained home visitor? _____YES _____NO

(continued)

10. Have you ever used a computer? _____YES _____NO

11. If yes, how? _____Games _____Word processing _____Work related _____Internet
_____Seeking information _____Email _____Library computer workshop

12. Do you have a computer in your home? _____YES _____NO
If yes, what type? _____

13. Do you have school age children? _____YES _____NO
If yes, do they use computers? _____YES _____NO
If yes, where? _____Home _____School _____Library _____Other

14. For what reason(s) does your child use computers? ___Information/Internet _____Games
_____Word processing _____Email

15. Do you use a computer with your preschool age child (if applies)? _____YES _____NO

16. Are you interested in sharing computer time with your 3–5 year-old child while learning early literacy skills from a certified teacher? _____YES _____NO

17. Please check any of the following that might prevent you from attending **PACTT**.
_____Transportation _____Child Care _____Work Schedule
_____Other (Please specify) _____

For childcare providers: Do you watch a child on a regular basis between the ages of 0–3? Yes _ No_
If yes, how many and what ages? _____

Would you like early literacy materials brought to your house by a librarian trained in early literacy techniques, that you could use with the children in your care? Yes _ No___

Thank you for your interest. If you would like to be considered for these special programs, please fill in the information below:

Name: _____

Address: _____

Name and age of child(ren), Birth-5 years old: _____

_____

Daytime Phone: _____ **Evening Phone:** _____

I am interested in (check all that apply): PCHP _____ PACTT _____ Library Links _____

PLEASE RETURN THIS FORM TO YOUR CHILD'S TEACHER BY SEPTEMBER 30, 2005 TO BE CONSIDERED FOR THESE PROGRAMS.

Index

About the Authors

Sandra Feinberg has devoted the past thirty years to public library service and, since 1991, has served as the director of the Middle Country Public Library, Centereach, New York. An advocate for improving the quality of life for families, she firmly believes in the ability of public libraries to be family- and community-centered institutions. She created the Parent/Child Workshop, which began as a local library program for babies, toddlers, and parents. Partnering with Libraries for the Future, she developed this innovative local program into the national Family Place Libraries™ initiative, a national model and change agent for libraries wanting to serve families in a dynamic and collaborative community environment. In addition to the development of Family Place Libraries, she has spearheaded the development of the Community Resource Database (CRD) of Long Island which includes over 12,000 health and human services on Long Island. She has also developed several Long Island networking organizations and coalitions, including the Suffolk Coalition for Parents and Children and the Library Business Connection. A leader in the support and development of programs for the interaction between parents, children, businesses, and libraries, she created the Middle Country Library Foundation and the Miller Business Resource Center. Under her leadership, the library received numerous awards, including the first annual Godfrey Award for Services to Children and Families in Public Libraries (2002). Ms. Feinberg graduated with a bachelor of arts degree from Western Michigan University and received master's degrees in library science from the University of Michigan and professional studies from the State University of New York, Stony Brook. She is the author of numerous articles and five books: *Running a Parent/Child Workshop: A How-To-Do-It Manual for Librarians* (Neal-Schuman, 1994), *Parenting Bibliography* (Scarecrow, 1994), *Serving Families and Children Through Partnerships: A How-To-Do-It Manual for Librarians* (Neal-Schuman, 1996), *Learning Environments for Young Children: Rethinking Library Spaces and Services* (ALA Editions, 1998), and *Including Children with Special Needs: A How-To-Do-It Manual for Librarians* (Neal-Schuman, 1999). She is an adjunct professor at the Palmer School of Library and Information Science, Long Island University, and lives in Stony Brook with her husband.

Barbara Jordan is assistant director for Grants and Special Projects at Middle Country Public Library, Centereach, New York. She is the principal grant writer for the library and is involved in the implementation and management of a variety of grant-funded library initiatives. A children's librarian for many years, Ms. Jordan was responsible for the development of a comprehensive, countywide, multimedia Parent/Professional Resource Center at Middle Country. She has been the coordinator of the Community Resource Database of Long Island, an online directory of health and human services for the Long Island region since its inception. The author of numerous directories, bibliographies, and articles aimed at increasing access to information for parents and family-serving professionals and the role of libraries in the family support movement, Ms. Jordan is coauthor of *Including Families of Children with Special Needs: A How-To-Do-It Manual for Librarians* (Neal-Schuman, 1998) and *Audiovisual Resources for Family Programming* (Neal-Schuman, 1994) and a contributor to *Serving Families and Children Through Partnerships: A How-To-Do-It Manual for Librarians* (Neal-Schuman, 1996). Ms. Jordan was involved in the national implementation of the Family Place Libraries project and has spoken in a variety of forums on topics related to families, libraries, and community coalition building. She is active in numerous initiatives and organizations focused on children, youth, families, and business. Ms. Jordan has a degree in sociology from Adelphi University and a master of library science degree from Queens College School of Library and Information Studies. She lives in Coram, New York, with her husband and son.

Kathleen Deerr is assistant director/Family Place Libraries™ coordinator at Middle Country Public Library, Centereach, New York. Her library work with children and families spans more than twenty-five years. Recognizing early on that children's most important role models are parents, caregivers, and teachers, she has developed many innovative, interdisciplinary programs which focus on parent-child interactions. As a children's librarian, she brought programs such as the Partners for Inclusion Project, Reach Out and Read, the Parent Child Home Program, Learning English a Family Affair, and Family Place Libraries to community families. She has served as a guest lecturer at the Palmer School of Library and Information Science and is the coauthor of *Running a Parent/Child Workshop: A How-To-Do-It Manual for Librarians* (Neal-Schuman, 1994) and *Including Families of Children with Special Needs: A How-To-Do-It Manual for Librarians* (Neal-Schuman, 1999). Other publications include numerous journal articles as well as contributions to *Play Learn and Grow* (Bowker, 1992), *Youth Services Librarians as Managers: A How-to Guide from Budgeting to Personnel* (ALA, 1995), and *Partners for Inclusion: Welcoming Infants and Toddlers with Disabilities and Their Families into Community Activities: A Replication Guide* (NYS Dept. of Health, Bureau of Child and Adolescent Health, Early Intervention Program). A lifelong advocate for children, Ms. Deerr has presented workshops and lectures at the state and national levels on the role of the public library in serving and supporting children and families as well as lectures on the administration and management of children's and parents' services in public libraries. As the Family Place coordinator she oversees the training and technical assistance for the more than 200 libraries within the network. Ms. Deerr has a degree in sociology from Dowling College, New York, and a master of library science degree from the Palmer School of Library and Information Science of Long Island University. She lives in Westhampton, New York, with her husband and son.

Marcellina Byrne has over ten years of experience as a children's librarian and currently serves as the Coordinator for Clearinghouse, Parenting and National Family Place Services at the Middle Country Public Library in Centereach, New York. In her role as Coordinator for Clearinghouse and Parenting Programs, she supervises library staff, oversees collection development, schedules and organizes parent and professional programs, and outreaches to new family audiences. As the National Family Place Training Coordinator, Ms. Byrne facilitates the National Family Place Training Institutes. In addition, she is a member of and collaborates with various national and local organizations, including Libraries for the Future, Family Support America, the Suffolk Coalition for Parents and Children, Cornell Cooperative Extension, the Suffolk Education Clearinghouse and Regional Family Place. Ms. Byrne has coauthored an article in *American Libraries* (September 2003) entitled "Book a Play Date: The Game of Promoting Emergent Literacy," which discusses the importance of emergent literacy and the role of the public library. Ms. Byrne holds a bachelor of arts degree in English literature from St. Joseph's College and a master's degree in library and information science from Long Island University. She lives in Ridge, New York, with her husband.

Lisa G. Kropp has worked as a children's services librarian for over fourteen years, with a focus on early childhood, parenting, and emergent literacy services. Currently serving as coordinator of Early Childhood and Regional Family Place Services for Middle Country Public Library, Ms. Kropp supervises library staff, oversees collection development, schedules and organizes programs for young children, and works with libraries on Long Island to implement Family Place. Ms. Kropp is a reviewer for *School Library Journal* and has written articles and columns for national periodicals, including co-authoring an article in *American*

Libraries (September 2003) entitled "Book a Play Date: The Game of Promoting Emergent Literacy." She received a bachelor of arts degree in English literature and education from Adelphi University and a master of library science degree from Queens College. She lives in Centerport, New York, with her husband and two sons.